WOMEN

A Bibliography on Their Education and Careers

WOMEN

A Bibliography on Their Education and Careers

Sponsored by University Research Corporation and the Institute of Life Insurance

Helen S. Astin
Nancy Suniewick
Susan Dweck

BEHAVIORAL PUBLICATIONS, INC.
New York

Ref.
HD
6051.2
.A75

Library of Congress Catalog Number 74-5124
ISBN: 0-87705-701-X
Copyright 1971 by University Research Corporation
Copyright 1974 by Behavioral Publications, Inc.

All rights reserved. No part of this work may be reproduced or utilized in any form or by any means, electronic or mechanical, including photocopying, microfilm and recording, or by any information storage and retrieval system without permission in writing from the publisher.

BEHAVIORAL PUBLICATIONS, Inc.
72 Fifth Avenue
New York, New York 10011

Printed in the United States of America
456789 987654321

Library of Congress Cataloging in Publication Data

Astin, Helen S   1932-
    Women; a bibliography on their education and careers.

    "Sponsored by University Research Corporation and the Institute of Life Insurance."
    Reprint of the 1971 ed. published by the Human Service Press, Washington.
    1. Woman–Employment–Bibliography. 2. Education of women–Bibliography. I. Suniewick, Nancy, joint author. II. Dweck, Susan, joint author. III. Title.
Z7963.E7A86   1974   016.3314   74-5124

Preface

The impetus for this volume was a grant made by the Institute of Life Insurance to facilitate our work in the development of a data base on women's education and career development. It was mutually agreed that an overview of the research in this area was needed to begin to identify the state of knowledge and to suggest directions for the future.

Nancy Suniewick and Susan Dweck searched the literature for relevant articles, monographs and books; they were also responsible for the preparation of all abstracts and annotations. Helen S. Astin directed the total project, approved the materials to be included, and read all abstracts and annotations to ensure accuracy and clarity. The primary emphasis was on research conducted during the last decade; however, several articles from the fifties that were considered important were also abstracted and included.

Most of the publications identified in our search are based on empirical research. However, we did include some historical accounts, policy papers, and articles containing information on today's women's liberation movement. The abstracts and annotations are classified according to their main theme or purpose.

There are seven main categories. An eighth category covers miscellaneous materials such as syllabi on women's studies, commentaries and informational articles on the women's liberation movement. The seven major categories are:

1. *Determinants of Career Choice:* This category includes studies by researchers who describe and discuss the characteristics of women who choose fields of study related to future careers.

2. *Marital and Familial Status of Working Women:* This section includes works that describe and discuss working women and their interaction with their families, their husbands' attitudes, their marital adjustment, etc.

3. *Women in the World of Work:* This is the largest category and incorporates studies that describe women in different types of work and work settings—women in the professions, women in higher education, women in business and government, and women in executive roles. The final section in this category includes studies that describe the various characteristics of women workers.

4. *Developmental Studies:* These studies are by authors who have conducted research on sex roles, identification, socialization processes, etc.

5. *History and Economics of Women at Work.*

6. *Commentaries and Policy Papers:* Studies in this section are not based on empirical data, but the authors comment on women and work. Also included are papers that have implications for policy making.

7. *Continuing Education of Women:* Studies on aspects of continuing education are classified under this heading.

We used our best judgment in classifying the abstracts and annotations. However, as in any work this size, readers may find occasional cause to challenge our judgment. For some articles, varying interpretations of purpose or theme would have been possible.

The volume includes an author and subject index. Key subject headings are provided for each abstract to assist the reader in quickly determining the nature and subject matter of each without having to read through the entire abstract to make these determinations.

Two introductory chapters precede the abstracts themselves. The first is an *Overview of the Findings* by Dr. Astin. The second, *Beyond the Findings: Some Interpretations and Implications for the Future*, contains reflections by Nancy Suniewick based on her close examination of all the works abstracted in this document.

We would like to thank Carolyn Davis for editing all the abstracts and for supervising the production of this volume. Her painstaking editorial help has made the abstracts very clear, enabling the reader to get accurate and adequate information

PREFACE

without necessarily having to refer back to the original publication.

We would also like to thank Dr. Jacob R. Fishman, the president of University Research Corporation, for his continuous support of this effort. We appreciate the interest and support of Barbara Auerbach of the Institute of Life Insurance.

We hope that this volume will prove to be a useful resource to researchers, educators, and policy makers concerned with the education and career development of women.

—The Authors

Contents

Preface *The Authors* — i

Overview of the Findings *Helen S. Astin, Ph.D.* — 1

Beyond the Findings: Some Interpretations and Implications for the Future *Nancy Suniewick* — 11

Abstracts
  Determinants of Career Choice (1-82) — 27
  Marital and Familial Status of Working Women (83-100) — 79
  Women in the World of Work (101-212) — 93
  Developmental Studies (213-239) — 157
  History and Economics of Women at Work (240-288) — 175
  Commentaries and Policy Papers (289-330) — 201
  Continuing Education of Women (331-342) — 221
  Miscellaneous (343-352) — 229

Author Index — 233

Subject Index — 239

Overview of the Findings
By Helen S. Astin

Today there is much interest in and concern about women's educational and occupational development.

The decade of the sixties saw the emergence of a new women's liberation movement with its major objectives of making women aware of who they are as human beings and helping them to recognize their potential and to define means and ways of actualizing themselves.

The movement has focused on two issues:
- The bind that women are in because of early role stereotyping which continues to be reinforced throughout their lives, preventing them from searching for alternative and/or multiple roles and from engaging in a variety of tasks.
- Discrimination against women in education and work.

The effort and work of feminine activists has led to some recognition on the part of the larger society of the inequities and to an emergent willingness to find ways and means to remedy the wrongdoing. One such example is the investigation by the Department of Health, Education, and Welfare of higher educational institutions and the subsequent request that such institutions develop affirmative action plans to improve the status of women students, faculty, and staff.

We have also witnessed the establishment of special committees within professional organizations to examine their respective professions and to make recommendations for the improvement of the status of women. Moreover, some colleges and universities have encouraged the development of specialized curricula that will contribute to knowledge and greater understanding of women and their multiple roles in society.

Along with all these recent efforts and growing awareness of the status of women, we have also witnessed the need for better communication and exchange of ideas, and the development of means of transmitting information to those who work on committees and boards concerned about the status of women, as well as to those planning women's studies and to researchers considering new directions for research in women's educational and career development. Moreover, those in position to legislate or recommend changes in institutional policy need information about the state of knowledge—where we are and where we ought to be.

This general need for information and our own continuing research efforts on the career development of women prompted us to undertake the task of reviewing the literature on this subject. We focused primarily on research done in the sixties, with the inclusion of some classical studies produced prior to 1960. We felt that such a review could be of great value to a variety of individuals.

The abstracts are self-contained, so a reader can acquire general knowledge very quickly. Each abstract presents the findings and conclusions, lists the instruments used, and describes the sample and the methodology. Moreover, the abstracts are classified by topic for easy reference.

AN OVERVIEW OF CONTENTS

The bibliography includes more than 350 abstracts and annotations. Only 16 of the original books or articles were written prior to 1960, and the majority were written or published after 1966. Although we made every effort to locate all the relevant references originally identified for inclusion, we were unable to obtain 64. We had difficulty locating earlier writings. Interest in research in this subject area has increased in recent years, and 124 of the articles abstracted in this volume were published in 1970 and 1971.

We made a judicious effort to classify studies by subject matter or in terms of special emphasis. We identified seven major categories: 1. *Determinants of Career Choice*, 2. *Working Women and Their Marital and Familial Adjustment*, 3. *Women in the World of Work*, 4. *Sex Roles and Early Socialization*, 5. *Historical and Economic Accounts of Women's Education and Work*, 6. *Policy Studies and Commentaries*, and 7. *Continuing Education for Women*.

One of our interests was to examine the trends over time with regard to the types of studies produced on the basis of emphasis in the content and subject matter of the various studies. For example, we asked whether the studies in the early sixties were concerned more often with the determinants of career choice than with the characteristics of working women. Was the emphasis during that time on sex role and socialization rather than on marital and familial adjustment of working women?

An inspection of all the abstracts by year of research indicates that there was not a great shift or change over time in emphasis in the types of subject matter considered in studies on women's career development. The greatest interest during all the years covered was on women in the world of work. Next in emphasis came the determinants of career choice. Third in line were historical and economic accounts and policy papers and commentaries.

However, an increase in interest in determinants of career choice can be observed over time. Three times more studies on this subject appeared between 1967 and 1971 than had appeared in the preceding years. On the other hand, about the same number of studies on sex role and early socialization were published in the late sixties and in the early and middle sixties. Most studies on women are conducted by women themselves, but a sizeable number (about one third) are conducted by men. The authorship of articles abstracted in this document is: female, 58 percent; male, 29 percent; unidentifiable, two percent; committees or boards, five percent; and the Women's Bureau of the U.S. Department of Labor, six percent.

STUDIES ON CAREER DETERMINANTS

A very close examination of the studies on determinants of career choice suggests that most researchers and investigators have attempted to identify the characteristics of women who have a career orientation rather than the more traditional homemaking orientation. The characteristics on which most comparisons are made are within the domain of aptitudes and achievements, personality, and measured or expressed interests. Moreover, many investigators have attempted to identify the family backgrounds of career- and noncareer-oriented women, the relationships of subjects with parental figures, and the manner in which women perceive what is expected of them.

The dichotomy between career orientation and homemaking orientation in itself has implications in that it suggests limits on the options available to women. Nevertheless, differences can be observed among women with respect to career plans and aspirations, degree of interest in careers, and career commitment.

Aptitudes and Achievement

There is no conflict or contradiction in the literature regarding the differential aptitudes and achievements of women with career aspirations and plans and those who expect and plan for traditional roles of marriage and family. Women with career orientations tend to be high achievers and to score high on test measures of need achievement. They have more academic accomplishments and usually score higher on aptitude measures. Moreover, women interested in sciences, medicine, business—that is, careers that are more often chosen by men—tend to score higher on mathematical and computational aptitudes.

Personality

All the researchers who have examined the impact of intellectual orientation and achievement on the career development of women are in general agreement, but there is controversy and conflict in the reported findings regarding the personality dimensions of career-oriented women and homemaking-oriented women. However, some of the contradictory findings regarding the personality characteristics of career-oriented and homemaking-oriented women tend to be a matter of interpretation of study results and of assumptions about what is "healthy" or appropriate behavior rather than discovery of conflicting evidence.

Most of those who have investigated the personality characteristics of gifted and high achieving women agree that gifted women who do not achieve tend to be immature, as reflected in personality measures, while those who achieve are more insightful and psychologically healthy. Although most authors report that career-oriented women and high achieving women score higher on measures such as endurance and intraception and that they are more independent and responsible and more insightful on all measures reflecting psychological health, there is still a great deal of tendency to talk about women's occupational or educational interests in terms of the dimension of masculinity/femininity and to describe career-oriented women as women with masculine interests or with a masculine orientation. Unfortunately, the present clinical interpretation of a person who has interests and/or talents in areas that are descriptive of the opposite sex, is that such interests and aptitudes reflect one's lack of acceptance of his/her sexuality and that the person is in some kind of psychological conflict. This interpretation warrants reconsideration in light of evidence that great numbers of women desire careers that have traditionally been viewed as careers for men.

Regarding expressed or measured interests, studies have classified women on the basis of patterns of interests such as artistic or socially oriented (teaching, nursing, social work) rather than the more atypical interests for women such as scientific and business interests.

However, investigators who have used standardized interest instruments such as the SVIB-W (Women's Form of the Strong Vocational Interest Blank) have come to question to some extent the validity of such instruments primarily because they are limited in the options they offer. Moreover, the instruments have been found to lack validity regarding long term plans and behavior of career-committed and homemaking-oriented women.

Family SES and Relationships with Parental Figures

Studies that focus on family socioeconomic status (SES) and its impact on career aspirations of women suggest that parents of high educational and occupational level tend to exert a positive influence on the daughter's educational and career plans. Moreover, a working mother or one with an occupational orientation tends to influence a daughter in the direction of occupational planning and commitment. Regarding the relationships of daughters with parents, there is some indication that a close relationship with both parents and some identification with the father are positive predictors of a career orientation among young women.

Women's Perceptions of Male Attitudes and Expectations

This area of inquiry has been of concern to a number of investigators. Most seem to agree that a woman's perception of whether men approve of working women or whether men expect women to center their efforts primarily around the home influences her aspirations and career planning. Often, if a woman experiences or anticipates conflict between the working and homemaking roles and if she feels that men expect her to be passive and primarily a homemaker, she is likely to forego any career plans and opt for homemaking.

Unfortunately, the research thus far has been primarily descriptive and no one has addressed the question of how and why differences exist between women who decide to work and those who become or remain homemakers. New questions need to be considered: Why are some women comfortable about making career choices and showing a career commitment while others feel conflict about making such choices? What individual differences or early socialization experiences account for these observed differences in behavior and attitude? These questions represent unexplored areas.

When we examined the presentation and interpretation of findings of the various studies on career determinants during the early sixties, middle sixties, and 1969-1971, we observed some interesting differences in general orientation. In the early sixties, many of the studies were exploratory of the characteristics of women with different orientations, and compared women and men on interest measures. During the middle sixties, however, a greater emphasis began to appear on the conflicts women experience in making choices. There was a greater tendency on the part of investigators to talk of career-oriented women as having "masculine" interests or "masculine orientation." Interestingly, the later studies in 1969, 1970, and 1971 reflect a more positive attitude toward career-oriented women. Women who plan or choose careers are described as having interests in mathematical or computational areas, for example, rather than as having masculine interests. This may indicate that researchers have become more liberated. Or could it mean that the women they study are indeed more liberated than earlier cohorts of women?

Most of this discussion so far has been influenced to some extent by my clinical judgment of the manner in which study findings are presented and interpreted by different investigators. However, the fact cannot be denied that researchers are influenced by the times, and that choices for research inquiries and topics are often made because of the researcher's individual interests, concerns, and biases. Thus, we hope that this analysis can be useful not only in pointing out the need for some caution in the implementation of research findings in action, whether in counseling young women, in promoting educational change, or in making legislative decisions, but also in suggesting new directions for future research. For example, what are some of the facilitating experiences in women's career development? What are indeed some of the external as well as psychological or internal barriers that prohibit women from full self-actualization?

MARITAL AND FAMILIAL STATUS OF WORKING WOMEN

Although the research in this area has not been abundant, interest has been consistent throughout the decade. Most research on this subject has centered around three basic issues: the happiness and/or emotional adjustment levels of husband and wife when the wife works, the impact of the mother's work on the adjustment and happiness of the children, and how the tasks and roles within the home are defined, divided, and assigned. In brief, the findings appear to be somewhat conflicting on the issue of "happiness," although some new directions have been suggested for studying marital happiness in couples in which the wife works. That is, one observes differences on this dimension in couples of different SES and educational level. In addition, the wife's reasons for working and the degree of satisfaction she derives from work are important variables in work and marital adjustment. Thus, it is not the wife's working or not working per se that influences happiness and adjustment. Other personal and demographic factors are important in the assessment of marital adjustment.

There is greater agreement among investigators regarding the effect of working mothers on the children's behavior, adjustment and growth. For example, most studies report that there is no support for a position that a mother's working has negative effects on her children. Moreover, some studies indicate that working mothers tend to have more positive attitudes than nonworking mothers toward children.

Regarding the definition of roles, tasks, and activities within the home, research results suggest that working women are more involved than nonworking women in decision making and that husbands of working women are more willing than other husbands to help with domestic tasks. Moreover, working women spend less time on leisure activities in order to have adequate time for the family.

Although the husbands of working wives have more liberated attitudes, professional men in general hold negative attitudes toward professional women who are trying to fulfill the dual role of career woman and homemaker.

WOMEN IN THE WORLD OF WORK

The studies on women at work comprise the largest single category included in our bibliography. An examination of how highly trained women fare in the world of work indicates the following: women have been choosing and preparing through advanced training for occupations that have been called feminine occupations. For example, only one percent of all engineers are women, but women comprise the majority of personnel in the field of education and constitute more than a third of all persons working in social sciences and the arts and humanities. Nevertheless, it is important to note that highly educated women (i.e., those with doctoral degrees working as physicians, lawyers, engineers, and the like) demonstrate a high degree of career commitment. A very high proportion of these women (between 80 and 90 percent) are in the labor force.

In spite of the dedication and involvement of highly educated women, and despite their enormous contributions, the rewards they receive are not commensurate with those received by men. They receive lower salaries than men for the same work, and it takes them longer to achieve status as measured by rank and position. In addition, they report experiences with other discriminatory practices such as nepotism regulations which are applied in a way that affects the woman more than her husband. Lack of benefits for the woman who works part-time because of family responsibilities, as well as other forms of subtle discrimination, are also reported.

Characteristics of Women Workers

Most of the studies that describe women workers in general have been concerned with three basic issues: motivation for work, demographic characteristics of women workers, and rewards as measured by salaries, promotions, etc.

Economic factors are very important in the decision of a woman to enter the labor force, according to findings in most studies of the characteristics cf women workers. Moreover, women who value economic security are more likely to work. However, other important factors that cause women to work include the characteristics of the community in which a woman lives, the size of her family, her field and/or her past training, and her educational level. The more education a woman has, the more likely she is to enter the labor force.

Regarding the general demographic characteristics of women, married women are more likely than widows to work, but they are less likely than divorced, separated, or single women to be in the labor force. Fewer married women with children under six work than women with school-age children. Moreover, married women with family responsibilities and women over 65 prefer part-time employment.

On the question of rewards received by women workers, the majority of the studies report great salary differentials between female and male workers, even when controls such as the length of time on the job, type of job, training and education are used. Women's salaries are between 40 and 60 percent of men's salaries for the same work. Moreover, 60 percent of women workers earn less than $5,000 compared to 28 percent of the men. On the other hand, studies on turnover and absenteeism indicate very small differentials between men and women workers. That is, women lose 5.7 days a year compared to 5.5 days for men. There is a slightly higher turnover rate for women workers of the same age, although the turnover of older women tends to be lower than that of younger men. In summary, although women workers constitute a third of the labor force, are motivated by the same economic factors as men, and show extensive commitment to work, they still do not receive the salary and status they deserve and they experience a great deal of discrimination, not because of reasons such as incompetence or lack of motivation but because of their sexual status.

SEX ROLE, IDENTIFICATION, AND EARLY SOCIALIZATION

A close examination of the findings reported in studies dealing with the issues of sex differences, sex role, identification and aspects of socialization suggests some need for caution in their interpretation or implementation of their findings. A number of studies in the literature include biases in design, frame of reference and style of presenting findings. To be more explicit, some investigators present their findings indicating great sex differences in behavior, aptitudes, interests, and skills in the most definitive way without concern for individual differences or determinants of such behavior. For example, they indicate that women evidence greater need for affiliation than males, are more dependent on the external context of a situation, are more reluctant to deviate from the given, and tend to be more receptive to standards held by others. The careful reader notes that the authors not only present their findings in definitive terms but also proceed to make recommendations without regard for the implications of these recommendations. Often, their recommendations are based on questionable assumptions. For example, one author concludes that teaching and nursing are appropriate career choices for women because women have great interest in people and an ability to perform many tasks simultaneously. Why should one assume that such traits are necessary or essential for desirable job performance as a nurse or teacher? Moreover, might it not also be possible to ascertain that a man's "analytic ability" could be very useful in teaching or handling patient problems?

In the literature on sex role, identification, and early socialization, studies can also be found that discuss sex-role stereotyping and suggest that characteristics thought of as feminine are not necessarily valued by the larger society and are not thought of as indicative of "maturity," "strength," or "mental health," qualities held in high esteem in our culture. These studies suggest some of the researchers' stereotypic thinking with regard to issues of normal behavior or mental health. And they highlight some negative attitudes about women's behavior and perceived traits. These studies stand in sharp contrast to extensive works demonstrating how women perceive themselves and their role. Similarly, there are sharp differences in women's view of the ideal woman and their view of what the man perceives the ideal woman to be. Women tend to see the ideal woman as an active woman, but man's ideal woman as passive. However, when men are questioned about their ideal woman, they do not necessarily suggest that she be passive. These findings not only suggest the existence of potential conflict in women on this issue but also indicate some of the problems of communication between the sexes and suggest that our expectations of appropriate feminine behavior are quite limited by the tendency to think in stereotypic ways without regard for individual differences.

The fourth category of studies dealing with issues of sex role and sex differences are those by investigators who point out sex differences and make an effort to identify the potential sources for the observed differences. For example, studies on sex differences in intellectual functioning discuss the manner in which differential personality characteristics—impulsivity, independence, activity, aggressiveness, etc.—influence the development of differential aptitudes. However, these discussions are highlighted by the need for better understanding and exploration of the socialization process and of the impact of inherited and hormonal differences upon personality and aptitude differentiation.

HISTORICAL ACCOUNTS AND COMMENTARIES

Most of the historical accounts on women's education and work give rise to some optimism about changes that have taken place in women and work as well as in the larger society. More women, especially married women, are participating in the labor force today than in former years. Changes in attitudes have also occurred about the care of children by substitute mothers when women work. Some of the positive changes affecting women and work have resulted from larger changes in society such as advanced technology, improved health and increased educational facilities (kindergartens, nurseries, etc.).

However, along with those who view the present situation of working women optimistically, there are those who look into historical accounts with great pessimism about the future of women with respect to higher education and careers. They report that the educational participation of women has not changed. Sometimes they interpret the changes in Ph.D. productivity (from 20 percent in the 1920s to 10 percent in the 1950s) as a drop in the educational aspirations of women. They also report with pessimism the lack of change in the kinds of jobs women engage in today compared to two or three decades ago. Women still work primarily in the typical feminine occupations of teaching, nursing, and social work. Moreover, they point out the myths that still persist to the effect that "women want jobs and not careers" and that "women control the national wealth."

The commentaries tend to be individualistic and subjective. Because of the lack of data to support positions presented, the reader is cautioned to be very careful in drawing conclusions from the commentaries, especially when one takes into account the variety of interpretations and conclusions drawn even in the studies that are based on data.

SUMMARY

This brief overview of studies on the education and career development of women suggests new directions for research. New emphases are essential that include:
1. Better understanding of the dynamics of women who make different kinds of educational and vocational decisions.
2. A greater understanding of the influences of heredity, physiology, and socialization in the formulation of different aptitudes and interests by men and women.
3. A greater understanding of the manner in which the educational structure and the woman's own experiences affect her self-concept and her educational and vocational aspirations and behaviors.
4. Action research that includes well thought-out programming and the evaluation of its impact on women, their families, and the larger society.

For example, action programs can include the development of day-care facilities with an educational emphasis, the establishment of special scholarships to encourage women to enter new fields, the allowance of part-time graduate and professional study, and part-time work with benefits similar to those provided for full-time work, etc. The development of such programs could have an impact on the decisions of women about education and work as well as an impact on the family structure and the socialization process. Programs like this should be evaluated through research again in order to understand how our society and its institutions affect women's education and career development. In essence, we propose structural changes that will affect women and help them make new choices and lead to greater options for women in developing their life styles. Accompanying these should be evaluative research to determine their effect on society that can begin to point the way to improvement and continued refinement of the new structures.

Beyond the Findings:
Some Interpretations and Implications for the Future

By Nancy Suniewick

Any discussion of women today runs the risk of becoming emotion-charged. Men who write about women run the risk of being immediately censured because, their critics claim, they will never understand the subject. Women who write about women are often called hysterical, and the suggestion is frequently made that they are "not ready" for equal status with men. Even the scientific findings of serious students of human behavior can give rise to strong emotional reaction. Review of the works abstracted in this document suggests that researchers need to reconsider not only their approaches to the study of women but also their interpretation of their own findings.

Consider what the results of the studies covered in this document tell us about women. Here are some of the findings:
- Women are, by nature, less aggressive than men.
- No real differences can be found in the aggression levels of men and women.
- Women have made great strides in achieving equal opportunity in the world of work in the last 50 years.
- Women have suffered setbacks in the pursuit of equal opportunity in the world of work in the last 50 years.

- No real differences can be found between the behavior of children whose mothers work and children of nonworking mothers.
- Differences can be documented in the behavior of children of nonworking mothers and the behavior of children of working mothers.

Different researchers, all using scientific methods, have arrived at contradictory findings about women.

Which findings are we to believe? Empirical analysis of the findings of research studies designed to answer questions about women, their work, and their place in the world leads the observer to several conclusions, not the least of which are that not all the "evidence" on women is in yet, and that new tools are needed for the investigation of women, their education and career development.

WHY THE CONTRADICTIONS?

Some of the instruments used in research on women have been designed for use with men. In many cases, they are dysfunctional for the study of women.

For example, a frequently used instrument is the Strong Vocational Interest Blank (SVIB), a test designed to predict career patterns on the basis of nonspecific interests. Until recently, it consisted of two forms, one for men and one for women.

Researchers using this test have had considerable difficulty predicting career behavior for women, but considerable success in predicting for men. Why?

The men's form of the SVIB has many more categories than the women's. The categories in the most widely-used women's form are very limited. They range from teacher to social worker to seamstress, and that's about it. In other words, many of the career categories open to selection by men are not open to selection by women who attempt to indicate their career interests on the SVIB. It is impossible for the woman interested in being a banker to obtain an accurate assessment by this test.

The SVIB was originally designed to predict vocational interests of men; the women's form came later. It is considered by many to be worthless because of its limitations in scope regarding the career fields women can enter. Yet some researchers are still attempting to predict the career interests of women using this form.[1] Some investigators have found it increasingly necessary to use the men's form for the prediction of women's

---

[1] Apparently the inappropriateness of the SVIB-W and other tests similar to it was initially taken by many as confirmation of the conventional notion that women do not aspire to careers. As the belief came under scrutiny, people began to suggest that women did not aspire to careers because of the vicissitudes of socialization. What is becoming more evident because of new research and reevaluation of existing literature is that women have always aspired to careers but that discriminatory practices in business and other institutions have kept them out.

career choices, and there are efforts to update and revise the women's form.

The research language used in testing women's career goals and patterns suffers from the same kind of bias, and carries with it the notion that the scope of women's career aspirations is inherently very limited. For example, in many research studies, women are classified as being either career-oriented or home-making-oriented. No other possibilities exist, and women who want particular kinds of careers are considered "deviant." Now, it may be true that in actual fact today, the woman who wants to be a banker deviates from the great majority of women in the numerical sense. But classifying someone as deviant carries with it a connotation that something is inherently wrong with or lacking in that person—the woman who does not choose nursing, housewifery, teaching or social work as a career goal.

Even the terms "masculine" and "feminine" are weighted against women. That is, on many tests, women who demonstrate high career motivation are said to be "more masculine" than women in general. Again, this type of statement carries with it a judgment that the "masculine" woman is a deviant person, an incomplete person. (Men suffer from the use of the designations, too. The man who chooses to be a nurse is considered "feminine" even though he is choosing a field in which the tasks performed are similar to those performed by a physician, whose career choice is considered quite "masculine.")

Classification as "more masculine" or "more feminine" is not necessarily bad in itself. Often, however, interpretations of masculine-feminine scales are linked to concepts or notions of sexuality beyond the framework of the tests. If our increasing racial and ethnic awareness has done nothing else for us, it has taught us that such distinctions or stereotypes never remain free of value and judgment.[2] Researchers need to reconsider the language they use.

There is also a great variability among studies in definition of terms and use of terminology. Such disagreement makes comparison of findings virtually impossible. For example, "career-oriented" is defined by investigators such as Angrist to mean women who aspire to academic careers. Others use it to describe women who aspire to careers as doctors, lawyers, journalists, social workers, etc., sometimes including academicians. Still others mean any woman who remains on a given job for a given period of time and who has probably had some academic preparation for that job as a medical technician, a nurse, a secretary, a teacher, or—a banker. Agreement on definitions is needed.

By the late sixties, researchers had begun to reach several conclusions that are becoming universally agreed upon and that can be easily documented.

---

[2]The era of rigid sex-role conformity that our country is emerging from today as described by many theoreticians (Millet, Friedan, Riessman, etc.) was probably extended and confirmed by empirically-demonstrated and "objective" sex-role distinctions.

First, there is general agreement that *women are people*. To understand the newness of this concept, read any publication about women written early in this century or read Mable Newcomer's work, *A Century of Higher Education*. The kinds of discrimination characteristic of this earlier era may be less evident and susceptible to documentation today, but they still exist. For example, if you are a single woman, try to buy a house yourself. If you are pregnant, try to get an abortion. If you are single and pregnant and want your child, just try to keep it. If you are a secretary, just try to get out of fetching your boss' coffee. If you are beautiful, try to conduct a serious, intellectual discussion with a group of men. If you are not beautiful, try to engage in any kind of social interaction with them. And, if you are a female college professor with tenure, try to become the head of a department. In any of these cases, you are likely to find that you are not thought of as a person, but rather, as a woman, with different rights and abilities and without the ability to make decisions for yourself.

Second, there is general agreement among research findings that *in every category of work—education, higher education, medicine, domestic labor, factory work, office work—qualified women have lower status and lower income than men performing the same jobs.*

Third, research study results agree that *women can be more than wives and mothers.* (Labor-force participation rates of married women have been going up since 1967 in spite of the high level of unemployment in the country and prevailing economic conditions.[3])

Finally, there is agreement among many researchers and documentation to show that, from cradle to grave, *women are discriminated against in the arenas of education and work.* From the time early learning begins at home, girls are taught to behave as women, in ways that may later make them reject any but those patterns of education and career routes considered appropriately feminine. Many options that could be open to women are blocked out of their thinking by the educational process.

SCHOOLS OF THOUGHT

Anyone who reads extensively the research findings on women, education and work will discover that ideological considerations of the researchers contribute to inconsistencies and uncertain conclusions. The reader will give his own classifications to the schools of thought that can be identified. We call the two most common ideological positions of the researchers the *moderate-equivalent* and the *progressive-equal*. These classifications can be made on the basis of the hypotheses developed and the resulting interpretation of findings by researchers.

---

[3] As reported in the April 1971 issue of *Personnel Journal*, page 260.

THE MODERATE-EQUIVALENTS

Most of the works covered in this publication fit into the *moderate-equivalent school*. The hypotheses on which they are based and the interpretations given to their findings support the concept that women are capable of much more than has traditionally been believed or permitted, and, in fact, have potential in educational or vocational endeavors that is equivalent to the potential of men.

In these studies, researchers develop hypotheses and concepts of occupational, educational, and personality development that favor expansion of women's roles to include the provider role as well as the nurturer role. These studies invariably show that no harm comes from the employment of wives and mothers or of scientific or business education for girls and women. In fact, these researchers suggest, benefits may come to the woman and her family if she engages in fields of study and work not traditionally entered by women.

Such studies also have the effect, often stated as a desired outcome, of refuting what Germaine Greer has called the "eternal feminine." They show that women in atypical occupations (meaning occupations other than teaching, nursing, or social work) are still women, that women out of the labor force for ten years or more have higher achievement motivation than young women in college, and that girls who become committed to a career in college are not necessarily emotionally maladjusted, and so on.

Some of the findings of the "moderate-equivalent" studies have the effect of attacking time worn moral codes. One author found that female nursing students who behaved in a manner defined by school administrators as "indecorous" (i.e., smoking, drinking in public, etc.) were the girls who stayed with hospital nursing. Of those whom the administrators considered model students, only one became a hospital nurse. The others got married immediately after graduation and left the field or took positions in private practice.[4]

The moderate-equivalent approach increases our knowledge and understanding of what is. It also increases historical perspective and understanding of evolution and changing human behavior. And because the goal is to increase and expand the parameters of acceptable behavior for women, it can only help speed up change and refute stereotypic concepts about women.

THE PROGRESSIVE-EQUALS

Studies in the "progressive-equal" school start from the premise that men and women have the same or equal potential for human development, intellectual growth and performance. While the distinction between the two schools may seem so

---

[4] Krueger, Cynthia. DO "BAD" GIRLS BECOME GOOD NURSES? *Trans-Action*, 1968, 5(8), 31-36.

slight as to be niggling, careful examination proves otherwise. Proponents of this school, like those of the moderate-equivalent school, believe that women are capable of much more than has generally been believed, permitted, or condoned. But they are not out to prove it. They know that women suffer discrimination.

Their studies investigate relationships between people and institutions. The findings of the studies are left to stand by themselves, with no interpretation. Recently, however, such studies have begun to be interpreted to demonstrate institutional discrimination against women.

For example, studies in the prediction of college attendance reveal that sexual status is a very important variable in predicting attendance. That is, men are more likely than women to go to college and persist in college work. Such studies, instead of analyzing the reasons why or making the findings a basis for action, are left to stand. Such findings often become tools in the hands of radical feminists as they develop their arguments for women's liberation and the change of educational curriculums and programming. In fact, modern feminists such as Kate Millet or Germaine Greer could be classed as progressive-equals except for the emphasis they place on institutional change.

APPLES AND ORANGES ...

Because of the differences in the schools of thought, research reports have to be read with an understanding of the school they represent. For example, the affiliation of the moderate-equivalent school with the theory of role and position and its need to examine the individual in relation to the institution leaves no room for the study of the institution itself. In other words, no attempt is made to find out what things about colleges or about the manner in which young people are prepared for college affect the differences in rates of college attendance or success by men and women.

The moderate-equivalent school is predicated on the belief that institutions, being dominant entities and thus rigid, cannot change, and that individuals, being adaptable, singular entities, are required to modify their behavior.

Many proponents of this school acknowledge that women have a decidedly inferior position in relation to men. Their minority status is well documented in social stratification studies. They also acknowledge that no one body of research shows beyond doubt that there is or is not a biological reason for women's inferior position. Some believe that women's status should change and probably will some time in the future when humankind becomes able to take equality of the sexes for granted. Others say nothing should be done because women's current status is a natural state. They believe that women should not take their inferiority to heart or that they should accept their status and endeavor, by embracing their womanhood ever closer to their psyches, to help the world appreciate their natural qualities.

They usually point to the virtues of modern men and women and suggest that the relationship between the two should be a complementary one, in business, in school, and at home. They call on men and women to live as superior and inferior beings for their own and society's good. From an objective perspective, this approach to the issue gives rise to the claim that research conducted under the moderate-equivalent school is biased against women.

The inability of moderate-equivalent researchers to advance much beyond examination of woman except in relation to her family is one example of such bias. Study after study describes those factors that facilitate a mother's going to work, that hinder a mother's going to work, what working does to the mother's position within the family, what the community's attitude and the husband's attitude means to the working mother. While valuable, such research is always governed by considerations of what the "system" can bear in the way of deviation from it by women and takes for granted that the "system" requires normative behavior by women.

Another example is that researchers studying marital dissatisfaction in working-wife families continue to squabble over whether the wife works because of dissatisfaction at home or becomes dissatisfied after she begins to work. No one has designed or executed a study on the question that we know of, however. Such studies should be undertaken over time to add to our understanding of the dynamics of marriage. But they should also include consideration of the effect of family life as set forth by the system on the lives of women. And, they should question why some husbands work 40 hours a week and some 80. Is the father who works 40 hours a week demonstrating marital satisfaction, the father who works 80 hours a week, marital dissatisfaction? Or is it possible that anyone who chooses to work, whether male or female, simply is highly motivated to work? Why should female employment be considered a major factor in marital discord?

Some researchers, while finding greater marital dissatisfaction in working-wife families have stressed that not all the evidence is in yet, and that maternal employment may be but one small factor in a complex structure of interrelationships within an institution changing in form. In one study,[5] researchers

---

[5] Nye, F. Ivan, and Hoffman, Lois Wladis. THE EMPLOYED MOTHER IN AMERICA. Chicago: Rand McNally, 1963. 406 pages. Nye and Hoffman undertook studies to provide researchers with a compendium of research done on maternal employment from 1957 to 1962 and to fill the gap in empirical data on the topic so as to counteract conservative notions within the social sciences about working mothers. Specifically, they were attempting to refute researchers, such as Lundberg and Farnman, Bossard, and Bowlby, who declared that mothers who worked were depriving their children. Nye and Hoffman make it clear that these researchers were generalizing from findings drawn from institutionalized and otherwise severely deprived children to reach their conclusions.

discovered that when they controlled for marriage position (first marriage or remarriage), no marital dissatisfaction was found in working-wife families that were remarriages. This finding is in line with other family-life researchers' discovery that the age of the partners at time of marriage is a very important factor in marriage permanence. These researchers, however, called the finding a matter of serendipity, and attributed success in marriage to the age of the partners. But—they simply let the finding stand. Had they taken the clue of their serendipitous finding and tested for age of partners at time of marriage in first marriages, they might have found a crucial factor in marriage success that is completely unrelated to the wife's educational or career aspiration but, rather, to the age of partners at time of marriage. Using their results in this way could help to overcome the guilt that women feel about working outside the home.

Results in another study demonstrate the bias in the moderate-equivalent school. Broverman and colleagues (1969), who could be classified as proponents of the progressive-equal school, found that clinical practitioners (psychiatrists, social workers, psychologists) have perceptions of men and women that parallel the traditionally held stereotypes; their perception of what constitutes a healthy woman is definitely less healthy than their perception of what constitutes a healthy man.[6] Although the study has yet to be replicated on a larger sample, the finding is enough to question the objectivity of the moderate-equivalent school which is comprised of people from an educational and professional milieu that is similar to that of the practitioners.

Many speculations of theoreticians of the moderate-equivalent school in the middle sixties on the nature of women reveal the moderate-equivalent bias in no uncertain terms. For example, Robert Lifton[7] suggests that American women are the conservationists of the "human condition," because of the "close identification with organic life and its perpetuation" and because of the procreative function. And, because of their instinct to nurture, their function may simply be to give soul to the male world they live in, something they have always done. Although many American women today are strongly opposed to war and destruction, their opposition is not necessarily related to their procreative function, any more than to men's. Many American men today are opposed to war. Perhaps they, too, have a nurturing, procreative function.

A particularly revealing example of the moderate-equivalent bias appears in the writings of Mervin Freedman. For example,

---

[6]Broverman, Inge K.; Broverman, Donald M.; Clarkson, Frank E.; Rosenkrantz, Paul S., and Vogel, Susan R. SEX-ROLE STEREOTYPES AND CLINICAL JUDGMENTS OF MENTAL HEALTH. *Journal of Consulting and Clinical Psychology*, 1970, 34(1), 1-7.

[7]Lifton, Robert J. WOMAN AS KNOWER: SOME PSYCHOHISTORICAL PERSPECTIVES. In Lifton, Robert J., Ed. *The Woman in America*. Boston: Houghton Mifflin, 1965, 27-51.

in one article,[8] Freedman attempts to refute the assertion that women have been discriminated against, particularly the assertion by Betty Friedan that "American women have been brainwashed into acceptance of housewifery, motherhood, and conventional feminine behavior as the 'be-all and end-all' of women's existence." He reported in 1965 that women, in fact, reject conventional feminine roles but almost all of them want to get married. Sixty-nine percent of the Vassar students he surveyed said, "I would like a career."

But, although nearly 70 percent of his subjects were shown to be career-motivated, he concluded—because they also wanted to get married—that marriage and motherhood are the primary goals of the great majority of young women. His own conflict in interpretation brings into sharp focus the central conflict facing women over careers and marriage.

He does note that the "standard pattern that students envision is work in their fields or professions until children arrive, the foregoing of this work for some suitable period while the children are young, and then resumption of it." He notes that over half of the career-minded women in his sample do not anticipate conflict "when the time comes to interrupt their careers." But, one of his students says, "Deep down, marriage is more important." However, others said, "I don't want to devote all my time to my children, but I have to." Or, "It may make life miserable for my husband, but I intend to continue my career."

According to Freedman, the girls who want careers are "somewhat more intellectual, unconventional, independent (perhaps rebellious), and flexible in thinking and outlook. They are also somewhat more alienated or isolated socially."

One is tempted to ask, "If the number of girls who want a career is about 70 percent of the total, is it possible that they could all be isolated socially or alienated?" It is staggering to think that 70 percent of any group is isolated or alienated. Perhaps the 30 percent who do not want careers are the isolated group. At the least, the statement suggests that reconsideration should be given to the belief that women are not really interested in careers, and research should begin to be based on the goal of identifying patterns that will enable the majority of women to have careers if they want them.

Freedman also notes that differences between career and non-career-oriented women are sharpened by college attendance, as shown by their responses on the Ethnocentrism Scale in his study. But he never really discusses the significance of this finding. The reader is left to determine the implications of the finding. Does it mean that "rebellious" girls should not go to college? That the predilection to a career is established before girls embark on their college careers? That there is a correlation between a girl's rebellious, unconventional nature and her desire

---

[8]THE ROLE OF THE EDUCATED WOMAN: AN EMPIRICAL STUDY OF THE ATTITUDES OF A GROUP OF COLLEGE WOMEN. *The Journal of College Student Personnel*, March 1965, 145-155.

for a career? Perhaps the real significance of this finding is that if a young woman wants a career, she is forced to be rebellious and unconventional in relation to traditional standards of behavior and that colleges and universities need to reexamine their curriculums to make them more appropriate to the needs of women who want careers.

Freedman also notes that most women students "are content with the current status of educated women in the United States." However, they "recognize certain kinds of professional discrimination against women or attempts to restrain women intellectually. They are aware of these things, but they matter little to the students. The prevailing attitude is that no barriers to a woman's development are insurmountable. Any woman can manage to do whatever she wishes, provided that she possesses the appropriate capabilities." Finally, he notes that the students he surveyed in 1958 foresaw a time of greater independence and equality for women in the future and that they regarded the fervor of the feminists of the 19th century as passe, and a little odd. "The feminist ethos somehow belongs with bustles or cloché hats, a thing of the past. The sense of membership in something of an underpriveleged group, the feeling of being involved competitively with men in professions or occupations no longer move students. They do not perceive society or its chief agents, men, as imposing restrictions upon their development or behavior."

Freedman concludes by noting that the images frequently presented of dissatisfied suburban women, unhappy homemakers, and bored mothers are based on "special samples who frequent psychotherapists' offices or who bare their souls to social sicentists and journalists." He concludes that the home and family are returning to a position of primacy in American culture. In effect, he suggests that women are happy in their roles as wives and mothers, and that even though the majority of them indicate they want careers, they really do not. He suggests that there may be "considerable wisdom in the reluctance of many educated women to commit themselves to conventional careers and work after the fashion of men."

It is not our intention to take advantage of one writer among the many whose work we surveyed for this document. But his work shows the conflict that was apparent as we read and studied this literature: On the one hand are the statistics which show that women are discriminated against in their pursuit of education and in their attempts to find careers. On the other, we are told of the conflicts they face as they attempt to enter worlds formerly the province of men and as they endeavor to change their image and status. The obvious interpretations are too often missed.

It will be clear to any clear-thinking person who reads these abstracts or the works themselves that obvious implications of research findings are seldom mentioned. We refer to the implication that changes need to occur in the institutions that educate women, in the world of work, and in women themselves as they deal with the conflict between career and marriage. The obvious finding is that women are not being helped to resolve the conflict; rather they are being asked to accept their roles as wives and mothers and to make their career goals secondary to the other "natural" functions of women in society. For example, Kruger[9] reported that despite the increase in number of women entering the labor force, it is unlikely that the utilization of womanpower will improve. Sex-labeling of jobs, woman's responsibility for children and family, prejudice against women in the world of work, and other cultural limitations will continue to hinder woman's equal access to work, he said. He suggested, in conclusion, that each woman should endeavor to live as an individual and as she sees fit. How is it possible for the woman, under the conditions he described, to live as she sees fit?

Little evidence was found of change occurring in educational institutions to assist women in gaining access to fields of study normally open only to men. And the need for the professions and vocations to accept qualified women on an equal basis with men was also clearly shown.

That the researchers may be reading women all wrong is apparent from statements such as the one made by Freedman as recently as 1965 to the effect that women are no longer interested in the feminist movement. One has only to look at a newspaper or magazine to see the extent to which women today are involved in the drive for equality of opportunity and equality of results in the academic world and the world of work.

THE MEANING AND USES OF RESEARCH FINDINGS

When an investigator completes a study and formulates his conclusions, he prepares a paper for presentation at a meeting of colleagues or for publication in a professional journal. In either case, it appears that there is very little monitoring of the research effort itself as described by the investigator.

The readership of professional journals seldom comb articles for errors. More often, unless the article covers a subject with which the reader is familiar, it is read superficially. But, only a careful reading of the research on women today can provide the reader with an understanding of the procedural and interpretative wrinkles in published materials. Thus, misinterpretations of research findings pass into the consciousness of countless numbers of practitioners who, in turn, incorporate them into day-to-day ministrations to the detriment of countless students and society in general. People who refuse to believe the interpretations cling to their own biases, and some researchers base further study on information derived from superficial reading.

---

[9] Kruger, Daniel H. WOMEN AT WORK. *The Personnel Administrator*, 1964, 9(July-Aug.), 7-15.

The misuse of research tools or the failure to test them adequately before drawing conclusions is common. Take the case of the work of Lorraine Eyde[10] who attempted to measure work values and work motivation in college-educated women. She is to be commended for using the answers and attitudes of women to develop new instruments, something that had not been done before in research on women. What she discovered was that women with high motivation for work valued mastering skills and keeping and staying abreast of new developments in their fields in relation to work, which is different from the assumed reasons men work.

Eyde makes no outsized claims or conclusions for her instrument or her findings, which, one could speculate, are not sex-specific, especially when controlling for level of education. But, her measures must be used on a sample of men with similar educational and class background to discover if this is so or not. In the face of the change in college populations today, one could suggest that the work values and commitment of male college graduates would be similar to those of females. There is anecdotal and research evidence to support this.

For example, businessmen complain rather frequently of an inability to draw high-powered college graduates into their firms because of the students' interest in serving the welfare of the community. Ralph Nader's very large volunteer staff is another case in point. And Maslow[11] reports in his study of new federal employees that men and women have the same job priorities.

Unfortunately, Eyde's instrument has been used in another study to reach some very outsized conclusions. The rationale for the recent research, conducted by Helen Wolfe in 1970,[12] was to give educators and counselors of women some real idea, which they have not had previously, of the educational and counseling needs of the majority of women who will be looking for jobs within the next ten years in the entire state of New York. (The research was sponsored by the State Department of Education.) Wolfe used a much larger sample population than Eyde—1,874 women working in various organizations throughout the state; Eyde's sample consisted of 188 college graduates. The findings were similar to Eyde's and in some ways more startling: the women consistently indicated, much more so than the women in Eyde's sample, that they valued mastery-achievement

---

[10]Eyde, Lorraine Dittrich. WORK VALUES AND BACKGROUND FACTORS AS PREDICTORS OF WOMEN'S DESIRE TO WORK. Bureau of Business Research Monograph Number 108. Columbus, Ohio: The Bureau of Business Research, College of Commerce and Administration, The Ohio State University, 1962. 88 pages.

[11]Maslow, Albert P. JOB FACTORS, ATTITUDES, AND PREFERENCES AFFECTING THE RELATIVE ADVANCEMENT AND TURNOVER OF MEN AND WOMEN IN FEDERAL CAREERS. American Psychological Association, Washington, D.C. Paper presented at the APA convention in Miami, 1970. 11 pages.

[12]Wolfe, Helen Bickel. WOMEN IN THE WORLD OF WORK. University of the State of New York, The State Education Department, Division of Research, 1969. 65 pages.

in relation to work, and that they showed no interest in work for its economic rewards—at all. (The latter finding of no interest in economic rewards is much more striking than Eyde's findings, and contradicts findings of many other investigators.)

Wolfe's information is valuable for the educator and counselor of women. They can now design retraining programs for older women, vocational programs for younger women, and all other job-related programs for women with this in mind. But Wolfe takes it one step further, noting that most of the jobs that women will be entering in the next decade will be low-paying, low-status jobs (which she determined on the basis of government data) and that since they do not seem to mind and, in fact, show a pathological avoidance of jobs requiring supervisory skills and leadership qualities, the training of women should not provide them with these skills and qualities. Wolfe interprets the findings this way without endeavoring to use Eyde's instruments on a similar male sample. She interprets the findings this way even though, by her own admission, the sample was over-represented with middle- and lower-class women who were middle-aged, married, and living with their husbands. In fact, 83 percent of the sample population was made up of these women, a figure which does not correspond at all to the statistical number of such women in the country.

One can fault Wolfe on her interpretation of her findings. She may believe that there is nothing wrong in her subjects' work goals. Or she may think it wrong, but that one should not upset the apple cart and throw such people into stressful situations. Whatever her motivations, we can await the outcome of further research to gain greater insight.

However, her findings and interpretations have been described in a position paper put out by Harcum Junior College, in Pennsylvania, without any mention of the sample population breakdown. An uninformed reader has no way of weighing the merits of the study without going back to the original report. And from the "tenor" of the study description, the unaware reader would have no reason to question the study. Thus, another half-formulated insight, filtered through existing misapprehensions concerning women, passes into the "scientific" psyche. Because it confirms conventional wisdom it will be embraced vigorously by those who desire and need "hard data" to secure their position and will be rejected out-of-hand by those who desire aggrandizement of women's status.

What of the scientific impurities of the progressive-equal school? The adherence of its proponents to the notion of equality between the sexes would seem to be proof of bias if one did not subscribe to that notion. Objectively speaking, however, bias is not the better noire of the progressive-equal school. Rather, overzealous promotion of the ideology and rejection of existing theory in the face of entrenched traditions may well be. But this fault, if it is in fact a fault, is move evident in dissertations on theories of equality vis-a-vis other theories of stratification and their effect on institutions. Examples of this that come to mind immediately are Millet's *Sexual Politics*, Germaine Greer's *The Female Eunuch*, several articles in *The Voices of the New Feminism,* and others. In some instances, progressive-equal theorists abandon as totally worthless all existing research and findings. This abandonment may be self-defeating. What could do justice to the issues concerning women would be clearly conceived analyses of existing research with a view to developing new research designs that are as objective as possible. The first step that must be taken to achieve this is complete reevaluation of conceptual models for research.

TOWARD OBJECTIVITY AND ACTION-BASED RESEARCH

Several research reports abstracted in this volume reflect objectivity. They also fall under the ideology of the progressive-equal school. Lorraine Eyde's is one of them. Matina Horner has found that some individuals evidence a need to avoid success, and that the women in her sample evidenced such a need much more frequently than men, especially in competitive situations with men. Rather than offering her findings as proof of some sex-linked characteristic peculiar to women, Horner suggests that it is more evidence of the damage that double-standard socialization can have.

Torrance, in the course of investigating creativity, attempted to examine how 11-year-old boys and girls figured out the principles of scientific toys.[13] He encountered a major problem, however. The little girls refused to participate because girls "were not supposed to know anything about things like that." Rather than force them into it then or leave it at that, he spoke to school administrators and parents about the need for them to disabuse girls of their notions about sex-specific traits. The parents and school administrators cooperated, and after a year, Torrance ran the experiment again without any trouble. As Rossi notes, the second time around, the girls participated gladly. Both boys and girls enjoyed themselves and did equally well with the toys. The only difference that remained was that "both boys and girls thought the contributions the boys made were better than the contributions the girls made."

A follow-up investigation of the sample to determine the effect of altered attitudes or "social action," as Rossi calls it, in parents and children would be interesting and highly valuable. Similarly, it would be interesting to see if "social action" or intervention would increase our understanding of Horner's findings. Perhaps some "consciousness raising" would change the outcome of *her* test.

---

[13] Rossi, Alice. BARRIERS TO THE CAREER CHOICE OF ENGINEERING, MEDICINE, OR SCIENCE AMONG AMERICAN WOMEN. In *Women and the Scientific Professions: The M.I.T. Symposium on American Women in Science and Engineering.* Cambridge, Mass.: The M.I.T. Press, 1965. 250 pages.

The book, *The Development of Sex Differences*, edited by Eleanor Maccoby, is an excellent resource document. For the most part, it is free of any bias against women. The conclusions that can be reached from reading the papers compended in this book on sex differences is that we do not really know whether these differences are biologically determined. But, in a discussion of the effects of socialization, Maccoby notes that the same environmental factors affect boys and girls *differently*.

"The brighter girls tend to be the ones who have not been tied closely to their mothers' apron strings, but have been allowed and encouraged to fend for themselves. The brighter boys, on the other hand, have had high maternal warmth and protection in early childhood."

She goes on to state that, based on the research she reviewed, it appears that

"The two sexes have somewhat different intellectual strengths and weaknesses, and hence different influences serve to counteract the weaknesses and augment the strengths."

It would be interesting to hear Maccoby's definition of "apron strings" and how it really differs from "high maternal warmth and protection." High maternal and *paternal* warmth and protection are probably both necessary to the upbringing of boys *and* girls. To assume, as she does, that girls who evidence incipient autonomy are getting something different than boys similarly inclined comes depressingly close to the "separate but equal" theory of racial accommodation. It is probable that early socialization has a greater impact on individuals than we imagine now since all individuals, male and female, have to sort out all kinds of complex expectations and anticipations and realities as soon as they enter this world.

So where are we now? There are several other examples of objective research in this volume. They generally appear as surveys and statistical investigations, with little interpretation included. Some leaders of the progressive-equal school of research have developed strong arguments for looking at the world as it really is and developing mechanisms *now* for eradicating the double standard.

In her paper given at the MIT Symposium cited earlier, Rossi makes some pertinent points related to educational and career development of women in the 1970s. She, for one, has decided to stop worrying about the role of biology in such development. She has noted, as have others, that even if it is a factor, what it has to do with humankind in a very complex society must be minimal in terms of intellectual development. She also makes a very strong case for educating the public to actual job requirements of many careers. Noting that many people still think engineering requires complete outdoor living and doctoring requires complete abstinence from "normal" pursuits, she shows how such stereotypic thinking keeps many women (and men) out of fields in which there are desperate needs for skilled manpower.

Astin, a co-author of this bibliography, has repeatedly demonstrated the worthlessness of myths concerning women in the world of work, specifically women with doctoral degrees, such as the myth that women are too emotional to be productive in any professional endeavor; that women are bad workers because they leave the job as soon as they marry or have a baby; that women cannot become experts in any kind of endeavor because they are too busy doing other things, and so on. Her research and findings are always presented within the framework of the fact that women constitute more than half the world's population, and that it is no small matter that they are discriminated against from cradle to grave. It is very easy to lose sight of this little statistic in everyday activities, and much research evidences almost no realization of the fact.

In terms of future research, one could say that the sky is the limit and Dr. Astin has treated this topic at great length elsewhere in this publication. What is *the* most crucial factor in the development of intellect in men and women? Is there such a factor, or do many factors combine to create intellect? What really goes on between parents and children in terms of socialization? How immutable is gender identification? What effect does intervention have on sex-role attitudes *and* intellectual functioning? What happens to women and men who get their consciousness raised with respect to women? Is existing research susceptible to re-evaluation in more objective light? How much of the "mothering" role can be taken over by institutions and mother surrogates? And so on.

There are several comprehensive surveys of existing literature on women, their education and careers. As a starting point, they are invaluable. But whatever research is undertaken from now on must acknowledge that women are people with great competence and that to discriminate against them is unjustified under any circumstances. There is no longer time for clucking about the injustices of the world when they are uncovered during the course of research. We have ample evidence that our institutions, one and all, are changing. Whether we are passing into a state of anarchy, as many would have it, is highly questionable. The many changes that have occurred in the last 50 years, we must remember, were often met with admonitions from countless experts that the downfall of the American ideal was imminent. The working man reduced his hours on the job from 60 to 50 to 40 and now to 35, women got the vote, children now instruct themselves with machines in the classroom, and so on.

History tells us that the downfall did not occur. Similarly, as women continue to press for change in their status, the world will not collapse in total chaos. As more organized women's groups act to eradicate the double standard, their number will increase, and still more changes will occur. Whether the changes are for the better depends on one's perspective. But certainly, just as it is true that time waits for no man, nor men for time, women will wait for neither.

Determinants of Career Choice

1

Almquist, Elizabeth and Angrist, Shirley S. CAREER SALIENCE AND ATYPICALITY OF OCCUPATIONAL CHOICE AMONG COLLEGE WOMEN. *Journal of Marriage and the Family*, 1970, 32(2), 242-249.

Deviance Hypothesis. Enrichment Hypothesis. Occupational Choice.

College graduate women who plan careers in occupational fields dominated by men are not necessarily different—in terms of dating, level of participation in extracurricular activities, relationship to parents, and work values—from non-career oriented women who choose traditionally feminine occupations. A woman's propensity for a career may be a reflection of the effects of broadening and enriching experiences such as her mother's work history, her own work experience, or the influence of occupational role models on her plans for a career in an atypical occupation rather than a reflection of deviant experiences such as disruptive family experiences, low dating frequency, etc. More research is needed into the nature of the "deviance hypothesis" and the "enrichment hypothesis" as measures of career planning of college women.

To obtain these findings, researchers conducted a four-year longitudinal study of 110 students in the same class in a women's college of a coeducational university. Questionnaires about adult role perceptions, occupational choice, career plans, work experience, school activities, and dating and social life were administered to the subjects each Fall. Interviews were conducted twice with each student during the four years.

2

Almquist, Elizabeth and Angrist, Shirley S. ROLE MODEL INFLUENCES ON COLLEGE WOMEN'S CAREER ASPIRATIONS. Paper Presented at the American Sociological Association annual meeting, 1970. 33 pages. In press, *Merrill-Palmer Quarterly*.

Career Motivation. Role Influences.

Career-salient women (those completing four years of college and planning careers) perceive their professors as having a more positive evaluation of their academic ability than non-career-salient women do. They were most strongly influenced by college professors and occupational role models. Career salience is also related to choosing fields of work chosen by male peers and to choosing male-dominated occupations. Career-salient women are likely to have more work experience in a greater variety of jobs than non-career-salient women. Career salience is not significantly associated with the educational level of either parent or with the father's occupational level, but career-salient women are more likely to have working mothers, while non-career-salient women have mothers who tend to be more active in leisure pursuits.

Non-career-salient women are likely to feel that peers, family members, or no one influenced their decisions not to have careers. Non-career salience in women is associated with: sorority membership, being married, being engaged, going steady and positive perception of parental characteristics. It is not strongly related to the amount of dating in college.

To obtain these findings, the researchers administered questionnaires every Fall (from freshman to senior years) to 110 students in one class of a women's college in a private coeducational university. Tape-recorded interviews were also conducted among a sample of the class every Spring.

3

Anastasi, Anne and Schaefer, Charles E. BIOGRAPHICAL CORRELATES OF ARTISTIC AND LITERARY CREATIVITY IN ADOLESCENT GIRLS. *Journal of Applied Psychology,* 1969, 53(4), 267-278.

Creativity. Academic Superiority.

Creative adolescent girls in the fields of writing and art exhibit a high degree of continuity and pervasive interest in their chosen fields. They become involved in creative activity during childhood; receive early recognition of their efforts from parents and through exhibits; experience unusual, novel and diverse experiences in early chilhood (i.e., imaginary companions); come from educationally superior family backgrounds, and exhibit greater identification with their fathers than with their mothers. When the creative writers, creative artists, and control groups are compared, the writers differ significantly more from the controls than the artists.

This finding supports previous research findings on the biographical correlates of creative adolescent boys (Schaefer and Anastasi, 1968). It was undertaken to describe the antecedents and correlates of creativity in the female high-school population. The sample of 400 high school girls identified by their teachers as creative and academically superior was divided into four subgroups: creative-art, control-art, creative-writing, and control-writing. A biographical inventory including 166 questions on physical characteristics, family history, educational history, and leisure time activities was administered to each subject along with three standardized tests, including the Guilford Alternate Uses and Consequences test.

4

Angrist, Shirley S. CHANGES IN WOMEN'S WORK ASPIRATIONS DURING COLLEGE (OR WORK DOES NOT EQUAL CAREER). Paper presented at the Ohio Valley Sociological Society annual meeting, 1970. 26 pages.

Career Motivation. Marriage Aspiration. Sex Roles. Higher Education.

During their four years in college, women tend to develop a flexible approach to combining their interests in advanced education, work, and family life. Their plans revolve around meshing schooling and careers according to their family situations. In the freshman year, the women have a low desire for a career, and this declines even more until the junior year. Only among seniors is a conversion to career salience evident; of the 42 percent of seniors who wanted careers, only seven percent wanted them all four years.

Work motivation of the female students increased steadily and sharply under conditions of familial convenience or need during the four years. Nearly all students surveyed wanted to marry and have children, and most preferred to delay marriage until after graduation. The preference to "marry later" declined, however, after the freshman year. As sophomores, the women chose atypical, male-dominated occupations, but by the senior year, over half chose typically feminine jobs, most in professional fields. Commitment to an occupation deepened each year, but over the four years, most students vacillated between decision and indecision, and 35 percent were still undecided as seniors. The number of students planning advanced education after graduation increased over the four years, and three-fourths of the students were oriented toward seeking advanced education by their senior year.

To obtain these findings, the researcher examined data from a questionnaire administered to the students in one class of a women's college of a coeducational, technically oriented university. Panel analyses were carried out on a core group of girls to provide key information on changes occurring during the four years.

See also: Angrist, Shirley S. THE STUDY OF SEX ROLES. Margaret Morrison Carnegie College Reprint No. 15, Carnegie-Mellon University, Pittsburgh, Pa. 15213, 1967. 17 pages.

In a discussion of the implications of these research findings on current sex-role theory, the author examines the finding that women learn to operate on the basis of contingency orientation, with marriage as the key contingency. The author submits that sex role is made up of four elements—label, behavior, expectations, and social location—and that the changing sex role norms in society justify observing actual role involvement by actors as a complex phenomenon rather that as a series of individual roles.

5

Angrist, Shirley S. PERSONALITY MALADJUSTMENT AND CAREER ASPIRATIONS OF COLLEGE WOMEN. In press, *Sociological Symposium*, 1971. Mimeo. 16 pages.

Deviance Hypothesis. Career Motivation.

College girls who want careers are not necessarily emotionally maladjusted, despite existing research that suggests that career-salient women are deviant in terms of normative role expectations and behavior. This conflict in findings points up the need for social scientists to observe caution before equating personality differences with personality maladjustment. This finding partially supports the hypothesis that no association exists between college maladjustment and career aspiration and refutes the conclusion that career aspiration is associated with deviance.

Responses were analyzed of 87 women students in one class of the women's college of a large, coeducational, technically oriented university to questionnaires and tests used in a larger, longitudinal study of another class. The sample included majors in physical and biological sciences, home economics, social sciences, and humanities. The extent to which a girl foresees work as an integral part of her adult life was measured with the 11-item Life Style Index. Maladjustment in college was measured by the College Maladjustment Scale (Kleinmuntz, 1960 and

1961), a 43-item scale derived from the Minnesota Multiphasic Personality Inventory. Subjective measures of health status (Rossi) and personality (Bass, 1962) were also used along with data on those subjects who sought school counseling services.

6

Angrist, Shirley S. SOURCES OF INFLUENCE ON WOMEN'S CAREER ASPIRATIONS: FAMILY, COLLEGE, AND SELF. Paper prepared for the School of Urban and Public Affairs, Carnegie-Mellon University, 1970. Mimeo. 30 pages.

Life Style Aspirations. Role Influences. Higher Education. Employment.

Career and non-career life-style aspirations of women college students are influenced by factors within and outside of college. Mothers and teachers have influence, and college experiences strengthen the college women's own inclinations, goals, and values. A girl will become more career salient if she values higher education and a high-level occupation, is self-oriented, prefers to enter an atypical field for women, chooses a liberal arts major, and favors a modern concept of family life.

Although the impact of college on career aspirations manifests itself between freshman and sophomore years, the greatest impact is in the senior year. The many factors that influence life-style aspiration suggest viewing career-oriented women as products of enriching and varied life experiences, rather than as products of negative experiences. A woman college student who chooses a vocational or applied field for her major usually indicates a movement away from career commitment; a choice of professional field does not necessarily imply career commitment.

In this study, subjects interested in academic fields which require advanced education showed the most evidence of career commitment. Undertaken to expose those factors that affect a woman's willingness to incorporate career pursuits with family roles in adulthood, the study is based on analysis of a core group of 87 women students who entered the women's college of a large, coeducational, technically oriented university as freshmen and graduated in four years.

7

Angrist, Shirley S. THE IMPACT OF HIGHER EDUCATION ON WOMEN. Paper prepared for the School of Urban and

Public Affairs, Carnegie-Mellon University, 1970. Mimeo. 44 pages.

Higher Education. Life Style Aspirations.

Review of existing literature on the impact of higher education on women fails to support the conclusion that college has no influence on a woman's later life styles. But it does reveal the lack of a clear picture of the precise effects college has on women. Life style, in terms of social class, income, and occupation, is predictable. But life style, in terms of the priority placed on advanced education, marriage, family, leisure, and work, is less predictable. The ability to predict the extent to which an adult woman will pursue a career on the basis of career salience in college is low. The author reviews the research on the effects of college on both men and women. She points out the need for more research on the influence of college on later life styles of women.

8

Astin, Helen S. CAREER DEVELOPMENT OF GIRLS DURING THE HIGH SCHOOL YEARS. *Journal of Counseling Psychology*, 1968, 15(6), 536-540.

Career Prediction.

This study, utilizing the Project TALENT Data Bank, was designed to predict the career plans of 817 female high school seniors from their personal characteristics as ninth graders and from selected environmental characteristics of their high schools. Twelfth grade girls who planned college careers either in sciences or in teaching were differentiated from girls who planned either to become housewives or to do office work on the basis of their families' higher socioeconomic status, their greater mathematical ability, their more frequent choices of a college preparatory curriculum, and their strongest measured interest in physical science. Moreover, girls who anticipated scientific or teaching careers in the twelfth grade had been more likely than those choosing other careers to report in the ninth grade that they had already had counseling regarding college plans. When some of the high school characteristics were examined, girls who attended larger high schools were more likely to plan careers in the professions and sciences; girls who attended smaller high schools were more likely to aspire to teaching and office work.

9

Astin, Helen S. FACTORS ASSOCIATED WITH THE PARTICIPATION OF WOMEN DOCTORATES IN THE LABOR FORCE. *Personnel and Guidance Journal*, 1967, 46(3), 240-245.

Higher Education. Employment. Career Commitment.

Ninety-one percent of the women who received doctoral degrees in 1957 and 1958 were in the labor force in 1965, and 81 percent of them were working full time. Fewer women trained in the natural sciences were in the labor force than women in other disciplines. Among married women with doctorates, those who married after receiving the degree were less likely than those who married during or before graduate school to be working full time seven to eight years later. Women who worked full time on their first job after receiving the doctorate were more likely to be employed full time later, even if they had children of preschool age. These findings emerged from a survey of all women U.S. doctoral degree recipients of 1957 and 1958.

10

Astin, Helen S. STABILITY AND CHANGE IN THE CAREER PLANS OF NINTH GRADE GIRLS. *Personnel and Guidance Journal*, 1968, 46(10), 961-966.

Career Planning. Career Prediction.

Changes in career plans made between the ninth grade and one year after high school were examined in a sample of 7,061 girls from the Project TALENT Data Bank. Longitudinal changes for five career groups (natural sciences, professions, teaching, office work, and housewife) were examined as functions of selected aptitude and interest measures. Girls who changed career plans differed from girls who maintained the same plans over time in each career group on most of the measures employed. There is a tendency for brighter girls to change from initial careers in office work and housewife more frequently than the less able girls. Those who shift out of the career-oriented groups—sciences, professions, and teaching—are scholastically less capable than those who maintain the same plans over time. The results suggest that the career changes that take place during the high school years result partly from a greater self awareness and from the development of more realistic views about various occupations. Thus, as girls mature, their vocational plans become more appropriate. Brighter girls tend to raise their occupational aspirations and less capable girls aspire to less intellectually demanding careers.

11

Astin, Helen S. and Myint, Thelma. CAREER DEVELOPMENT AND STABILITY OF YOUNG WOMEN DURING THE POST HIGH SCHOOL YEARS. Monograph in press, *Journal of Counseling Psychology*, 1971.

Secondary Education. Career Prediction. Higher Education.

An investigation of the personal characteristics of female high school seniors and their career development experiences during five years after high school reveals that prediction of career choices of such women is possible. The best environmental predictors of career outcome were education and marital status—receiving a B.A. degree predicted pursuit of careers in the natural sciences, the professions and teaching. Being married and having children right after high school was predictive of housewife status later on.

Personal characteristics of the subjects as high school seniors could be used to predict career outcomes five years later and to differentiate among girls with different career goals. That is, girls with high scores on tests of scholastic aptitudes (especially on tests of mathematical ability) and girls who early aspire to an advanced degree usually choose fields that require greater career commitment—the natural and social sciences, the professions and teaching. Girls with lower scholastic aptitude and fewer academic interests usually aspire to be office workers or become housewives. Girls of this orientation who get married plan to be housewives; those who remain single tend to pursue office work. An early interest in business and management, a B.A. degree, full-time employment after high school, and unmarried status are all predictive of the pursuit of a career in business. Artistic interests and aptitudes and earlier plans to become an artist predict later plans to remain in the field of art.

Although almost half of the women studied changed their career plans between their senior year in high school and five years later, counselors and educators can rely on early patterns and interests to predict later career outcomes. Since scholastic ability appears to be an important factor, counselors should help girls with high aptitudes to plan for future education. They should also assist and encourage girls with high ability but low aspiration to recognize their skills and the possibility that office work and marriage may not meet their needs completely at a later date. These results were obtained through multiple discriminate analysis of longitudinal data from the Project TALENT Data Bank on 5,387 women who were tested in the national program in 1960, 1961 and 1966.

12

Bailyn, Lotte. NOTES ON THE ROLE OF CHOICE IN THE PSYCHOLOGY OF PROFESSIONAL WOMEN. In Lifton, Robert J., ed., *The Woman in America.* Boston: Houghton Mifflin, 1965. Pages 236-246.

Higher Education. Occupational Choice. Work Satisfaction.

Women with high levels of education and training are confronted with choices that differ significantly from choices faced by men in similar circumstances. These choices create problems that also differ from those faced by men. Men do not have problems related to choosing to work, since society assumes that they will do so. Women professionals, in contrast, have to choose to work. Because of traditional attitudes toward woman's role in relation to the family, the woman who makes this choice does not have the options of mobility and autonomy that men have. This lack of options undermines the effectiveness of professional women. Highly trained women have the freedom to choose, but this choice leads to confusion and lack of work satisfaction. In order to examine this situation (which has not been done to date), investigators must acknowledge the need to hold constant the environmental factors that differentiate between women professionals who work and those who do not.

13

Bott, Margaret M. MEASURING THE MYSTIQUE. *Personnel and Guidance Journal*, 1968, 46(10), 967-970.

Role Influences. Methodologic Problems.

The learning of the feminine role is reflected both in interest and personality measures in a manner consistent with Gough's description of "psychological femininity" (1952). That is, in contrast to men, women prefer white-collar work and the conventional female role. They demonstrate feelings of sensitivity, responsiveness to social interaction, and a sense of compassion and sympathy. Women who express preferences most typical of other women have learned well that woman's role is to please and earn approval from others. Women who express interests more typical of men than women are highly psychological-minded, more responsible, less reliant on the approval and support of others, less likely to conform to social demands, more sensitive to inner needs and characteristics, and more likely to carry through in responsibility.

Further study of the hypothesis that existing instruments used in research on women may be measuring different rather than the same aspects of a complex phenomenon resulting from learned behavior will shed more light on the problem of aspiration and achievement of women. This study lends support to the belief that personality differentiation based on ranked masculine-feminine (M-F) scores is possible. However, there is no relationship between educational goal choices and similarity of interest to the measured femininity pattern. These findings were obtained by analyzing, in relation to M-F scores and rank, the personality characteristics (as measured by the California Psychological Inventory) and the educational goal variables (collected from existing data) of 517 freshmen women enrolled in a large state university in 1962.

14

Brown, Donald R. VALUE CHANGE IN COLLEGE WOMEN. *Journal of the National Association of Women Deans and Counselors,* 1962, 25 (June), 148-155.

Higher Education. Educational Counseling. Value Change.

College women experience value changes as a result of value conflict and individual growth. But because they make a culture-approved and supported commitment at an early age to narrow and perhaps false images of femininity, their metamorphosis from adolescent to adult is different and probably more conflict-ridden than that of college men. To reduce conflict and maximize growth, educators must acknowledge the demands of child bearing on women and fit the higher educational process to these demands. Women college students should also have more models to identify with such as women educators who have equal status with men and who are successfully handling the roles of scholar, teacher, wife and mother. An increase in the acceptability and availability of part-time employment and education will provide women with families an opportunity to gratify their needs as intelligent adults in a setting larger than the home. Empirical research shows that different student subgroups seek and have different college experiences and that colleges are able to accommodate this pluralism. Educators must seek to accommodate one more subgroup—women. The author cites existing research and theory, specifically the Carnegie-Mellon Vassar Study, to develop his argument.

15

Campbell, David P. THE VOCATIONAL INTEREST OF BEAUTIFUL WOMEN. *Personnel and Guidance Journal*, 1967, 45(9), 968-972.

Career Motivation. Employment.

Women who choose modeling as their career prefer the dramatic to the routine, the unstructured to the structured, are verbally rather than mathematically oriented, and generally have exhibitionistic life styles. Interviews with photographers, agency directors and models revealed that many have over-exaggerated ideas of self-worth, marital problems, and troubles. Despite the limitations of the sample, evidence suggests a negative relationship between beautiful women and science. The 100 fashion models in the sample had a median age of 27 and were working part time as models, usually because full-time work was not available. All subjects were administered the Strong Vocational Interest Blank for Women to distinguish specific interests and dislikes.

16

Clark, Edward T. INFLUENCE OF SEX AND SOCIAL CLASS ON OCCUPATIONAL PREFERENCE AND PERCEPTION. *Personnel and Guidance Journal*, 1967, 45(5), 440-444.

Career Motivation. Occupational Choice.

Middle-class boys (53%) and lower-class girls (85%) showed a significant preference for white collar and professional occupations; only 30% of lower-class boys and 68% of middle-class girls exhibited this preference. Ten percent of both middle- and lower-class boys chose doctor or lawyer as a future occupation with middle-class boys choosing baseball player and engineer as their second and third choices. In comparison, lower-class boys expressed a preference for fireman and policeman. Overwhelmingly, both middle- and lower-class girls chose either nursing or teaching. However, more middle- than lower-class girls selected housewife. There was very little overlap in occupational preference of the boys and girls. The investigator cautions against generalizations since these conclusions reflect only a present conception of occupational choice and, thus, are not indicative of the children's adult aspirations. The sample for the survey consisted of 159 boys and 139 girls of lower socioeconomic status (90% black) in grades three through six of a New York City school and 206 boys and 204 girls in the same grades in suburban New York schools. The city school subjects were in a Higher Horizons program and the suburban school subjects scored above the national norms on standardized tests. All subjects were administered the Vocational Apperception Test, and Hollingshead and Redlich's Occupational Scale, and all were interviewed.

17

Cook, Barbara Ivy Wood. ROLE ASPIRATIONS AS EVIDENCED IN SENIOR WOMEN. Doctoral Dissertation (Purdue U.), 1967.

Marital Status. Career Aspiration. Career Motivation. Higher Education.

Marital status is the most significant determinant of the expectations senior college women have about careers and homemaking. When women who wanted careers were compared with those who wanted to be homemakers, the career-oriented women were found to be: mostly single, less conforming on religious beliefs, more likely to have working mothers, and more committed to using their academic competencies. They scored higher than the homemaking-oriented women on independence and confidence-attitude scales. The homemaking-oriented women were more likely to be: married, liberal arts majors, more influenced by men in decision-making, less committed to future working. They scored high on the "need for security." Differences were found among the women in different academic areas. For example, science majors were generally found to be hard workers; home economics and liberal arts majors were more homemaking oriented. The 296 senior college students in this 1966 study were administered a questionnaire on role preferences and academic areas. They were divided into groups: strong career (10%), preference toward career (30%), combined career and homemaking (41%), strong homemaking (8%), preference toward homemaking (7%), and other (5%). Groups were compared on variables such as: home background, marital status, academic and professional expectations, adult role models, etc.

18

Davis, Natalie Zemon. A STUDY OF 42 WOMEN WHO HAVE CHILDREN AND WHO ARE IN GRADUATE PROGRAMS AT THE UNIVERSITY OF TORONTO. Preliminary Report, Graduate Students' Union, University of Toronto, May 1966. Mimeo. 25 pages.

Higher Education. Career Planning. Marital Status.

Married women graduate students with children seemed deeply interested in their fields of study and determined to get their degrees. Encouragement from professors was not a significant factor in the decision to pursue graduate studies, but their husbands' attitudes were. Even though these women had problems combining study with domestic responsibilities, most had found ways to manage. Usually they had to realign priorities so that family and work came first, entertaining and housekeeping second. These findings and other characteristics of the women were derived from the responses of 42 married women with children to a mailed questionnaire and from verbal comments made during a general discussion. More than half of the women were under age 35; most had children under 10.

19

Elton, Charles F. and Rose, Harriett A. SIGNIFICANCE OF PERSONALITY IN THE VOCATIONAL CHOICE OF COLLEGE WOMEN. *Journal of Counseling Psychology*, 1967, 14(6), 293-298.

Occupational Choice. Career Motivation.

Vocational guidance counselors should be aware that differences in intellect and personality influence vocational choices of women who appear to have similar perceptions of feminine roles. A discriminant analysis (with interpretations based on Deutsch, 1944) of the vocational choices of freshmen women revealed that passively feminine women can be expected to enter artistic and aesthetic vocations; actively feminine women to choose social service occupations; and women with more masculine interests to choose occupations in business-finance, science, or medicine. Brighter girls choose the arts and humanities, while those less academically able enter secretarial arts. Further research among mature women in various fields is needed. Undertaken because of a scarcity of research on factors affecting women's vocational choices and because so many college-educated women are now entering the labor force, the study replicated the research of Bereiter and Freedman (1962) except for the use of a different population and different variables. The sample was 637 freshman women at the University of Kentucky. All subjects were administered the Omnibus Personality Inventory, Form C, which measures five personality factors, and the American College Test (ACT). All selected their primary vocational choices from a list of 83 academic majors.

20

Empey, Lamar T. ROLE EXPECTATIONS OF YOUNG WOMEN REGARDING MARRIAGE AND A CAREER. *Journal of Marriage and Family Living*, 1958, May, 152-155.

Vocational Counseling. Role Expectations.

It appears that young women still favor traditional female roles rather than occupational equality. Among young high school and college women surveyed, the majority preferred marriage over a career or marriage with a traditionally feminine career. High school girls had more specific occupational plans than high school boys and the college women and men were at the same level. The tendency for young women to view themselves as filling a dual role seems to be growing, but the average age at marriage is falling. Educators and counselors should develop ways to help young women plan for careers before the last year of high school. This is especially important since the majority of women in this study aspired to professional female occupations, positions that few would attain. These findings were obtained from probability samples of 1,981 (about one-tenth) of all public high school seniors in Washington State in the Spring of 1954 (1,004 girls and 977 boys) and of 403 undergraduates (190 girls and 213 boys) at the State College of Washington in 1952-1953.

21

Entwisle, Doris R. and Greenberger, Ellen. A SURVEY OF COGNITIVE STYLES IN MARYLAND NINTH GRADERS: 4 VIEWS OF WOMEN'S ROLES. The Johns Hopkins University, Center for the Study of Social Organization of Schools, Report No. 89. Baltimore, Md.: Johns Hopkins University Press, 1970. 26 pages.

Role Perceptions. Secondary Education.

The educational system appears to promote wide differences in the concepts young men and women have of female work roles. In this study on whether women should work, hold the same jobs as men and derive satisfaction from problem-solving, girls expressed more liberal views than boys. However, both groups responded negatively when questioned about women holding men's jobs. The greatest disparity existed on the question of whether women should work at all, with girls responding positively and boys negatively. Among the boys, blacks were more liberal than whites. Blue-collar whites were more conservative than middle-class whites. A greater discrepancy was found between middle-class girls and boys than between blue-collar girls and boys. The middle-class sex difference is especially marked among the high IQ group. This suggests that girls with greatest work potential will face strong opposition from their future mates. To obtain these findings, the authors analyzed the responses made by 270 boys and 305 girls to questions on women's role. Subjects were ninth graders in seven schools of various socioeconomic and ethnic composition in Baltimore. This was part of a larger survey on the relationships of social class and cognitive style variables.

22

Eyde, Lorraine D. WORK MOTIVATION OF WOMEN COLLEGE GRADUATES: FIVE-YEAR FOLLOW-UP. *Journal of Counseling Psychology*, 1968, 15(2), 199-202.

Career Commitment. Work Values. Higher Education.

The work commitment of 10-year college alumnae was more closely related to the self-rating obtained five years earlier than was the work commitment of five-year alumnae originally studied as seniors. Work values for both groups remained fairly stable. These findings differ significantly from previous research (Baruch, 1966), indicating a need for more research. To analyze the stability of women's commitment to paid employment and the stability of their personal reasons for working outside the home, the researcher tested 51 graduates of 1953 and 55 graduates of 1958 of Jackson College on their work motivation in 1958; she retested 106 of the women in 1963. Instruments used were two experimental scales: Desire-to-Work Scale, a measure of work commitment, and the Ranked Work-Value Scale, a measure of the reasons women work for pay.

23

Eyde, Lorraine Dittrich. WORK VALUES AND BACKGROUND FACTORS AS PREDICTORS OF WOMEN'S DESIRE TO WORK. Bureau of Business Research Monograph Number 108. Columbus, Ohio: The Bureau of Business Research, College of Commerce and Administration, The Ohio State University, 1962. 88 pages.

Career Motivation. Commitment Prediction. Work Values. Higher Education.

Undertaken to develop a means of predicting work motivation of women, the study reveals work-motivation patterns of seniors and five-year alumnae of Jackson College that relate to marital and financial success and to number and age of children. The study was also designed to test the validity of the instruments developed by the investigator to measure work motivation.

Specific findings included: 1) involvement in college activities was associated with work motivation in seniors, but not in alumnae; 2) lower middle-class background—as measured by father's occupation and mother's education and work experience—was associated with high motivation in alumnae but not in seniors; and 3) desire for graduate level education in seniors and the actual attainment of a graduate degree by alumnae were associated with high work motivation. Perceived adequate and minimum income of husband was related to work motivation. That is, highly motivated alumnae, and some seniors, indicated relatively lower salaries as being adequate for their husbands more often than the less motivated women. Alumnae with high motivation indicated a need for variety in activities and a need for a sense of achievement in work outside the home.

To obtain these findings, the author constructed a Work Value Scale (drawing on existing theory and previous research and on a preliminary questionnaire) to measure such values as Dominance-recognition, Economic independence, Interesting activities-variety, Mastery-achievement, Social. The sample population consisted of 70 seniors (class of 1958) who responded to the developmental questionnaire, 58 of the same seniors who responded to a final questionnaire, and 60 alumnae (class of 1953).

24

Farley, Jennie. GRADUATE WOMEN: CAREER ASPIRATIONS AND DESIRED FAMILY SIZE. *American Psychologist*, 25(12), 1099-1100.

Career Aspiration. Family Size.

The importance a woman attaches to a career may affect her other plans and aspirations considerably, especially the future size of her family. Career women want small families with two or fewer children; noncareer women anticipate larger families, with three or more children. These results are based on a questionnaire survey, sponsored by the National Organization of Women (NOW), of 530 women enrolled in graduate programs at large universities in May 1969. Half of the questionnaires (263) were returned and the women were categorized as career or noncareer on the basis of their responses to a question about the importance of a career to their life style. Of the sample, 65 percent of the respondents were single, 73 percent were in their first or second year of graduate school, and most did not anticipate conflict between marriage and career.

25

Farmer, Helen S. and Bohn, Martin J., Jr. HOME-CAREER CONFLICT REDUCTION AND THE LEVEL OF CAREER INTEREST IN WOMEN. *Journal of Counseling Psychology*, 1970, 17(3), 228-232.

Career Commitment. Marital Status. Career Conflict.

The level of vocational interest among women, regardless of their marital status, would be raised if home-career conflict were reduced, according to these authors, who used the SVIB-W to measure the effect of home-career conflict on the level of women's vocational interests. Fifty working women, 25 married and 25 single, took the SVIB-W twice, the first time with standard instructions and the second with experimental, home-career conflict-reducing instructions. It was predicted, and substantiated, that scores on Career scales would increase and scores on Home scales would decrease after the experimental instructions and that marital status would not be a significant variable in home-career conflict reduction.

26

Faunce, Patricia Spencer. PERSONALITY CHARACTERISTICS AND VOCATIONAL INTERESTS RELATED TO THE COLLEGE PERSISTENCE OF ACADEMICALLY GIFTED WOMEN. *Journal of Counseling Psychology,* 1968, 15(1), 31-40.

Higher Education. Educational Commitment.

Comparison of the personality characteristics and vocational interests of freshmen women who later graduated from college and freshmen women who did not revealed that the nongraduates had less insight into their own personality structures, greater difficulty in interpersonal relationships, more problems with impulse control, and greater inner tensions. Graduates were more insightful, conventional, temperate, modest, and self-confident. They were also relatively free from tension and had better ego strength and psychological integration. The findings were obtained through analysis of the results of MMPI tests administered to 723 gifted freshmen women graduates and 526 nongraduates. The SVIB scores of graduates were higher on the Author, Librarian, English Teacher, Social Science Teacher, Psychologist and Lawyer scales; nongraduates had higher scores on the Buyer, Stenographer-Secretary, Office Worker, Business Education Teacher, and Dietician scales.

27

Flanagan, John C. QUALITY EDUCATION FOR GIRLS. *Women's Education.* 1966, 5(4), 1-7.

Employment. Educational Aspirations. Higher Education.

Today's education for girls is not adequate to prepare them for world-of-work occupations or for roles as parents and citizens. In this age of science and mathematics, most girls do not take enough courses in these subjects to prepare them for occupations in such fields. High school girls tend to aspire to typically feminine occupations such as teaching, nursing, and social work rather than to professional or scientific occupations. Although almost as many girls as boys continue education beyond high school, many fewer girls than boys plan to obtain college degrees. Lack of financial support seems to be an important factor in this. These conclusions were based on the findings from Project TALENT, a long-range study of a sample of 440,000 of the nation's high school students. Tests of academic aptitude and achievement were administered to all students along with a questionnaire on present and future educational and career goals. Two follow-up surveys were done, one in 1961 and one in 1966. Two more follow-ups are planned, ten and twenty years after high school graduation.

28

Freedman, Mervin B. THE ROLE OF THE EDUCATED WOMAN: AN EMPIRICAL STUDY OF THE ATTITUDES OF A GROUP OF COLLEGE WOMEN. *The Journal of College Student Personnel*, 1965, **March**, 145-155.

Role Expectations.

Examination of the attitudes of a group of college women concerning woman's role revealed little interest in the matter on the part of the women. Most of the women wanted careers or work outside the home, but they wanted them when they are compatible with family life. They evidenced no real dedication to careers. Like many college men, they wanted to live in a world without conflict between countries, races, or sexes. It may be that college women are preparing for a future in which the conventional work ethic loses meaning because of technological advances. The women demonstrated a desire to be subordinate to their husbands and to avoid competition with men. They all expressed the belief that they would be able to fulfill themselves and combine marriage and career without much difficulty. These findings are based on conversations over four years with 49 seniors at an Eastern women's college and on test data on three classes of students enrolled in the same college.

29

Gysbers, M.C., Johnston, J.A., and Gust, T. CHARACTERISTICS OF HOMEMAKER- AND CAREER-ORIENTED WOMEN. *Journal of Counseling Psychology*, 1968, 15(6), 541-546.

Career Motivation. Life Style Satisfaction.

When the two groups are compared, career-oriented women are more intellectual and enterprising, and homemaker-oriented women are more social and conventional. In contrast to homemaker-oriented women, for example, career-oriented women are more apt to be single, less patient when personal needs conflict with needs of other persons, more skeptical about religion, more interested in news magazines than women's magazines, and less content with their own emotional adjustment. They also are likely to have completed more education and to have more highly educated parents. They describe themselves as moderately attractive physically, and they derive more satisfaction from social interactions with men than they do with women. The subjects, students at the University of Missouri, were tested with the SVIB-W between 1958 and 1964. In 1967, they took the SVIB-W again, and filled out an Occupational Questionnaire and a Homemaker-Career Opinionnaire. The sample for the first test session was 52 homemaker-oriented and 29 career-oriented women; in the second, there were 34 homemaker-oriented and 15 career-oriented women.

30

Harmon, Lenore W. ANATOMY OF CAREER COMMITMENT IN WOMEN. *Journal of Counseling Psychology*, 1970, 17(1), 77-80.

Career Motivation. Commitment Prediction.

Women in this study became committed to careers after entering college, and they did so for motivational rather than circumstantial reasons. At age 18, there were no differences in the career plans of career-committed and noncareer-committed women. Similarly, these women indicated no differences in levels of satisfaction in home life or accomplishment of husbands 15 years later. However, career-oriented women do stay in college longer, earn higher degrees, and work more. To obtain these findings, the researcher analyzed the questionnaire responses of women who had entered the University of Minnesota between 1953 and 1955 and had scored high on the Social Worker Scale on the Strong Vocational Interest Blank. Respondents were classified as career-committed or noncareer-committed on the basis of the reported "usual career" whether they were employed currently or not. Of the 169 subjects, 94 were classified as career-committed and 75 as noncareer-committed.

31

Harmon, Lenore W. PREDICTIVE POWER OVER TEN YEARS OF MEASURED SOCIAL SERVICE AND SCIENTIFIC INTERESTS AMONG COLLEGE WOMEN. *Journal of Applied Psychology*, 1961, 53(3), 193-198.

Career Prediction. Methodologic Technique. Vocational Counseling.

The response to "usual occupation" on the Women's SVIB can be used to determine the predictive validity of earlier results of vocational interest tests. After 10 to 14 years had elapsed, the Social Worker scale of the SVIB was shown to be 70 percent accurate in predicting commitment of women to social service work. The Laboratory Technician scale of the SVIB, also taken earlier, was 61 percent accurate in predicting future commitment to work in science occupations. However, early SVIB profiles did not differentiate significantly between career- and homemaker-oriented women.

In view of these findings, counselors using the SVIB for women should know that a high score accurately predicts future occupational behavior for all women rather than just for those who actually become career women later; the scores suggest choices, whether a woman has plans for a career or not. The sample consisted of two groups of women who scored A or B+, 196 on the Social Worker scale and 125 on the Laboratory Technician scale. They were tested in 1953 and 1955 as entering students in the University of Minnesota and retested in 1966 and 1967. Subjects also furnished information on their vocational history and current vocational status.

32

Harmon, Lenore W. STRONG VOCATIONAL INTEREST BLANK PROFILES OF DISADVANTAGED WOMEN. *Journal of Counseling Psychology,* 1970, 17(6), 519-522.

Methodologic Technique. Occupational Choice.

The Strong Vocational Interest Blank for Women can be useful in recognizing individuality in disadvantaged women and helping them choose job-training experiences. Pattern analysis (Stephenson, 1961) of the profiles of culturally different and educationally disadvantaged women participating in job training programs was used to obtain this conclusion, contradicting an earlier hypothesis that the SVIB-W scales of such women would be flat and/or all the same. Although most of the profiles had identifiable interest patterns, the majority of the women had high scores on the Medical Service and Nonprofessional Occupational groups. At the scale level, considerable diversity was noted among women who had high scores on the Nonprofessional group of occupations.

33

Harmon, Lenore W. THE CHILDHOOD AND ADOLESCENT CAREER PLANS OF COLLEGE WOMEN. *Journal of Vocational Behavior,* 1971, 1(1), 45-56.

Occupational Choice. Career Prediction. Vocational Counseling.

The occupations considered by a group of women during different developmental periods in their lives suggest that counselors of college women should encourage women to consider occupational choices that cross over cultural and sexual stereotypes. And, attention should be paid to unusual occupational preferences of adolescent girls because they provide clues to future occupational behavior.

As preadolescents, the freshmen college women in this study had expressed more varied and sophisticated occupational preferences than they did by the time they got to college. By the time they were freshmen, their choices were in typical feminine fields of work. Thus, interest in professional and technical occupations in girls at this age should be encouraged, rather than discouraged on the basis of not being women's fields. The most popular and persistent vocational preferences, after housewife, were educational and social service occupations. The least persistent occupational preferences involved unusual talent, long periods of training, or short noncollege training (i.e., physician, actress, dental assistant).

The sample was 1,188 freshmen women at the University of Wisconsin who completed the Life Planning Questionnaire for Women which is designed to ascertain the educational and occupational level of family members and the attitudes of family members toward maternal employment. A list of 135 occupations (drawn from the occupation list of the SVIB-W) was also utilized to ascertain all occupations they had ever considered and record the age when they first considered them as well as the reasons for the change.

34

Harmon, Lenore W. WOMEN'S INTERESTS—FACT OR FICTION? *Personnel and Guidance Journal,* 1967, 45(9), 895-900.

Methodologic Technique. Career Prediction. Marital Status.

Measurements of women's vocational interests on the Strong Vocational Interest Blank (SVIB) have not been as accurate as measures of men's interests. A review of the attempts to measure women's vocational interests (Hogg, 1928; Manson, 1931; and Strong, 1943) produced the conclusion that women were basically working as a stop-gap until marriage and motherhood. However, the influx of married women into the labor force in recent years suggests that work is not only a stop-gap measure but also an indication of career commitment. Vocational directions of married women can be differentiated from those of women in general by altering the key for the SVIB, using different item selection and weighting. Findings support the hypothesis that marital status per se is not the only factor affecting career interest and that high vocational interest scores can be obtained through the use of different item selection and weighting. The study suggests the heterogeneity of women's interests and the resulting difficulties in measuring them. The sample consisted of a married subgroup of Strong's original Psychologist and Laboratory Technician group of 1959. The data included their SVIB scores and personal histories.

35

Harmon, Lenore W. WOMEN'S WORKING PATTERNS RELATED TO THEIR SVIB HOUSEWIFE AND "OWN" OCCUPATIONAL SCORES. *Journal of Counseling Psychology,* 1967, 14(4), 299-301.

Career Prediction. Methodologic Issues.

Women who have worked for long periods of time score no higher than housewives or women who have never worked on the Strong Vocational Interest Blank section on work patterns. The vocational interests of women were tested and compared after they had been classified in five groups based on the amount of time they had worked over a 25-year period: consistently working, not working at all, working until marriage or first child, working most of the time, and recently returned to work. The work patterns of the women were related to their scores on the SVIB Housewife scales and to their scores on the scales in the occupations in which they had worked. Undertaken to demonstrate the validity of the women's SVIB, the study neither proved nor disproved its validity. The sample was a subgroup of 98 subjects from the University of Minnesota classes of 1933 through 1936 who had served as the sample for the Williamson and Bordin (1940) and Campbell (1965) studies. Data included family histories, analysis of work patterns, and classification into one of five vocational groups.

36

Harmon, Lenore W. and Campbell, David P. USE OF INTEREST INVENTORIES WITH NONPROFESSIONAL WOMEN: STEWARDESSES VERSUS DENTAL ASSISTANTS. *Journal of Counseling Psychology,* 1968, 15(1), 17-22.

Methodologic Validity. Career Prediction.

Differential measurement of vocational interests of women at nonprofessional levels is feasible using an updated version of the SVIB-W, although some technical problems remain. Using criterion groups of 440 airline stewardesses and 417 dental assistants to develop mean SVIB profiles and scales, researchers found that the dental assistant profile had peaks on the Nurse, Housewife, and Office Worker scales. The stewardess profile peaked on the Music Performer and Model scales. Overlap of scores between the criterion groups and a Women-In-General

(W-I-G) group (Campbell, 1966) was 26 percent when the Dental Assistant scale was used and 17 percent when the Stewardess scale was used.

37

Hawley, Marjorie J. THE RELATIONSHIP OF WOMEN'S PERCEPTIONS OF MEN'S VIEWS OF THE FEMININE IDEAL TO CAREER CHOICE. Doctoral Dissertation (Claremont Graduate School and University Center), 1968.

Role Perceptions. Career Motivation.

Married women and unmarried women have different views of men's attitudes toward women's roles and behavioral differences between the sexes. Married women tend to believe that men are not inclined to differentiate between the sexes in intellectual capacity and appropriate use of intelligence. But they also believe that men view competitive behavior as "unfeminine." Women engaged in traditional feminine occupations—homemaker, teacher, social worker—more frequently view behavior as an outgrowth of biological differences between the sexes. Women in careers usually pursued by men are less likely to believe that behavior is related to sexual status. The researcher classified 86 subjects into three career styles: Homemaker Career, Feminine Career, and Androgynous (traditionally male) Career. Using a 35-item Likert-type scale to measure perceptions of male views of the feminine ideal, the researcher used multivariate analysis of variance to make three comparisons: Married versus unmarried, homemakers versus androgynous careerists, and homemaker and feminine career groups versus the androgynous group.

38

Heist, Paul. MOTIVATION OF COLLEGE WOMEN TODAY: A CLOSER LOOK. *Journal of the American Association of University Women*, 1962, 56(1), 17-19.

Career Motivation. Career Achievement. Higher Education.

Since 1900, traditional expectations of the "fairer sex" have been breaking down. In spite of the great number of women attending college today, they do not seem to be achieving or performing at expected levels in relation to college enrollment and completion of a college education. The reasons for such underachievement are complex, including lack of motivation, too many social activities, too much dating, etc. The author describes five types of women college students: 1) the socially oriented student who lacks serious academic goals and who is looking for a husband, 2) the career-oriented student concerned primarily with gaining skills to make a living after college, 3) the nonconformist intellectual who is politically active and generally more scholastically oriented than the first two types, 4) the young scholar who tends to devote her energy to a single discipline or subject, and 5) the general student looking for a well-rounded college education. The nonconformist intellectual and the young scholar appear to be the types who enter graduate and professional education most frequently. If marriage does not interrupt their education, many general students will continue their graduate and professional education.

39

Helson, Ravenna. PERSONALITY CHARACTERISTICS AND DEVELOPMENTAL HISTORY OF CREATIVE COLLEGE WOMEN. *Genetic Psychology Monographs*, 1967, 76, 205-256.

Creativity. Higher Education. Role Influences.

Young women identified as creative—showing considerable potential for creative work in the arts, sciences, and humanities—have personality characteristics like those of creative men. Their parents are also likely to have the same characteristics. Creative subjects seemed to have modeled themselves after their fathers more than their mothers, but most were close to both parents. Non-creative women, in contrast, seemed to have had more companionable relationships with their fathers.

Creative women had stronger symbolic interests and higher levels of aspiration in childhood, and these characteristics put them at an advantage during periods when ego-building was rewarded and at a disadvantage when sex-role learning was rewarded. As college seniors, most creative women planned to combine career and marriage. They married men with whom they had creative values in common and who tended not to be domineering. Those who were inactive five years after graduation appeared to be finding fulfillment as wives and mothers and to have fewer strong creative traits than those who were active.

As a group, the creative women increased more than others in flexibility, complexity of outlook, and the "expression of impulse in conscious action and attitude." Similarity between these findings and previous findings (Helson, 1967) would tend to support their generality. In this study, senior women regarded as highly creative by the faculty of Mills College were compared with the rest of the class and with a smaller group of seniors in 1958 and 1960.

40

Horner, Matina S. THE PSYCHOLOGICAL SIGNIFICANCE OF SUCCESS IN COMPETITIVE ACHIEVEMENT SITUATIONS: A THREAT AS WELL AS A PROMISE. Unpublished manuscript, Harvard University, June 1970. Mimeo. 18 pages. Available from author.

Success Avoidance. Sex Roles. Achievement Motivation.

The anticipation of success, especially in interpersonal competitive situations, can sometimes be regarded with mixed feelings, if not outright fear. Anticipation of success over a male can provoke anxieties in women such as fear of loss of femininity and self-esteem. Thus, fear of success can inhibit positive achievement and directed motivation and behavior. The anticipation of success over a male may even pose a threat for some men. Research is needed on the psychological significance of success as a function of sex. Research is also needed into the function of intrinsic and extrinsic motivation to achieve in interpersonal competitive situations. The goal of this study was to increase understanding of the determinants of motivation for achievement. The researcher observed the performance of 88 men and 90 women (predominantly freshmen and sophomores at a major university) in one interpersonal competitive situation with a member of the opposite sex and one with a member of the same sex. In addition, each subject was observed in one noncompetitive achievement-oriented situation in which he worked alone. Verbal cues were used in further experimentation to measure success-avoidance motivation.

See also: Horner, Matina S. FAIL: BRIGHT WOMEN. *Psychology Today,* 1969, 3(6), 36-41.

41

Houts, Peter S. and Entwisle, Doris R. ACADEMIC ACHIEVEMENT EFFORT AMONG FEMALES: ACHIEVEMENT ATTITUDES AND SEX ROLE ORIENTATION. *Journal of Counseling Psychology,* 1968, 15(3), 284-286.

Sex Role Perceptions. Educational Prediction. Achievement Motivation.

A significant relationship was found between achievement and school grades in girls who consider masculine competitive behavior to be appropriate to the female role. High achievement and, to a lesser extent, high grades can be predicted for girls demonstrating a masculine sex-role orientation. Further research into the question of what attitudes are related to achievement in women who have a traditional perception of the female sex role is needed. Undertaken to replicate previous studies (French and Lesser, 1964; Lesser et al., 1963) and to develop a direct test that could predict academic performance, the study is based on the results of a questionnaire administered to 405 tenth-grade girls from four high schools. Subjects were divided into high and low verbal ability groups for purposes of analysis.

42

Hoyt, Donald P. and Kennedy, Carroll E. INTEREST AND PERSONALITY CORRELATES OF CAREER-MOTIVATED AND HOMEMAKING-ORIENTED COLLEGE WOMEN. *Journal of Counseling Psychology,* 1958, 5(1), 44-49.

Career Motivation.

Homemaking-oriented women score higher on interest in occupations such as buyer, housewife, elementary teacher and secretary; career-oriented women score higher on interest in occupations such as artist, author, librarian, psychologist or physician. The women who want to be homemakers score higher on measures of heterosexuality and succorance, but career-oriented women score significantly higher on achievement and endurance. These were the findings among 386 freshman women at Kansas State College in 1956-1957 who were administered a questionnaire designed to distinguish women who wanted careers and marriage from those who planned to work only until marriage. All subjects were administered the Strong Vocational Interest Blank and the Edwards Personal Preference Schedule.

43

Johnson, Ray W. PARENTAL IDENTIFICATION AND VOCATIONAL INTERESTS OF COLLEGE WOMEN. *Measurement and Evaluation in Guidance,* 1970, 3(3), 147-152.

Career Motivation. Sex Role Identification.

Career interests of college women do not necessarily reflect masculine identification, but their mathematical-scientific interests may. This finding was obtained by administering two independent measures of parental identification (Heilbrun, 1965) to 139 women volunteers from introductory psychology classes at a state university. Results were divided into high and low identification groups, and SVIB scores were compared.

44

Jones, Paul W. SEX DIFFERENCES IN ACADEMIC PREDICTION. *Measurement and Evaluation in Guidance,* 1970, 3(2), 88-91.

Academic Prediction. Methodologic Issues.

More research is needed before a sex differential can be assumed in the prediction of academic performance from achievement scores. To obtain this finding, scores on the STEA and SAT and the academic grades of 284 male and 263 female seventh-grade students were analyzed, with the result that better academic prediction for females was not suggested. This conflicts with findings of significant sex differences in favor of females in other attempts to predict academic performance.

45

Krueger, Cynthia. DO "BAD" GIRLS BECOME GOOD NURSES? *Transaction,* 1968, 5(8), 31-36.

Nursing. Commitment Prediction.

Describes the behavior of student nurses in a hospital school of nursing in two self-selected social subgroups—the "wild group" and the "ideal group"—and the administrators' treatment of each group. Administrative rules governing nonacademic behavior and expected student attitudes may relate to being a good student nurse, but not to being a good working nurse. All the students judged by the administration as "wild" took jobs after graduation in hospitals. Of the students judged as "ideal," all except one took jobs in private practice, which is less demanding, or left the profession for marriage. The traditional emphasis on virtue seems completely irrelevant and should be abandoned, especially in light of the great need for more qualified nurses.

46

Kuvlesky, William P. and Lever, Michael. OCCUPATIONAL GOALS, EXPECTATIONS, AND ANTICIPATORY GOAL DEFLECTION EXPERIENCED BY NEGRO GIRLS RESIDING IN LOW-INCOME RURAL AND URBAN PLACES. Paper presented at the Southwestern Sociological Society Meeting, Dallas, Tex., March 1967. 25 pages.

Career Expectations. Occupational Choice. Goal Deflection.

Undertaken to replicate research on occupational goal expectations of youth from differing socioeconomic backgrounds, the study indicated that rural and urban Negro girls had similar occupational goals and expectations. However, both groups also expected that they would be deflected from achieving their goals. Responses of the subjects indicated that most girls in each group wanted and expected to get high-status, white-collar jobs. They did not want or expect to become housewives, operatives or unskilled workers. Rural girls had lower occupational goals and higher rates of anticipated deflection from the achievement of these goals. These findings support theories of high achievement orientation within our society (Merton, 1956). The low prospects for occupational mobility for these members of an economically disadvantaged racial minority will probably lead the subjects to become either "innovators" or drop-outs, thus increasing tension in society. The authors analyzed the responses of 99 rural and 170 urban subjects to two open-ended questions designed to indicate occupational goals and expectations. Anticipated deflection was measured by comparing measures of goals and expectations.

47

Leland, Carole. WOMEN-MEN-WORK: WOMEN'S CAREER ASPIRATIONS AS AFFECTED BY THE MALE ENVIRONMENT. Doctoral Dissertation (Stanford U.), 1966.

Role Influences. Sex Role Perceptions. Career Planning.

The post-graduation plans and the factors which affected these plans were compared in 559 women from a state college and a private university. Most women in both groups planned to marry and have children, but only a few expected marriage to be their only commitment in life. Almost half expected to do graduate work, and a third planned careers. Both groups denied the influence of other people on their specific career plans, but women who were closely associated with a male (husband, boyfriend, etc.) were more likely to have been influenced in their career planning. Other influences included parents, professors, and the women's own interests in work or involvement in a particular field of study. The two groups differed most on their attitudes toward the feminine role. Women at the private university exhibited a stronger commitment to both marriage and career. Generally, the findings indicated that women's aspirations or expectations are altered throughout life by the desires and careers of men and that decisons about marriage and work are often based on family and friendship experiences. Findings were based on data from questionnaires, interviews, and test measures.

48

Leland, Carole A. and Lozoff, Marjorie M. COLLEGE INFLUENCES ON THE ROLE DEVELOPMENT OF FEMALE UNDERGRADUATES. Paper prepared for the Institute for the Study of Human Problems, Stanford University, Stanford, California, 1969. 100 pages.

Higher Education. Educational Counseling. Life Style Prediction. Autonomy.

In this study of "able college women," the variation in backgrounds and college experiences of the subjects tends to refute the widely-held notion that college women can be classified in terms of educational needs because of homogeneity of background. The level of individual development in autonomy among the subjects ranged widely. Analysis of the subjects' scores on the Scholastic Aptitude Test, the Omnibus Personality Inventory Scale, perceptions of feminine role, and interview protocols from previous research (Katz, 1967 and 1969) revealed similarities of backgrounds and motivation among the subgroups, however. Data were also provided on a variety of educational interventions and on the prediction of life styles after college. A critical survey of two decades of research in educational and occupational development of women precedes the report. To obtain the findings, the authors examined the interview protocols (spanning a period of four years) of 49 able women students at Stanford University. The subjects were classified in terms of autonomy or the individuals' assumption of personal responsibility for self-definition and self-development. The interview data on the subjects were analyzed in detail.

49

Lewis, Edwin C., Wolins, Leroy, and Yelsma, Julie J. THE ACADEMIC INTERESTS OF COLLEGE WOMEN: A FACTORIAL STUDY. *Personnel and Guidance Journal*, 1967, 46(3), 258-262.

Higher Education. Methodologic Technique. Educational Prediction.

It is generally assumed that college women do not differ greatly in their educational goals and their reactions to educational experiences. This assumption derives from the seemingly homogenous interest patterns found by many researchers among college women. However, when the factor analytic technique is used, consistent attitude differences can be validly identified.

Based on the assumption that differences in attitudes toward the same academic experiences would reflect differences in educational needs and goals, this study was designed to measure the attitudes of women college students toward various courses. An attempt was made to locate factors that would suggest meaningful variations. The subjects were 94 juniors, 105 seniors, and 103 alumnae in the College of Home Economics at Iowa State University. Researchers used an IBM 7074 computer to determine significant interactions on a seven-question attitude scale (based on the certainty method) of a three-way factorial design ("person-course-question"). Because of differences in variance components, subsequent analyses were designed to reliably estimate a person's general attitude toward the courses. Intercorrelations were developed for the factor analysis which was conducted by the method of maximum likelihood (Wherry, 1959; Hemmerle, 1965).

50

Lovett, Sarah Lee. PERSONALITY CHARACTERISTICS AND ANTECEDENTS OF VOCATIONAL CHOICE OF GRADUATE WOMEN STUDENTS IN SCIENCE RESEARCH. Doctoral Dissertation (U. of California), 1968.

Career Prediction. Occupational Choice. Sex Role Perceptions.

Data indicates that women scientists are consistently more nonperson oriented, that they identify more with their fathers than their mothers, and that they report tomboy activities as children. Social workers, in contrast, are people-oriented, exhibited feminine play activities as children and experienced less consistent, impersonal discipline processes as children. There was no significant difference between the scientists and social workers regarding feminine role, and both groups were similar on achievement, endurance, and autonomy. A large number of women in each group had working mothers and parents who encouraged independent, self-reliant children. Investigators examined the women's personal characteristics and vocational choices using a questionnaire, the Adjective Check List, and a Personal Interest Inventory Identification Scale.

51

Lubetkin, Barry S. and Lubetkin, Arvin I. ACHIEVEMENT MOTIVATION IN A COMPETITIVE SITUATION: THE OLDER FEMALE GRADUATE STUDENT. *Journal of Clinical Psychology*, 1971, 27(2), 269-271.

Graduate Education. Achievement Motivation. Role Perceptions.

Older women enrolled in graduate school after a substantial time lapse in their education exhibit greater achievement motivation than younger women or undergraduate students. As previous research has indicated, older women have been more successful in throwing off cultural inhibitions related to women's achievement. The "Zeigarnik Booklets" were administered to 95 male and female subjects in five groups of 19 each to obtain the findings. Four groups consisted of paired graduate and undergraduate students. The fifth group consisted of female graduate students enrolled in a program for older women returning to graduate school at Kent State University and one male "stooge." Because previous research (Atkinson, 1953; Weiner, 1966) has shown that high achievement motivation is revealed when individuals remember more incompleted than completed tasks (the Zeigarnik Effect), the authors measured achievement motivation by the percentage of incompleted tasks recalled minus the percentage of completed ones. The Newman-Keuls Sequential Range Tests and other techniques were used to confirm the findings.

52

Lunneborg, Patricia W. SEX DIFFERENCES IN APTITUDE MATURATION DURING COLLEGE. *Journal of Counseling Psychology*, 1969, 16(5), 463-464.

Sex Differences. Higher Education.

Men and women college students mature in aptitude at the same rate. This finding extends previous research on maturation rates of high school students (Droege, 1967). Tests are needed to see whether men and women mature the same during the ages of 17-23 when they are not in college. The author retested 59 female and 67 male seniors (all highly intelligent) with the multi-aptitude precollege battery they had taken as high school seniors in Washington state. Although sex differences usually exist on tests taken by university freshmen, with females superior in verbal abilities and males in nonverbal abilities, the verbal differences in this sample were absent and the nonverbal differences were present when the subjects were high school and college seniors.

53

Lyon, Ella Rhee. CAREER INTERESTS OF MARRIED WOMEN WITH COLLEGE DEGREES. Doctoral Dissertation (Northwestern U.), 1967.

Occupational Choice. Higher Education. Family Responsibilities.

Responses of college-educated women to a national survey suggest that most women are primarily family-oriented and prefer traditionally female educational and occupational choices. Many women indicated the arts and glamour occupations such as fashion design or advertising as their career choices. However, as occupations that would best fit their present interests and family responsibilities, most chose fields in which they were already trained. Very few women chose jobs or fields without consideration of family responsibilities and their training. For this study, 400 married women aged 24-45 with college degrees were selected randomly from the membership of the American Association of University Women. Five groups of women were identified: negative worker, positive worker, career-oriented housewife, satisfied housewife, and ambivalent housewife. One conclusion was that if conventional career patterns hold true, these women will re-enter the job market at age 40.

54

Masih, Lalit K. CAREER SALIENCY AND ITS RELATION TO CERTAIN NEEDS, INTERESTS AND JOB VALUES. *Personnel and Guidance Journal*, 1967, 45(7), 653-658.

Sex Differences. Career Motivation.

In a comparison of men and women on the degree (high, medium, low) of career saliency, men appeared to have a generally higher degree of career saliency or direction than women.

Women with high career saliency showed strong needs for achievement, endurance and fame. There were more women in the low-salient group than in the high or medium group. Thus, few women exhibited needs for achievement, endurance and fame. It appears that women are less career-oriented than men and that high career saliency is typically masculine. However, the same criteria were used to evaluate both men and women, and these were biased in favor of men's occupations. The sample was 68 male and 118 female junior and senior college students who were administered the Edwards Personal Preference Schedule, the Guilford-Zimmerman Temperament Survey, and the Strong Vocational Interest Blank. All subjects were also interviewed.

55

Matthews, Esther and Tiedeman, David V. ATTITUDES TOWARD CAREER AND MARRIAGE AND THE DEVELOPMENT OF LIFE STYLE IN YOUNG WOMEN. *Journal of Counseling Psychology*, 1964, 11(4), 375-383.

Life Style Motivation.

An examination of the relationship between attitudes toward career and marriage and the life styles of girls and young women reveals that attitudes toward career and marriage differ during developmental stages. A pseudo-career drive seems to appear in some women during early adolescence. Major themes that affect a woman's life style during early maturation are (in order of importance): 1) a consideration of the male's reaction to the use of her intelligence; 2) the struggle over the possible position of dominance of men at work and the "place" of women at home; 3) conflict between the demands of family and work on the time of a wife and mother; 4) dilemmas of timing in dating and marriage, and 5) general acceptance of the feminine role. A cross-sectional representation of the developmental stages of early adolescence, adolescence, and young adulthood is included. Life styles are represented by high school curriculum elected and plans for education, career and marriage during the decade ahead. The research sample included 1,237 girls and young women.

56

Metzger, Sherrill M; Bollman, Stephan R.; Hoeflin, Ruth M; and Schmalzried, B.A. COMPARISON OF LIFE STYLES OF HONORS, NON-HONORS WOMEN. *Personnel and Guidance Journal*, 1969, 47(7), 671-674.

Higher Education. Career Commitment. Career Aspirations. Life Style Aspirations.

In this study, women in a college honors program showed greater commitment to careers than non-honors women. They planned to continue working after marriage and parenthood and to earn advanced degrees. They hoped to raise themselves to higher occupational levels. In comparison, non-honors students were more satisfied with home responsibilities and with their present life styles. They were more active as volunteers in community activities. Marriage and a shift from rural to urban residence provided the greatest post-college changes in the life styles of both groups of women. The sample was 81 women who had participated as freshmen (1958-1961) in a study of an honors program in the College of Home Economics at Kansas State University. The 35 honors students, who scored in the top ten percent on aptitude tests, were matched with a control group of 46 women on size of hometown, size of high school, and socioeconomic level of family. In 1966, all subjects were administered an 11-page follow-up questionnaire designed to obtain background information, occupational experiences and plans, college experiences, community activities, and future goals.

57

Mitchell, Elmer D. INTEREST PROFILES OF UNIVERSITY WOMEN. *Vocational Guidance Quarterly*, 1957-1958, Winter, 85-89.

Educational Motivation. Higher Education.

A 25-year study of men and women students at the University of Michigan suggests that men show greater interest in the sciences, shop work, economics and civics. Women show greater interest in English, history, foreign language, home planning and gift making. However, men and women who are interested in the same fields have similar interest profiles. The author compared the interest profiles of men and women in 13 major fields of university study and described the interest profiles of women in four occupational fields dominated by women. The profiles were drawn from data on 8,946 women students.

58

Norfleet, Mary Ann. PERSONALITY CHARACTERISTICS OF ACHIEVING AND UNDERACHIEVING HIGH ABILITY

SENIOR WOMEN. *Personnel and Guidance Journal*, 1968, 46(10), 976-980.

Achievement Motivation.

Gifted senior women identified as underachievers appeared to be less mature and less adequately socialized than gifted senior women identified as achievers. Using the CPI to measure the extent of socialization and the Adjective Check List to measure self-perceptions, the original hypothesis of the study was supported—achievers scored higher than underachievers on the CPI, and the two groups described themselves differently on the ACL. The sample group consisted of 55 senior women in good standing at a large state university. The sample was divided into two groups on the basis of cumulative grade-point averages and SCAT scores.

59

Perucci, Carolyn Cummings. MINORITY STATUS AND THE PURSUIT OF PROFESSIONAL CAREERS OF WOMEN IN SCIENCE AND ENGINEERING. *Social Forces*, 1970, 49(2), 245-258.

Minority Status. Engineering. Science. Career Patterns. Marital Status.

A comparison of social characteristics of women and men trained as scientists and engineers reveals that male and female graduates obtain similar employment on their first jobs after graduation from college. They have similar levels of technical and supervisory responsibility, but the men earn more than women. The differential in salary and job level increases over time. Some believe that the disparity between men and women in career paths and success stems from the "fact" that women, single or married, do not need or value income and prestige as much as married men do. But this study showed no discernible difference between the sexes on work values. A comparison of women with careers and without careers indicates that those with careers are less likely to be married, and are more likely to be childless if they are married or to have only one child. To obtain these findings, the author analyzed data on 3,589 science and engineering degree recipients (bachelor's, master's and doctor's degrees) at a large Midwestern university between 1947 and 1964.

60

Psathas, George. TOWARD A THEORY OF OCCUPATIONAL CHOICE FOR WOMEN. *Sociology and Social Research*, 1968, 52(2), 253-268.

Occupational Choice. Vocational Theory. Sex Role Differences.

Previous research by the author and examination of theories point up the need for development of a new theory of occupational choice for women based on the relationship between sex role and occupational role. Existing theories suggest that the average worker is male, despite increased female participation in the labor force. Vocational theories differ with respect to variables that affect occupational choice, however, and fail to accommodate those factors that affect women differently from men. Intention to marry, time of marriage, reasons for marriage, and husband's financial status and attitude toward a working wife have profound effects on a woman's occupational choice. For example, it is unlikely that a young woman who married early will choose an occupation that requires extensive and lengthy training. Research into the effect of "settings" on a woman's choice of occupation is needed. The author draws upon aspects of current occupational theory and his own research to support his discussion.

61

Rand, Lorraine. MASCULINITY OR FEMININITY? DIFFERENTIATING CAREER-ORIENTED AND HOMEMAKING-ORIENTED COLLEGE FRESHMEN WOMEN. *Journal of Counseling Psychology*, 1968, 15(3), 284-286.

Life Style Prediction. Career Prediction. Methodologic Issues.

Masculinity-femininity is a valid dimension for differentiating women as either homemaking- or career-oriented. Career-oriented freshmen women used characteristics of both sexes to define their sex role, while homemaking-oriented women had more traditional concepts of femininity. Career-oriented women also exhibited more masculine characteristics and behavior than homemaking-oriented women. With the measures used, career-oriented women had higher masculine personality and ability characteristics and higher feminine ability characteristics; homemaking-oriented women had high feminine personality and social-interest characteristics. The reason that career-oriented women scored higher than homemaking-oriented women on feminine ability characteristics could be that the instruments used to measure such traits are mislabeled. Further analysis with larger populations supported the validity of the masculine-feminine dimension in relation to the general college population. Because of their negative stereotypic connotations, a semantic search should be made for more objective terms than masculine and feminine. The sample consisted of 848 freshmen women enrolled in 28 colleges in 1964. Three hundred were identified as career-oriented and 548 as homemaking-oriented. Responses of the subjects to the American College Survey, an inventory of ideas, attitudes and experiences, supplied the data.

62

Resources Analysis Branch, Office of Program Planning and Evaluation, National Institutes of Health, U.S. Department of Health, Education, and Welfare. SPECIAL REPORT ON WOMEN AND GRADUATE STUDY. *Resources for Medical Research Report No. 13.* 1968. 94 pages.

Graduate Education. Educational Barriers. Educational Facilitators. Bio-Medical Sciences.

This is an examination of the obstacles women encounter in pursuing graduate study, especially in the field of health, and the factors that might encourage more talented women to complete advanced training. Of the 131,200 women who earned bachelor's degrees in 1961, 72% planned to attend graduate school and 42% had enrolled by 1964. Of the women planning medical careers in 1964, all had planned as early as 1961 to do graduate work, and 93% had actually enrolled. Of the women in scientific fields in 1964, 80% had anticipated graduate study three years earlier, and 65% had enrolled.

The major obstacles to graduate study reported by these women were financial (42%), family responsibilities (41%), lack of available graduate school (16%), lack of qualifications (13%), and disapproval of husband (3%). These women cited several factors that would facilitate the entry of more women into scientific and medical fields: greater availability of part-time training and employment, establishment of child care centers or allowances, increase in training stipends, and greater recognition of women successful in these fields. To facilitate entry of more women into the biomedical sciences, the National Institutes of Health should seek to dispel the "inferiority myth" concerning women by instituting action programs aimed at young girls and their parents, educators, and counselors.

The report summarizes the results of a longitudinal study of 1961 college graduates conducted by the National Opinion Research Center. Follow-up surveys were conducted in 1962, 1963, and 1964. Questionnaires were used to gather the data.

63

Rezler, Agnes G. CHARACTERISTICS OF HIGH SCHOOL GIRLS CHOOSING TRADITIONAL OR PIONEER VOCATIONS. *Personnel and Guidance Journal*, 1967, 45(7), 659-665.

Career Prediction. Vocational Counseling.

By the end of the junior year in high school, it is possible to determine which girls will enter technical and scientific vocations (pioneers) and which will enter traditionally feminine occupations such as nursing and teaching (traditionalists). Differentiation can be made on the basis of the girls' interests, personalities, and academic records. Hobbies are not valid criteria for differentiation. Girls who choose pioneer vocations have greater abilities in computational and scientific areas, are more intellectual (earn higher grades), and are more masculine than girls planning to enter traditional occupations. Girls who choose traditionally feminine occupations, however, score higher on social service interest. Both the traditionalists and the pioneers have strong tendencies to change vocational plans during college.

Potential medical students, when compared to potential mathematicians and scientists, exhibit more people-oriented behavior and interest, are steadier in their vocational goals, and have more confidence in their ability to achieve goals. Potential teachers, when compared with potential nurses, have greater interest in literary, computational, and clerical activities. Thus, through use of interest, personality, and academic achievement profiles, the counselor can identify and give support to potential pioneer women. The sample was 515 junior and senior high school girls in a Catholic girls' high school in the Midwest. Data were derived from the California Test of Mental Maturity, Preliminary Scholastic Aptitude Test, Kuder Vocational Preference Record, and the Holland Vocational Preference Inventory.

64

Robin, Stanley. A COMPARISON OF MALE-FEMALE ROLES IN ENGINEERING. Doctoral Dissertation (Purdue U.), 1963.

Engineering. Sex Role Differences. Higher Education.

Male and female engineering students were compared to an ideal student (selected by engineering school faculty) with respect to attitudes, achievement, and grades. The "ideal" student had little tolerance of ambiguity and little concern with liberal arts training and extra-technical considerations and was concerned with efficient ways of gathering technical information. Male students were closer to the ideal student than females, but the male engineering role differed from the female engineering role just as the faculty's ideal role differed from the student's ideal role. Male students had consistently higher grades. Generally, the faculty felt that in a university setting, male engineering students earned higher grades and came closer to meeting the faculty "ideal."

65

Rossi, Alice S. MATERNALISM, SEXUALITY AND THE NEW FEMINISM. Paper presented at the 16th Annual Meeting of the American Psychopathological Association, New York, 1970. 33 pages.

Behavioral Motivation. Career Motivation. Feminism. Maternal Motivation. Sexuality.

Various research findings are discussed on the characteristics of feminists and on various aspects of sexuality and maternalism. The history of the feminist movement is traced, with emphasis on distinctions between the analytic approach of the National Organization of Women and the rage of the more publicized group, The Feminists. It is suggested that neurohormonal conditions may influence sex-distinguishing behavior; the author points out that androgen may account for variations in behavior within a sexual group as well as between the sexes. Androgen excess may trigger the physical energy needed to participate in strenuous activities.

The relationship between high career orientation or feminist commitment and low commitment to family cannot be explained as pragmatic adjustment-making, but tends to reflect discord of family origin. Writers in both traditional and feminist literature have concentrated on sexuality rather than maternalism. Research on sexual response and psychosexual stimulation is reviewed with emphasis on various erroneous views of female sexual satisfaction. The dichotomies between eroticism and affection and between "bad temptress" (sex) and "good woman" (procreation) are discussed. It is suggested that female arousal ratings are affected by social factors. The close relationship between childbirth, lactation, and sexual gratification is depicted, and the author concludes that only a strong assertive woman can counteract social barriers to achieve gratification in all three areas.

66

Schab, Fred. SOUTHERN COLLEGE WOMEN. *Journal of the American Association of University Women*, 1967, 60(3), 142-144.

Marriage Aspirations. Higher Education. Commitment Prediction.

Undergraduate women at the University of Georgia—141 arts and science majors and 136 elementary and secondary education majors—were randomly selected and compared with respect to career, domestic and educational values. Both groups expressed great interest in a combination of career and marriage, though arts and science majors were more confident of their preparation for careers and marriage. Women in both groups wanted to be married by age 25 and to have children, and both types of women intended to give up their careers when their first child was born. It can be predicted that more education majors will return to their careers when their children leave home. Social activities were considered the most important school activities by women in both groups.

67

Schissel, Robert F. DEVELOPMENT OF A CAREER-ORIENTATION SCALE FOR WOMEN. *Journal of Counseling Psychology*, 1968, 15(3), 257-262.

Career Prediction. Methodologic Technique.

Women can be ordered along a continuum of career orientations on the basis of interests. This finding stands in contrast to general experience and previous research. Interest characteristics of career-oriented women (women who had worked for five consecutive years since completion of their education and had received at least two promotions) and those of non-career women (women who worked for only two years after completing their education) differed significantly. The subjects were 200 employed and 200 unemployed females. All subjects were administered the Strong Vocational Interest Blank, Form M, and a Career-Orientation Scale for women designed by the investigator.

68

Schissel, Robert Francis. DIFFERENTIAL INTEREST CHARACTERISTICS OF CAREER WOMEN. Doctoral Dissertation (U. Nebraska Teachers College), 1967.

Career Prediction.

In a comparison of career-oriented women and noncareer-oriented women, the two groups appeared to lie along a bipolar interest continuum of "things" versus "people." Career women leaned toward the pole of "things" and noncareer women toward the pole of "people." Two hundred career women or working women were compared to 200 noncareer women; data was obtained from a Scale of Career and Homemaking-oriented Attitudes, Strong Vocational Interest Blank (Form M), and a background data sheet.

69

Schmidt, Marlin R. PERSONALITY CHANGE IN COLLEGE WOMEN. *Journal of College Student Personnel*, 1970, 11(6), 414-419.

Educational Aspirations. Personality Change. Occupational Choice. Life Style Prediction.

Women completing four years of study at a major state university undergo many personality changes during the four years, but further research is needed, using a noncollege control group, to determine whether such changes are a function of the college experience or the function of the general maturation process. In general, such women are less dogmatic and have greater interpersonal competence as seniors than as freshmen. Over the four years, they become more selective in their occupational choices and tend to prefer traditional feminine occupations such as teaching and social work. However, the subjects maintain the same aspirations about post-graduate work all four years. As seniors, they also appear to adhere more to nonconformist than to dominant campus life styles. Despite the majority of the seniors who are pinned, engaged, or married, senior women are less likely to believe that finding a mate in college is more important than finding a vocation. As seniors, the subjects are more critical of their college than as freshmen. Generally, they have a more positive regard for themselves. Subjects were 314 women who had completed the American College Survey (1964) as freshmen and who were still in college by the second semester of their senior year (1968) when several tests were administered: the American College Survey, the Vocational Preference Inventory (Holland, 1965), the Interpersonal Competency Scale (Foote and Cottrell, 1955), the Rokeach Dogmatism Scale (1956), the Student Orientation Survey, Form C (Farber and Goodstein, 1964), and several other instruments designed to measure traits and abilities (originality, scholarship, etc.) as well as the subjects' level of educational aspiration, their satisfaction with college choice, etc. Findings support research conducted at other colleges.

70

Siegel, Alberta E. and Curtis, Elizabeth Ann. FAMILIAL CORRELATES OF ORIENTATION TOWARD FUTURE EMPLOYMENT AMONG COLLEGE WOMEN. *Journal of Educational Psychology*, 1963, 54(1), 33-37.

Career Prediction. Life Style Aspirations.

No relationship was found between a woman's work orientation and her family's socioeconomic status, her parents' educational level, her parents' views on purpose of college, or her parents' attitudes toward the importance of education for their daughter. Only the mother's work orientation was found to significantly influence a female student's work orientation. Although most of the women studied planned to work after completing college, the majority intended to marry and give up employment for childrearing. Caution should be observed in making generalizations from these findings, however, because the sample was small and appeared extremely homogenous in many of the characteristics studied. The study was undertaken to examine whether young women were actually continuing to focus on home and family even though they are joining the work force in greater numbers every year. The sample was 43 sophomore women at Pennsylvania State University randomly selected to test work orientation and five characteristics of family background that might be significant in work orientation. All subjects were interviewed with open-ended questions on their purposes in attending college and their family background.

71

Tangri, Sandra Florence Schwartz. ROLE-INNOVATION IN OCCUPATIONAL CHOICE AMONG COLLEGE WOMEN. Doctoral Dissertation (U. Michigan), 1969.

Occupational Choice. Career Prediction.

Women who choose to enter predominantly male occupations (role innovators) express greater commitment to their jobs, aspire to higher levels of accomplishment, and are likely to have had educated working mothers as role models. In contrast, traditionalist women who enter predominantly female occupations tend to project their achievement values on their present or future husbands, are less committed to their jobs, and feared rejection as students. Both groups report many romantic relationships, but the role innovators report more nonromantic friendships than the traditionalists. A random sample of 200 women in a graduating class made up the sample. One third could be classified as role innovators, one third as traditionalists, and another third fell between the two classifications. Instruments used included a questionnaire and a test, Achievement and Motive to Avoid Success Measures.

72

Turner, Ralph H. SOME ASPECTS OF WOMEN'S AMBITION. *American Journal of Sociology,* 1964, 70(3), 271-285.

Achievement Motivation. Sex Differences.

Comparison of ambition in men and women suggests that they have different views of job rewards. Women's educational and material ambition is lower. Career and educational ambition are associated with material ambition among men much more often than among women. (However, the "minimum" occupational level women can accept for their husbands is associated with material ambition.) Women's decisions to pursue careers are not related to class values. They rate business success over family, and cultural enjoyment (music, books, art) over material benefits. Women tend to seek intrinsic benefits from their careers, but men seek both intrinsic and extrinsic benefits.

Sociometric ratings of the male and female subjects in this study indicate that ambitious men and women are rated as "big wheels" by peers. Orientation toward a career was related to "brain rating" (i.e., good in school work). In terms of popularity, those planning to combine career and homemaking roles were most often chosen as friends by their peers. Those planning only homemaking ranked in the middle, and the "career-only" women ranked lowest.

Although it is difficult to interpret the data on women's ambition, the findings support the notion that the key to the fundamental differentiation of women's ambition is related to direct and indirect pursuit of goals. Men seem to have the same differentiated elements of ambition that women do, but because men can pursue a greater variety of goals more directly, the differentiation is not as extreme. Several types of ambition were measured by means of questionnaires administered to 1,441 high school senior women representing various socioeconomic backgrounds.

73

Tyler, Leona E. THE DEVELOPMENT OF CAREER INTEREST IN GIRLS. *Genetic Psychology Monographs,* 1964, 70, 203-212.

Career Motivation. Career Prediction.

Girls' career interests begin to take shape at or before age 14 and may be influenced by temperamental factors. Career interest seems to develop more often in girls with above average ratings on mental ability tests. Comparison of 15 girls with career interests and 30 girls with noncareer interests was based on SVIB scores obtained in the 1st, 4th, 8th and 12th grades, scores from the California Psychological Inventory, and tests of special abilities and school achievement. The monograph also describes the results of other aspects of this longitudinal research project undertaken in 1946 in Eugene, Oregon. It traces the early development of differential interest patterns that appear in adult ratings on the SVIB.

74

U.S. Department of Labor, Wage and Labor Standards Administration, Women's Bureau. WHO ARE THE WORKING MOTHERS? Leaflet 37 (Rev.), May, 1970. 4 pages.

Maternal Employment. Employment Motivation.

Among the 29.9 million women in the labor force in March 1969, 11.6 million were mothers with children under 18. About 7.4 million of these women had children six to 17 years of age, 2.1 million had children three to five years of age, and 2.1 million had children under three. The great majority of these working mothers were working for financial reasons. Designed for people engaged in studies of working mothers, the pamphlet contains a statistical profile in question/answer format of mothers in the labor force. No citation of statistical source is included.

75

Watley, Donivan J. CAREER OR MARRIAGE?: A LONGITUDINAL STUDY OF ABLE YOUNG WOMEN. *National Merit Scholarship Corporation Research Reports,* 1969, 5(7), 1-16.

Career Prediction. Scholastic Ability.

Women who won National Merit Scholarships between 1956 and 1960 were followed up in 1965 to determine their marriage and/or career plans. Each of the 883 women was classified into one of five groups: marriage only, marriage with deferred career, marriage with immediate career, career only, or uncertain. The educational and career aspirations of these groups differed; and those seeking an immediate career scored higher on scholastic ability tests than those who either planned no career or who planned to delay entering careers. The groups also differed in their willingness to discuss problems derived from being women.

76

Werts, Charles E. SEX DIFFERENCES IN COLLEGE ATTENDANCE. National Merit Scholarship Corporation, 1966. Mimeo. 13 pages.

Sex Differences. College Attendance.

Reliability in the prediction of college attendance can be increased if the relationships among sex, social class, and ability are taken into consideration. Fifty percent more boys than girls attend college, but "very able" girls are as likely as boys to attend college, no matter what their socioeconomic background. Girls with fathers in occupations that require advanced academic degrees attend college nearly as often as boys of the same socioeconomic background. Among children of men with occupations that require little education, boys attending college outnumber girls two to one. Girls with relatively low grades in all classes are much less likely than boys to attend college, but low grades appear to discourage girls from low socioeconomic background more than girls from high socioeconomic background. The author used analysis of variance to examine responses on high school grade averages and fathers' occupations of 127,125 male and female students entering 248 four-year colleges and universities in the Fall of 1961.

77

White, Becky J. THE RELATIONSHIP OF SELF CONCEPT AND PARENTAL IDENTIFICATION TO WOMEN'S VOCATIONAL INTERESTS. *Journal of Counseling Psychology*, 1959, 6(3), 202-206.

Career Motivation. Sex Role Identification. Role Influences.

Girls whose self and ideal perceptions were similar to their parents' perceptions and ideals for them appeared to play more typically feminine roles and to be more satisfied with themselves and closer to their parents than girls who were career motivated. Career-oriented girls tended to come from homes in which the father was deceased or in which there was little communication between child and parents. Despite the low level of significance of these findings, evidence suggests that the relationship between a girl's self and ideal perceptions and her parents' perceptions affects the girl's vocational interest. The author tested 81 freshman women enrolled in a public junior college in California. Parents of 34 of the girls also participated in the study. Use of the Q technique revealed that girls identified more with their mothers than their fathers. Analysis of variance, tests, and product-moment correlations of the relationship between data from the Q sorts and personal data sheets and profiles from the SVIB-W revealed the effect of parental identification on career interest.

78

Wilson, Kenneth M. ASSESSMENT OF THE GRADUATE STUDY AND CAREER PLANS OF SENIORS AT THREE LIBERAL ARTS COLLEGES FOR WOMEN: A PILOT PROJECT. Paper prepared for the College Research Center, Vassar College, 1964. 24 pages.

Career Aspirations. Life Style Aspirations. Educational Aspirations. Higher Education.

This study is part of the continuing systematic research conducted by the author at the College Research Center, Vassar College, on the degree aspirations and career plans of women. The author feels that "women's colleges [have] a special responsibility and a unique opportunity to assess and analyze the career plans and the career-decision problems of their students and to introduce educational procedures designed to help young women deal more effectively with problems of career development and career planning." The research report includes tables and a discussion of findings from a survey of seniors at three women's colleges. Comparisons are made with data obtained from freshmen. About half the seniors planned traditional child-rearing futures, with slightly more than one third aspiring to marriage and career. About one third planned graduate study, a substantial increase over freshmen year plans. Preliminary analysis of career plans indicates that a majority of the seniors planned teaching careers or part-time work "until after the children are grown."

79

Wilson, Kenneth M. BLACK STUDENTS ENTERING COLLEGE RESEARCH CENTER COLLEGES: THEIR CHARACTERISTICS AND THEIR FIRST-YEAR ACADEMIC PERFORMANCE. *Research Memorandum 69-1,* College Research Center, Vassar College, Poughkeepsie, N.Y., 1969. 23 pages.

Career Aspirations. Educational Aspirations. Methodologic Validity. Higher Education. Racial Differences.

Black women who enter highly selective women's colleges as freshmen differ from their white classmates in several anticipated ways. For example, they are more likely to have graduated from large public high schools where less than half of the students go on to college. They are much more likely than white students to aspire to academic or professional careers in addition to marriage and family and are more likely to view college as preparation for a career rather than as development of the "well-rounded" individual. They are much more likely than white students to aspire to graduate or professional training and to be more liberal on social and economic issues. Traditional criteria for predicting freshmen achievement levels are as valid for black students as for white. More research is needed, however. The author analyzed data obtained from a comprehensive survey questionnaire administered to all freshmen entering Mount Holyoke, Vassar, Connecticut College and Trinity College and scores on measures of academic aptitude (SAT-Verbal, SAT-Mathematical, and CEEB achievement tests). Data on 150 black students entering the colleges in 1965, 1966, and 1967 were compared with data on 2,564 white students entering in 1967.

80

Wilson, Kenneth M. SOME PRELIMINARY FINDINGS: SURVEY OF CAREER AND GRADUATE STUDY PLANS, CLASS OF 1967, SELECTED LIBERAL ARTS COLLEGES FOR WOMEN. Paper prepared for College Research Center, Vassar College, 1967. 6 pages.

Educational Prediction. Higher Education. Methodologic Technique.

Among college women, achievement scores as expressed by grade point average may be a better predictor of advanced degree aspirations than standardized achievement tests. However, more research is needed to obtain reliable knowledge about degree plans as well as admissions criteria. A precoded questionnaire was administered to seniors at five women's colleges and the responses were collated with data from the Vassar College Research Center data bank. Institutional differences in graduate study plans were found. Relationships between selected variables and graduate study plans are presented for one college.

81

Wilson, Kenneth M., and Dunn, Frances E. REVIEW OF CENTER STUDIES: IV—SOME CONCOMITANTS OF WITHDRAWAL FROM COLLEGE: BRIEF REPORT OF A QUESTIONNAIRE SURVEY. *Research Memorandum RM 67-1*, College Research Center, Vassar College, Poughkeepsie, N.Y., 1967. Mimeo. 40 pages.

Educational Motivation. Educational Prediction. Educational Counseling. Higher Education.

This study suggests that two distinct patterns are followed by young women who drop out of highly selective women's colleges. Those who transfer to another college appear to be more academically oriented than those who simply drop out of college. Also, those who transfer seem to have a higher sense of academic values and intellectual interests and greater interest in atypical careers for women. The majority of young women who dropped out cited marriage as a major reason for leaving school and appeared to be more socially oriented than those who transferred. Generally, students who transferred were more likely to have attended public high schools and to transfer sooner than those who withdrew (who usually attended private high schools and left college later). It can be inferred that transfer students have a greater difficulty in adjusting to the social, cultural, and academic demands of the college they initially attended. Further research and examination of counseling procedures in relation to the "withdrawal phenomenon" is needed. To obtain these findings, the authors administered a questionnaire survey to 1,000 young women who had withdrawn from five women's colleges—Hollins, Mount Holyoke, Sweet Briar, Vassar, and Wheaton—between 1962 and 1966.

82

Withycombe-Brocato, Carol Jean. THE MATURE GRADUATE WOMAN STUDENT: WHO IS SHE? Doctoral Dissertation, (United States International U.), 1969.

Graduate Education. Educational Motivation. Sex Role Perceptions.

The typical mature woman graduate student is between 35 and 40 years old; married to an affectionate, intelligent man who has a B.A. degree and is a professional with an income of at least $13,000, and has two or three children. Her parents had higher than a high school education and are self-employed professionals. She attends graduate school because of a need for achievement as well as a need to develop career skills, engages in volunteer activities, and cares for her own family. She considers herself feminine but is more like an average male in her religious, political, social, and theoretical interests. She is more feminine than the average female in her economic and aesthetic interests. These conclusions resulted from an attempt to profile women over 25 years of age in masters' or doctoral degree programs in five universities throughout the United States. Three aspects of these women's lives were surveyed: family background, present home life, and self perception. The sample included 448 women who were administered a 180-item questionnaire designed by the investigator and the Allport-Vernon Lindzey Study of Values. Taped dialogue sessions were held with those women who volunteered.

Marital and Familial Status of Working Women

83

Angrist, Shirley S. ROLE CONSTELLATION AS A VARIABLE IN WOMEN'S LEISURE ACTIVITIES. *Social Forces*, 1967, 45(3), 423-431.

Marital Status. Leisure Activity. Lifestyle Influences.

Single and married women alumnae spend about the same amount of time on leisure activities, but marital and familial status significantly affect the type of activity undertaken. Single working women tend to participate more in fine arts activities such as going to concerts and plays. In contrast, young mothers with only preschool children usually undertake home-centered leisure activities, such as T.V. watching, hobbies, and informal visiting. As the mother and her children get older—from preschool to school age—the amount of time she devotes to leisure activities and participation in community welfare activities increases. Mothers with regular household and child care help are more active than mothers with little or no help. More research is needed to determine whether specific stages of a woman's life and specific sets of roles are related to the amount and type of her leisure activity. To obtain these findings, the researcher examined responses of 245 alumnae—from four classes (1949, 1950, 1959, 1960) of the women's college of a coeducational university—to a mail questionnaire, which included an Inventory of Leisure Activity (Searls, 1965). Respondents were categorized in terms of role characteristics. Mean scores were analyzed and tested for statistical significance.

See also: Angrist, Shirley S. LEISURE AND THE EDUCATED WOMAN. *Margaret Morrison Carnegie College Reprint No. 11*, Carnegie Institute of Technology, Pittsburgh, Pa. 15213. 1966. 3 pages.

A narrative description of this research effort and a discussion of the implications. The author also examines the findings in the slightly different light of the effect of the college experience on leisure activity.

84

Axelson, Leland. THE MARITAL ADJUSTMENT AND ROLE DEFINITIONS OF HUSBANDS OF WORKING AND NON-WORKING WIVES. *Journal of Marriage and Family Living*, 1963, 25(2), 189-195.

Sex Role Perceptions. Maternal Employment. Marital Adjustment. The Working Wife.

Husbands of working wives differ from husbands of nonworking wives in their perceptions of and attitudes toward working wives. The husband whose wife works seems to have a more liberal view of the wife's employment, her economic equality, and her privilege of individual sexual expression. Even though most of the husbands surveyed had reservations about the effect of a wife's employment on her role as wife and mother, the husbands of working wives were less likely to view the wife's employment as a threat to masculine status. Although evidence supporting previous research (Nye, 1961) indicated poorer marital adjustment on the part of husbands of working wives, the question of whether poor marital adjustment is the cause or the effect of the wife entering the labor force remains unanswered. To obtain these findings, the researcher examined the responses of 122 husbands living with their wives in a small community in the West to a mailed questionnaire, which included an altered version of a measure of marital adjustment (Nye, 1959). A Guttman-type scale was constructed for purposes of analysis.

85

Axelson, Leland J. THE WORKING WIFE: DIFFERENCES IN PERCEPTION AMONG NEGRO AND WHITE MALES. *Journal of Marriage and the Family*, 1970, 32(3), 457-464.

Sex Role Perceptions. The Working Wife. Racial Differences.

Undertaken because of evidence of significant differences between the Negro subculture and white culture, the study provides evidence that Negro and white males have different perceptions of working wives. Over half of the Negro males stated that a wife should work if she cares to, but less than half the white males expressed this view. Negro males were more likely than white males to state that a husband should feel inadequate when his wife earns more than he does. However, over one fifth of the Negro males were undecided about this issue and about who should manage family income. To obtain these findings, the author analyzed the responses of 67 Negro and 565 white males residing in Brevard County, Florida, to an individually administered, forced-choice questionnaire.

86

Bailyn, Lotte. CAREER AND FAMILY ORIENTATIONS OF HUSBANDS AND WIVES IN RELATION TO MARITAL HAPPINESS. *Human Relations*, 1969, 23(2), 97-113.

Marital Satisfaction. Life Style Motivation. Maternal Employment.

The husband's approach to integrating family and work in his life is as important to marital satisfaction as his wife's attempt to integrate career and family. Instead of continuing to study only the difficulties women face in integrating family and work, evidence suggests that researchers should also study the conditions that permit husbands to integrate family and work. In this study, marriages tended to be happier when the husband found satisfaction in both career and family than when the husband was either just career- or family-oriented. Also, marriages tended to be happier if the life style of the family was different from the one in which the husband grew up. The author analyzed the responses of 209 married couples to several items on a questionnaire (Rossi, 1965b), using the Conversational Mode Survey Analysis Program (Hawkins, Survey Analysis Ltd., London). The study is part of a larger study of highly qualified women and their careers (Fogarty, Rapaport and Rapaport, 1969). The women subjects were involved in a National Survey of 1960 graduates of British universities and were included along with their spouses in this study in 1968. They were categorized according to career-family orientation.

87

Blood, Robert O., and Wolfe, Donald M. HUSBANDS AND WIVES: THE DYNAMICS OF MARRIED LIVING. Illinois: The Free Press, 1960. 290 pages.

Marital Adjustment. Maternal Employment. Marital Decision-making.

This report on a major research project on modern American marriage is written from the perspective of the wife. More exploratory than definitive and more hypothesis-generating than hypothesis-testing, the report covers different aspects of the marriage such as: decision-making, working parents, economic factors, children, companionship, emotional well-being, love, stresses and strengths. The reasons wives work are discussed in detail: women are no longer dependent on their husbands for support, marriage is no longer an economic necessity for women, and divorce is no longer economically impossible. The investigators found that when both partners work, the husband is more likely to help around the house and the wife takes a more equal part in decision-making for the family. The final chapter discusses the stresses in marriage in detail. The sample was a cross section of 731 families living in the metropolitan Detroit area and a comparative sample of 178 farm families.

88

Finkelman, Jacob Jack. MATERNAL EMPLOYMENT, FAMILY RELATIONSHIPS, AND PARENTAL ROLE PERCEPTION. Doctoral Dissertation (Yeshiva U.), 1966.

Marital Decision-making. Maternal Employment. Role Perceptions.

This investigation of working mothers showed that more tasks are shared when both parents are employed and that homemaking mothers perform more family functions and make more family decisions. There was no significant difference in the children's perception of parental roles based on employment status of the mother and no significant social class difference in family tasks or decision-making. No significant difference was found in personality of mothers based on employment status, social class, or sex of child. The sample consisted of 96 fifth- and sixth-grade children and their mothers. The children were administered the Parental Authority-Love Statements and Projected Essential Needs Parental Authority-Love Statements (PALS) test. The mothers filled out a questionnaire on family tasks and decision-making. The mothers were also administered the Institute for Personality and Ability Testing Anxiety Scale.

89

Garland, Neal T. THE BETTER HALF? THE MALE IN THE DUAL PROFESSION FAMILY. Paper presented at the American Sociological Association annual meeting, 1970. 32 pages.

Dual-Career Families. Sex Role Differences. Sex Role Perceptions. The Working Wife.

Research indicates that in American society, there is continuing popularity among both sexes of the idea that "women's place is in the home." Hodge and Hodge (1965) showed that when women compete in the same occupational market as men, men's salaries tend to decrease. This decrease is probably due to cultural definitions of what women should be paid. This study was designed to determine if men feel threatened by working wives. An open-ended interview schedule, patterned after the Rapaport and Rapaport Schedule, was used on a sample of 53 presently married, professional couples. Findings suggest that matriarchal husbands whose wives had substantially higher incomes than they did were likely to be resigned to their wives' careers and to feel competitive. This group also had trouble keeping marital and professional roles separate. However, the research did not support the idea that a husband of a high-status wife automatically feels emasculated and dominated. But the wife's higher earnings in all cases seemed to produce negative effects on the husband. Only one couple was rated "egalitarian."

90

Gillette, Thomas Lee. THE WORKING MOTHER: A STUDY OF THE RELATIONSHIP BETWEEN MATERNAL EMPLOYMENT AND FAMILY STRUCTURE AS INFLUENCED BY CLASS AND RACE. Doctoral Dissertation (University of North Carolina), 1961.

Maternal Employment. Familial Roles.

Working mothers participate less and have more help from their husbands in household tasks. In comparison to nonworking mothers, they perceive the act of working as less disturbing to family life, and see certain characteristics of working as more attractive. Working mothers have fewer children, more years of formal education, and higher job status. Differences between working and nonworking mothers were greater than differences based on race or social class. A questionnaire with responses endorsing or rejecting attributes of maternal employment was administered to 668 mothers. Half of the sample was black, half white, all had intact families with the father present and half were middle class and half working class. Hollingshead's Two-Factor Index of Social Position was used in assigning class position.

91

Gover, David A. SOCIO-ECONOMIC DIFFERENTIAL IN THE RELATIONSHIP BETWEEN MARITAL ADJUSTMENT AND WIFE'S EMPLOYMENT STATUS. *Journal of Marriage and Family Living,* 1963, 25(4), 452-458.

The Working Wife. Marital Adjustment.

Undertaken because of conflicting findings about marital adjustment when wives work, this study, like previous research by Nye (1961), showed that unemployed wives had higher marital adjustment scores than employed wives. The difference was greatest between employed and unemployed working-class wives. Further analysis suggests that this difference is a factor of conventionally ascribed behavior within a geographical region, which could explain conflicting results of previous research. That is, in an area where conventional behavior calls for a wife to be unemployed and happily married, "nonconventional wives are more likely to score low on marital adjustment scales and [are] more likely to be employed than conventional wives." This hypothesis conflicts with existing theory—that working-class wives who are employed display lower marital adjustment because of the unsatisfactory nature of their work. Further research is needed in this area. Rebuttals by leaders in the field—Robert Blood, Jr., and F. Ivan Nye—are included in the discussion of the study findings. The results are based on the responses of 340 white women living with their husbands in Greensboro, North Carolina, to a questionnaire that included a seven-question General Evaluation of Marriage scale (Bowerman, 1957). Of these women, 177 were classified as working-class and 163 as middle-class.

92

Kaley, Maureen M. ATTITUDES TOWARD THE DUAL ROLE OF THE MARRIED PROFESSIONAL WOMAN. *American Psychologist*, 1971, 26(3), 301-306.

Role Perceptions. Career-Marriage Conflict. Career Barriers.

Married professional women have positive attitudes toward their dual role of career and marriage, while married professional men and case workers have negative attitudes toward their dual role. The sex and profession of the participants in this comparison produced significant differences in attitude toward the dual role of professional women; age, education, race, and professional experience did not. A review of research on the attitudes of professionally employed men and women toward women's dual role supports the hypothesis that negative attitudes held by both men and women inhibit qualified women from seeking higher education and professional careers. The sample consisted of 60 respondents including 35 females, 24 males, and one respondent not declaring sex. A questionnaire of the author's design, calling for demographic or personal history data and responses to six items concerning married professional women, was administered to measure attitudes. The sample included representatives of five professions: case worker supervisors, case workers, teachers, research psychologists, and consultants.

93

Nye, F. Ivan and Hoffman, Lois Wladis. THE EMPLOYED MOTHER IN AMERICA. Chicago: Rand McNally, 1963. 406 pages.

Maternal Employment. Role Theory. Role Influences. Life Style Satisfaction.

Maternal employment, which has only recently been recognized as a permanent and significant feature of American life, is a complex social phenomenon that can be successfully studied and examined within the conceptual framework of position and role. The authors' research leads to the formulation of several statements about the working mother: The assumption of the role of provider by a wife reduces tension by restoring her economic contribution and reducing the husband's role as provider. It also facilitates the achievement of upward mobility and a higher living standard. Such "contingent conditions" as age and number of children, occupation and age of mother, husband's income, and husband's family ideology all affect the roles of the wife-mother, as they do individual tension levels and attempts to reduce tension. While the provider role will affect the various wife-mother roles, it affects the roles of supervisor of children and housekeeper the most. Because it requires more time, the addition of the provider role to a wife's other roles represents a major structural change. Because the provider role is a dominant role, it will modify her other roles more than it will be modified by them.

Among more practical findings, the author notes that working and nonworking mothers have the same number of problems with their children, but that working mothers have more positive attitudes toward their children. They also have a more positive feeling about themselves as individuals although some feel inadequate in the role of mother. Working mothers appear to be in better health, and they tend to take a less active role in community activities and in nonfamilial acts such as visiting neighbors. They reserve their leisure time for activities with their families. Although working parents experience more husband-wife conflicts (the degree depending on the educational and financial level of the family), younger mothers express more satisfaction with their lives when employed. Much of the data and analyses reported in the volume are derived from several major research projects conducted by the authors and 17 other investigators who contributed to the book.

94

Orden, Susan and Bradburn, Norman. WORKING WIVES AND MARRIAGE HAPPINESS. *American Journal of Sociology*, 1969, 74(4), 392-407.

Marital Satisfaction. Life Style Satisfaction. Maternal Employment.

A woman's freedom to choose among alternative life styles is an important predictor of happiness in marriage. Both partners are less happy if the wife works because of economic necessity than if she participates by choice. This finding holds across educational levels, stages in the life cycle, and part-time and full-time employment. Among the less educated, the strain comes from an increase in tensions for husbands and a decline in sociability for wives; while among the better educated, husbands and wives both experience an increase in tensions and a decrease in sociability. A woman's decision to work strains the marriage only when there are preschool children in the family. At other stages in the life cycle, her decision to work makes little difference in an individual's assessment of her own marriage happiness. However, the decision to work is generally associated with a high balance between satisfactions and tensions for both husbands and wives. To obtain these findings, the authors analyzed the responses of 1,651 married (not necessarily to each other) men and women to questions on marriage happiness.

95

Pavalko, Ronald M. and Nager, Norma. CONTINGENCIES OF MARRIAGE TO HIGH-STATUS MEN. *Social Forces*, 1968, 46(4), 523-530.

Nursing. Marriage Access. Higher Education.

This study was undertaken to identify factors that affect a young woman's opportunity for marriage to men of high status—on the basis of the stratification theory that a woman's social status is governed by her husband's. Findings suggest that socioeconomic background is more important than occupation and educational attainment and community size. For girls who attended college, those who became nurses were more likely to marry high status men than others, regardless of socioeconomic background and size of hometown. Girls who became nurses without attending college were just as likely as college girls to marry high status men. To obtain these findings, the authors analyzed the results of a questionnaire survey on educational and occupational plans of Wisconsin high school seniors in 1957 and a follow-up survey of the former students in 1964. The sample for the study consisted of 296 women who were "nursing aspirants" and married.

96

Poloma, Margaret M. THE MYTH OF THE EGALITARIAN FAMILY: FAMILIAL ROLES AND THE PROFESSIONALLY EMPLOYED WIFE. Paper presented at the American Sociological Association annual meeting, 1970. 24 pages.

Sex Roles. Maternal Employment. Dual-Career Families. Familial Roles.

The author cites previous research to suggest that the traditional feminine role, in which the wife and mother is responsive largely to the will and needs of her husband and children, is not threatened by a married woman's employment outside the home. The sample was 53 women actively practicing in the fields of law, medicine, or higher education and their husbands. The sample was intended to represent "egalitarian" family units. Semi-structured interviews were taped, lasting between one and three quarters and two and one half hours. Four classes of families emerged: 1) traditional patriarchy (one family), 2) neo-traditional patriarchy (20 families), 3) egalitarian family (27 families), and 4) matriarchy (five families). Of the five wives who earned more than their husbands, two were happily resigned to this and three felt reluctant. Only in one instance did the husband perceive taking on equal responsibility for the homemaking function and child care duties as part of his role.

97

Safilios-Rothschild, Constantina. THE INFLUENCE OF THE WIFE'S DEGREE OF WORK COMMITMENT UPON SOME ASPECTS OF FAMILY ORGANIZATION AND DYNAMICS. *Journal of Marriage and the Family*, 1970, 32(4), 681-691.

Familial Roles. Marital Decision-Making. The Working Wife. Career Commitment.

Working wives with a high commitment to work see themselves as prevailing in decision-making, giving in in disagreements less often than their husbands do, having more freedom of behavior in and out of the home, and being satisfied with their marriage. Similarly, working wives with a low commitment to work see themselves as more equal members of an "equalitarian" model of family dynamics, but more by necessity than by choice. Even though such women work reluctantly because of financial need, the familial relationships change. Husbands help more often with household tasks and both husband and wife more frequently compromise in case of disagreements and share in decision-making. However, women with a low commitment to work have a restricted amount of personal freedom in and out of the home. Before a total picture of the relationship between the wife's working status and family dynamics can be developed, however, husbands of both types of women should be interviewed. The author analyzed interview data obtained from 549 nonworking wives and 347 working wives living in and around Athens, Greece. The interview schedule was designed to assess marital satisfaction, decision-making, division of labor, husband's permissiveness and wife's work commitment.

98

Safilios-Rothschild, Constantina. THE STUDY OF FAMILY POWER STRUCTURE: A REVIEW, 1960-1969. *Journal of Marriage and the Family*, 1970, 32(4), 539-552.

Methodologic Issues. Marital Decision-Making. Familial Roles. Research Needs.

Research into the nature and dynamics of family power structure during the 1960s is marked by a lack of sophistication in concept and method. There is little agreement on definition of terms from one study to the next. Generally, most studies have only been concerned with decision-making within the family as *the* dynamic of family power structure. By assuming that the spouse who makes most of the decisions holds the greatest power, investigators overlook possibilities such as subtle manipulation on the part of the other spouse. Too, no two studies have examined the same set of family decisions with the same degree of specificity, and analyses of data differ from study to study, so that comparisons are impossible. The almost exclusive reliance of investigators on the perceptions of wives and children as they study power structure provides little reliable information. Future investigations should view family power as a complex of many factors, with no single factor taken as a reliable measure by itself. The author examines existing research to develop her argument.

99

Stolz, Lois M. EFFECTS OF MATERNAL EMPLOYMENT ON CHILDREN: EVIDENCE FROM RESEARCH. *Child Development*, 1960, 31(December), 749-782.

Maternal Employment.

Some of the highlights of this research review include: • The problems of children of working and nonworking mothers are more often related to the mother's emotional adjustment than to her occupational status; • A study of 2,000 mothers of children in grades one through 10 reveals that employed mothers exhibit more favorable attitudes toward children; • Mothers who work are often found to have higher education or to be from lower socioeconomic status groups; • The proportion of widowed, divorced and separated women is higher among working mothers; • Working mothers tend to have smaller families and live in urban areas; • There is no significant incidence of delinquency in children of working mothers; • Regarding children's adjustment in school, children of working mothers are less often extremely aggressive or inhibited; • With respect to school achievement, children of working mothers are rated as low performers during grades three through six, but not in nine through 12, and • There are no significant differences on the dependence-independence dimension among preschool children of working and nonworking mothers. The author recommends that future research should focus on the personality of the mother and its effects on children rather than on her working status vis-a-vis children.

100

U.S. Department of Labor, Women's Bureau. 15 YEARS AFTER COLLEGE: A STUDY OF ALUMNAE OF THE CLASS OF 1945. Bulletin 283, 1962. 26 pages.

Life Style Aspirations. Higher Education. Career Aspirations.

An exploratory survey of college alumnae 15 years out of college shows that they aspire to develop means other than marriage and child rearing "to assert their individuality, attain personal recognition, and serve society." It is essential that employers, educators, and counselors develop ways to meet these women's needs. The great majority of the women surveyed indicated strong interest in future employment (less than one half of the women were employed at the time of the survey). The majority of women, especially those who were not employed, indicated a definite need for additional training. Of the women surveyed, 83 percent were married and over 90 percent of these had children. These findings are based on the responses of 580 alumnae of four colleges to a questionnaire.

Women in the World of Work

Women in the Professions	101-141
Women in Academe	142-156
Women in Business and Government	157-165
Women in Executive Roles (Academic, Business)	166-178
Characteristics of Working Women and Their Status	179-212

101

Astin, Helen S. THE WOMAN DOCTORATE IN AMERICA. New York: The Russell Sage Foundation, 1969. 196 pages.

Higher Education. Research Needs. Discrimination. Employment. Career Barriers. Career Motivation. Educational Counseling.

Undertaken to examine "folklore" about highly educated women, this work reveals that such women are very productive professionally. Among women who received doctoral degrees in 1957 and 1958, 91 percent were in the labor force in 1965 at the time of this study, and 81 percent were working full time. Women who interrupted their careers did so because of child bearing and child rearing; the median length of time for such interruptions was 14 months. The majority of the working women were teaching, 70 percent at the college level and 10 percent in junior colleges or at lower educational levels. Over one third reported that various discriminatory practices had hindered their professional progress. Those who felt they had been discriminated against by employers because of sex were also those who were most productive (they published more), most active professionally, and the highest earners, earning more than the median income of $11,330.

About half the women studied had domestic help, but most cited the inability to find adequate household help as the greatest obstacle to their career development. Autobiographical sketches indicated that parents had considerable influence on the women's career development. Parents' behavior, high expectations, and encouragement of their children, and the parents' own philosophies were important factors in the women's life decisions.

Over half the women had been or were still married at the time of the survey; the married women had smaller families than women in general. These and other findings suggest needed changes, including an increase in educational and guidance efforts designed to encourage young women to achieve advanced training in specialized fields and the establishment of special scholarships in career fields that women usually do not enter. Also needed are an increase in acceptability and availability of part-time study and employment; an increase in number of day-care centers; introduction of tax laws that permit deductions for household workers, and the elimination of discriminatory practices against women in higher education roles and the world of work.

The data also suggest new areas for research, including the use of a wider variety of early personal and environmental variables in the study of occupational and educational development of women; further research into the impact of parents' personality and aspirations on the occupational and educational development and aspirations of women. More research is also needed into the dynamics and general characteristics of career-oriented women in order to increase the understanding of the meaning of work and occupational achievement for all women. Finally, research is needed into the early life experiences that provide professional women with the high self-esteem necessary for professional achievement.

Data for the study were drawn from a questionnaire, "Survey of Women Doctorates," returned by 1,547 women who earned their doctorates in the United States during 1957 and 1958. An additional 106 women responded to a shorter version of the questionnaire, and a response rate of 86 percent was achieved. Additional data supplied by the National Academy of Sciences made possible a longitudinal design for the analyses. A smaller subsample of the women provided the research with autobiographical sketches.

102

Bowers, John Z. WOMEN IN MEDICINE: AN INTERNATIONAL STUDY. *New England Journal of Medicine*, 1966, 275(August 18), 362-365.

Medicine. Educational Barriers. Educational Facilitators. Discrimination.

Discrimination against women in medicine is more pronounced in the United States than in most other countries, according to findings from an examination of the status of women in medicine in the U.S., Europe, Australia, Asia, Africa south of the Sahara, and Latin America. The author points out the potential contributions of women, especially in pediatrics, psychiatry, and preventive medicine. Medical school administrators should be concerned less with women's higher drop-out rate (13.6 percent vs. 8.2 percent for men) than with providing arrangements for married women that facilitate their study. Internship and residency hours could be made more flexible, and nursery schools could be established. Moreover, medical schools should take a positive approach to informing young college women that they are wanted in order to change the current view that the medical profession presents insurmountable obstacles for women.

103

Bryan, Alice I. and Boring, Edwin G. WOMEN IN AMERICAN PSYCHOLOGY: FACTORS AFFECTING THEIR PROFESSIONAL CAREERS. *American Psychologist*, 1947, 2, 3-20.

Higher Education. Psychology. Career Patterns. Discrimination. Life Style Satisfaction.

A comparative study in 1946 of the career patterns of men and women psychologists with Ph.D.'s revealed that men tended to be researchers and writers and that women tended to be practitioners. Investigations of sex discrimination indicate various disadvantages for women but little discontentment. Women with the Ph.D. degree were more likely to have had educated parents, were less likely to be employed full time, were paid less (especially if married), and progressed less rapidly than men (except in educational and guidance jobs). Generally, both sexes reported satisfaction with their profession and with their marriages. Both men and women reported involvement in a variety of domestic duties and that they spent more time in domestic activities than in recreation. These and other findings related to development of professional interest, attitudes toward training, prejudice and employment, professional activities outside the job, activities outside the profession, etc., are based on a questionnaire survey of matched samples of 247 men and 245 women who received Ph.D.'s in psychology between 1921 and 1940.

104

Edisen, Adele E. Uskali. WOMEN IN SCIENCE. Report to the Conference of Professional and Academic Women, Professional Women's Caucus, June, 1970, Washington, D.C. Mimeo. 4 pages.

Science. Career Barriers. Discrimination.

Women scientists represented only about nine percent of the total membership of the National Science Foundation in 1968, and held about half the doctorates among the NSF membership. They generally earned about $3,500 less than male scientists, and were decreasing in total number. The greatest concentration of women in science worked in chemistry, psychology, mathematics, and biological sciences. The lowest paid field was education, which was also the largest employer of women. Likewise, there were few women in management, the highest paid category of work activity. Science as a field presents some distinct barriers to women. For example, home and motherhood responsibilities conflict with the amount of time necessary for professional development, and educational institutions often have policies against hiring wives of men employed in the institutions. Other barriers include lack of child care centers and insufficient income to cover child care expenses, discrimination, and the tightening job market for scientists. Recommendations are made to encourage and protect women who plan to enter scientific fields.

105

Epstein, Cynthia F. ENCOUNTERING THE MALE ESTABLISHMENT: SEX-STATUS LIMITS ON WOMEN'S CAREERS IN THE PROFESSIONS. *American Journal of Sociology*, 1970, 75(6), 965-982.

Career Barriers.

Women entering professional careers encounter many barriers that work to keep them out, despite the gains women have made in social and political rights since the turn of the century. Prestigious, male-dominated professions support traditional career development systems that limit a woman professional's achievements through the protegé system, sex-typing of occupations, use of peer-group relationships to establish performance criteria, and the use of sex, rather than credentials and achievements, to determine status. Women who overcome these obstacles are exceptions, not the rule. As status and prestige accrue to professions in public welfare and service, and traditional elite professions lose status, it is likely that new professional systems will evolve that will be more hospitable to women and to other minority group members. The new interest in achieving equal access to all spheres of society for women will also eliminate barriers to their full participation. The author draws on existing literature and previous research to develop her discussion.

106

Epstein, Cynthia Fuchs. LAW PARTNERS AND MARITAL PARTNERS: STRAINS AND SOLUTIONS IN THE DUAL-CAREER FAMILY ENTERPRISE. Paper presented at the 11th International Family Research Seminar, Tavistock Institute of Human Relations, London, September 1970. Mimeo. 53 pages.

Law. Dual-Career Families. Familial Roles.

Professional partnerships between husbands and wives seem to facilitate successful combination of work and family life. Such partnerships, however, are not free from cultural restraints. Often reflecting the prestige and division of labor system in the larger setting, these arrangements are often not equal; the wives assume subsidiary roles to their husbands. The alternatives developed by lawyer husbands and wives may be applicable to other situations where husbands and wives have the same occupational status. To obtain these findings, the author interviewed 12 women lawyers working with their husbands in New York City, a subsample of a larger study. The interviews ranged in length from one and a half to five hours. In some cases, other lawyer friends were interviewed for more information on the husband-wife relationships under study.

107

Fischer, Ann and Golde, Peggy. THE POSITION OF WOMEN IN ANTHROPOLOGY. *American Anthropologist*, 1968, 70(2), 337-344.

Anthropology. Discrimination. Career Barriers.

The field of anthropology is not the hospitable field for women that many believe it to be. With an annual growth rate for women that is four percent higher than the rate for men in the field (between 15 and 21 percent of the doctoral degrees in anthropology granted in recent years went to women), only about 10.4 percent of full-time faculty members in graduate departments are women. Of these, 31 percent are part-time faculty, and 19 percent are employed in research. As in other disciplines, many women anthropologists are employed by smaller educational institutions with less advanced students. The reasons for lack of advancement of women in the field include the fear on the part of educators that too many women in the field will downgrade the discipline and the feeling that many women will drop out of the field for marriage and home responsibilities. It appears that women can avoid discriminatory practices in the field by continuing steadily in the profession, without permitting any interruptions. The authors conducted a statistical analysis of existing data in various governmental and professional publications to support their argument.

108

Frithiof, Patricia. WOMEN IN SCIENCE: A THEORETICAL DISCUSSION IN PREPARATION FOR A FIELD STUDY OF

WOMEN SCIENTISTS IN SWEDEN. Paper prepared for the Research Policy Program, University of Lund, Sweden, 1967. Mimeo. 24 pages.

Science. Career Barriers. Research Needs.

A review of the literature on the development of scientific careers reveals how complicated the process can be for women. Several factors, such as attitudes against intellectually involved women, produce high levels of anxiety in creative women and inhibit their scientific development. Cultural and environmental factors such as tradition and lack of access to educational and vocational opportunities also have an inhibiting effect. All of these are reasons for the failure of women to achieve eminence in science in keeping with their potential, a phenomenon that afflicts many countries, such as the U.S., Sweden, and England. (The major exception is the Soviet Union.) In the U.S., the percentage of women in science has decreased, while the need for scientists has increased. Further research is needed on the nature and effect of such relationships as progesterone fluctuation and behavior, sociocultural/biological factors and different cognitive orientations and personality traits, field-dependence and direction of intellectual ability, motivation and perceptions of women's role, educational emphasis on the masculinity of science and loss of potential creative women scientists. The author describes a research study on such questions to be undertaken at the University of Lund, Sweden.

109

Giuliani, Betty and Centra, John A. THE WOMAN VETERINARIAN. *Personnel and Guidance Journal*, 1968, 46(10), 971-975.

Veterinary Medicine. Role/Sex Conflict. Career Patterns. Career Achievement.

The assumption that women veterinarians quickly become professionally inactive after graduation does not appear to be valid. Women who graduated from Michigan State University School of Veterinarian Medicine were in practice 78 percent of the total number of years they might have practiced. Ninety percent of them intend to continue or return to full-time practice in the future, and 96 percent are currently practicing in a veterinary specialty and most express a deep commitment to their work and obtain satisfaction from it. However, the career patterns of the 50 women surveyed were characterized by interruptions in practice, lower salaries, curtailment of activity, and participation in only a few of the specialties within the profession. Despite the need for career women to curtail professional activity for marriage and family, the tendency of women vets to engage in only a few of the specialties is probably an attempt to reduce professional role-sex conflicts. Undertaken to determine the similarities and differences of men and women graduate practitioners of Michigan State University in professional practice patterns, factors that influenced their choice of profession, and satisfaction with the field, the researchers compared the questionnaire responses of 50 women and 953 men.

110

Glancy, Dorothy J. HLS SURVEY WOMEN IN LAW. *Harvard Law School Bulletin,* 1970, 21(5), 22-33.

Law. Career Patterns. Success Avoidance.

Women graduates of Harvard Law School had more circumscribed job choices than men graduates, although no evidence was found to substantiate a wide-spread "negative" attitude on the part of employers toward women graduates. More than three-fourths of women graduates are employed. Those not working are kept from it by child-rearing responsibilities, and most intend to return to work. Upon graduation, almost three-fourths of the men went to work for law firms, but only about half the women did. Women graduates become consultants only half as frequently as men. Men and women in law both divert some time from practice to public service. Considerably more men than women engage in general practice, corporate law, litigation, and commercial law. Both men and women now practice poverty law, although positions in this field were formerly held mostly by women.

Women tended to practice corporate law in their initial postgraduate positions. Many of them leave this field of law, in contrast to men, who tend to stay in the field. Since graduation, over half of the women made no more than one change in employment; the comparable figure for men was 39 percent. More than one third of the women (but only 16 percent of the men) indicated that they are not now engaged in the occupation (within the field of law) of their first choice. Women lawyers have significantly fewer clients than men. While men and women lawyers receive the same salaries in their initial positions, fewer than 12 percent of the women are making more than $20,000 today, as compared with 57 percent of the men. The distribution of men and women graduates throughout the country is fairly equal except in the Midwest, where 12 percent of the men practice, but only five percent of the women. Women lawyers showed anxiety about success three or four times as frequently as the men (Horner, 1970). To obtain these findings, the researcher analyzed the responses of 400 men and 165 women graduates of Harvard Law School to a mailed questionnaire she designed. Only 66 percent of the women in the sample were married in contrast to 81 percent of the men. Of the married women, 63 percent were married to lawyers.

111

Harbeson, Gladys E. CHOICE AND CHALLENGE FOR THE AMERICAN WOMAN. Cambridge, Mass.: Shenkman Publishing Co., 1967. 185 pages.

Life Styles. Career Motivation. Career Planning.

For women, life planning is a new opportunity, a product of change. The former solitary goal for women, marriage and family, now exists alongside the goal of self-fulfillment through love, marriage and work. Today's woman is in the forefront of a revolution in life patterns, a revolution brought on by many factors or changes in attitudes and practice in recent decades. These include expansion of opportunities for women in higher education, advances of industry and technology that have reduced the demands of home responsibilities, the assumption of socialization training by schools and communities, and the consistently rising number of women entering and returning to the work force. Changes and suggestions for change that will help women who choose this new pattern of living include better counseling, better education, etc. The author draws on existing literature and research to develop her discussion.

112

Henschel, Beverly Jean Smith. A COMPARISON OF THE PERSONALITY VARIABLES OF WOMEN ADMINISTRATORS AND WOMEN TEACHERS IN EDUCATION. Doctoral Dissertation (U. Utah), 1964.

Education. Career Prediction. Career Motivation.

Women educators exhibit more masculine responses than feminine responses on the Edwards Personality Preference Schedule, indicating leadership qualities. They score higher than women in general in ability to analyze and predict behaviors in others, are less likely to feel inferior, and are not as likely to help others in need. The typical Midwest administrator in education exhibited strong leadership, high intraception, and high heterosexual activity, while the typical Midwestern teacher also scored high in heterosexual activity and intraception but scored higher than the administrator on endurance. The typical educational supervisor scored higher in leadership, intraception, endurance, affiliation and lack of opposition to change or novelty, while the typical teacher also scored high in leadership, intraception, heterosexual activity and exhibitionism. The sample for this survey included 136 women administrators, teachers and supervisors. All subjects were administered the Edwards Personality Preference Schedule and filled out a personal data sheet.

113

Honigman, Rhonda. WOMEN IN ENGINEERING. A report to the Conference of Professional and Academic Women, Professional Women's Caucus, June, 1970, Washington, D.C. Mimeo. 2 pages.

Engineering. Career Satisfaction. Career Barriers.

The barriers to women entering the field of engineering are diverse, ranging from an attitude that it is a masculine field to discrimination in promotion and lack of appropriate representation in professional organizations for engineers. In the United States, only two percent of all engineers are women. But there is also a positive side to the story including acceptance by most male engineers on the job, rewarding work, and income that exceeds that for other jobs that women find available. These findings are based on personal experience and observation.

114

Kaplan, Harold I., M.D. WOMEN PHYSICIANS: THE MORE EFFECTIVE RECRUITMENT AND UTILIZATION OF THEIR TALENTS AND THE RESISTANCE TO IT—THE FINAL CONCLUSIONS OF A SEVEN-YEAR STUDY. *The Woman Physician*, 1970, 25(9), 561-570.

Medicine. Educational Facilitators. Discrimination.

Prejudice against women physicians on the part of American medical educators is a significant factor in the low percentage (nine percent) of women physicians in this country. It is manifested often in the refusal of medical educators to admit women to medical school and in their resistance to making provisions for mothers already enrolled. In contrast, in countries where provisions are made to accommodate the special needs of student working mothers, the percentage of women physicians is considerably higher. In Russia, it is 65 percent and in England, 24 percent. Citing his own experience in a special residency training program in psychiatry for physician mothers, the author makes recommendations for modifying training to bring about the more effective recruitment of women into medicine. These findings were based on a mailed questionnaire to the deans of over 95 percent of American and Canadian medical schools and ministers of health in foreign countries.

115

Lewis, Edwin C. DEVELOPING WOMEN'S POTENTIAL. Ames, Iowa: Iowa State University Press, 1968. 389 pages.

Minority Status. Discrimination. Career-Marriage Conflict.

In this examination of research on women, the author demonstrates the lack of consensus in the field and the lack of real data to support extremist positions. Women have been studied and dissected in terms of their physiology, personalities, and spiritual qualities, but an element of mystery about women remains. Women have been viewed as a group and not as individuals. Fortunately, the modern feminist movement is concerned with women as individuals, their abilities, needs, choices, new roles. The modern woman faces the dilemma of striving to become a person without a clear self identity in the midst of rapid change. Women cannot be considered a minority numerically, but in terms of their psychological and sociological status in our society, they meet minority criteria—they suffer discrimination, they are kept at a "social distance" by men (the superior group), they encounter resistance when going against tradition. Women's life choices today include homemaker, career, community leader or some combination of these, but having to choose which can cause considerable conflict. The conflicts women face include traditional restrictions on individual development, discriminatory socialization practices in and out of the home, etc. The author surveys existing research and theory (some of it conflicting), without specifically citing sources in the body of the text, to develop his argument. An extensive bibliography is included, however, along with appendices describing specific research.

116

Lopate, Carol. WOMEN IN MEDICINE. Baltimore, Maryland: The Josiah Macy, Jr. Foundation, The Johns Hopkins University Press, 1968. 204 pages.

Medicine. Career Barriers. Discrimination. Higher Education.

Women physicians are successfully combining family and work, even with minimum help from society. The lack of scholarship aid to medical students, the need for flexible scheduling during training years, inadequate child-care facilities, and the lack of child-care tax deductions are several of the deficiencies in the system that make a woman's entry into the medical profession and completion of training very difficult. However, many women who enter medicine sense the bias against them and the pressures to prove they are "worthy" of the professional status. They are reluctant to ask for changes in the system that might help them accomplish their jobs of wife and mother more easily. The real need for more doctors, and the current interest in restructuring the medical profession will aid the situation and will enable many more able women to enter the field. As American society eliminates the sociological factors that inhibit young girls' career horizons to typically feminine occupations, the number of women interested in pursuing professional careers will increase.

The author treats the factors that affect women's entry into medicine such as attitudes of parents, teachers, counselors, medical educators, and the public; training and educational requirements; marital status, and sex-labeling of the discipline. She also describes the life of a woman as a medical student, intern, resident, and practicing physician. Data for the book, commissioned by the Josiah Macy, Jr. Foundation, resulted from a conference on women in medicine in 1966, existing research, and extensive interviews.

117

Mattfeld, Jacquelyn A. and Van Aken, Carol G. (Eds.) WOMEN AND THE SCIENTIFIC PROFESSIONS: THE M.I.T. SYMPOSIUM ON AMERICAN WOMEN IN SCIENCE AND ENGINEERING. Cambridge, Mass.: The M.I.T. Press, 1965. 250 pages.

Science. Career Barriers. Career Achievement.

This is a report of a conference held to: 1) convey to women that difficulties of entering a scientific field are surmountable and that satisfying careers can be attained; 2) bring together authorities to suggest ways of solving problems that keep women from entering scientific fields, and 3) attract favorable attention of industry, the public, and educational institutions to the contributions made by women scientists and the need to increase their number. Conference participants examined the high degree of commitment required of women who plan to enter a scientific profession, the cases for and against women in science, barriers that keep women from entering the field, and strategies for closing the gap between women's potential and the low number of women in science. Transcripts and panel discussions are included in the volume.

118

Matthews, Margie R. THE TRAINING AND PRACTICE OF WOMEN PHYSICIANS: A CASE STUDY. *Journal of Medical Education*, 1970, 45(12), 1016-1024.

Medicine. Role/Sex Conflict. Educational Facilitators. Educational Counseling.

Female physicians represent only about six percent of all practicing physicians in the United States today. Reasons for this small representation include circumstances unique to the medical profession, the traditional attitudes in America concerning women's place in the world of work, and women's conflict regarding multiple roles. The situation will change as women's attitudes change and as their interest increases. Change will also come from women's demands for innovations in existing systems to facilitate their advancement in the medical profession such as better counseling, child care centers, flexible residence schedules, and financial aid. Although 23 percent of the freshmen girls at the college studied indicated interest in medicine and 39 percent of their graduating class received degrees in science, only five percent applied to medical school. Nationally, female medical students have an attrition rate twice that of men. However, 95.7 percent of the licensed female physicians in this study were employed. To increase the number of female physicians, educators must provide better counseling services for able, interested females, innovative medical school practices and procedures, and more financial aid. Conducted at Duke University Medical Center in 1967 and 1968, the study focused on the training and work patterns of female physicians in the community.

119

McMurray, Georgia L. SOCIAL WORK. Report to the Conference of Professional and Academic Women, Professional Women's Caucus, June 1970, Washington, D.C. Mimeo. 3 pages.

Social Work.

The development of the field of social work paralleled the development of the feminist and pacifist movements of the late 19th and early 20th centuries and 68 percent of the members of the National Association of Social Workers (1968) are women. But they do not hold executive positions in this field. Women represent 41 percent of all case workers, but only 20 percent of all administrators. For males, the situation is reversed. In fact, present trends emphasizing the acknowledgement of social work as a profession include a push for attracting more males, which would increase salaries and prestige for the field. The implication is that as long as the field of social work remains a woman's field, the status of the field will remain low.

120

Morrow, L. HEALTH PROFESSIONS. A Report to the Conference of Professional and Academic Women, Professional Women's Caucus, June 1970, Washington, D.C. Mimeo. 2 pages.

Medicine. Discrimination. Educational Facilitators.

Women physicians represent only 10 percent of all physicians in practice in the United States (1970). Although more women are now being admitted to medical schools (five to nine percent) there are still proportionately fewer completing medical training. Of those completing training and entering practice, many have experienced discrimination in relation to salary and promotion. However, the trend is shifting, and more encouragement is being provided for women to enter the medical profession. There seems to be no lack of available positions for the trained physician, regardless of sex. Several medical organizations—the American Medical Women's Association and the American Medical Association—are increasing their efforts to promote medical careers for women. To facilitate the entrance of women into medicine, educators and other interested parties should promote the establishment of day-care centers and the acceptance of part-time study and practice.

121

National Academy of Sciences, Research Division of the Office of Scientific Personnel, National Research Council. CAREER OF PH.D.'S: ACADEMIC VERSUS NONACADEMIC. A SECOND REPORT ON FOLLOW-UP OF DOCTORATE COHORTS, 1935-1960. Career Patterns Report Number Two, Washington, D.C. 1968. 106 pages. (Chapter IV: CAREERS OF WOMEN. Pages 69-98.)

Career Patterns. Graduate Education. Higher Education.

A comparison of the career patterns of male and female Ph.D.s shows that the women receive lower salaries. Married women earn 25 to 30 percent less than men at the same time interval after earning the doctorate, and, on the average, single women with Ph.D.s earn more than married women with Ph.D.s, but never as much as men. Women progress less rapidly than men up the academic ladder and receive less support for their research. Many more women than men rely on a single source of support, and women do more teaching and less research than men. In pursuit of graduate education, single women provide more of their own support than married women, and women receive less support than men for graduate education, especially from government sources. The proportion of women in "always academic" positions is comparable to that of men, but more women shift to and from academic positions and fewer women remain in "always nonacademic" positions than men. The proportion of female Ph.D.s is fairly substantial in the social sciences and humanities, arts, and professions, but only a very small proportion of women hold Ph.Ds in the physical sciences. A larger proportion of women than men receive postdoctoral fellowships. This holds true particularly for nonscientists who follow academic careers later. Data were derived from a survey of 1,045 female Ph.D.s in all fields who earned their doctoral degrees between 1935 and 1960.

122

Parrish, John B. ARE THERE WOMEN IN ENGINEERING'S FUTURE? *Journal of the American Association of University Women*, 1965, 59(1), 29-31.

Engineering. Career Barriers. Career Achievement. Career Satisfaction.

Although employers rate female engineers highly in terms of performance and female engineers rate the field as a highly desirable one, women comprise only one percent of employed engineers. In this survey of 182 engineering firms, most of the employers of female engineers were large firms, with more than 12,000 employees, who had started hiring women only during the past eight years. Most employers ranked women's work as average or above average. Among reasons for not hiring women, these firms cited lack of women applicants, unsuitability of the women's field of specialization, the requirements of travel, irregular hours, lifting heavy equipment and materials, and women's lack of career orientation. In another survey of 266 members of the Society of Women Engineers (SWE), representing about one-fourth of all college-trained women engineers, 83 percent were employed. They reported very little prejudice among their employers but admitted this was because of the great demand for professionals in science and technology. Another factor mentioned was that many aerospace engineering tasks are short term, from one to five years, and women adapt more readily than men to these positions. Ninety percent of these women found engineering satisfying and strongly recommended the field to other undergraduate women. Of the 223 SWE respondents working at the time of the survey, 60 percent were married and 31 percent had children living at home. When asked why more women do not enter this field, the respondents cited lack of positive advice, education, and career information.

123

Parrish, John B. TOP LEVEL TRAINING OF WOMEN IN THE UNITED STATES, 1900-1960. *Journal of the National Association of Women Deans and Counselors,* 1962, 25(2), 67-73.

Graduate Education. Career Barriers. Higher Education.

Women who have earned doctoral degrees have distinguished themselves in almost all academic disciplines, but the total number of women earning these degrees is lower today (10 percent) than it was between 1900 and 1930 (15 percent). In addition to the decrease in the percent of doctorates earned by women, an extreme imbalance in their distribution was observed. That is, almost two-thirds of the doctorates awarded in 1960 were in education and the social sciences. Even in the academic areas that have been considered "women's" disciplines, such as home economics and library science, the percentage of female Ph.D. candidates has decreased while the percentage of male candidates has increased (50 percent). Thus, the future participation of women in higher education shows a definite trend toward a decline because of the diminishing number of women Ph.D. candidates and the serious imbalance among fields of specialization. Data for the survey were provided by the American Council on Education, National Research Council, Office of Education and several other sources of information on women Ph.D. candidates.

124

Parrish, John B. WOMEN IN TOP LEVEL TEACHING AND RESEARCH. *Journal of the American Association of University Women,* 1962, 55(January), 99-106.

Higher Education. Advancement Barriers.

At 20 selected institutions of higher education, women constitute only ten percent of the full-time faculty. At ten institutions with high enrollment, women faculty represented 11 percent of the full-time professional staff, and at ten highly endowed institutions, only seven percent. Descending the hierarchy of positions in higher education from full professor to lecturer, the percentage of women employed increases to a high of 16 percent as lecturers. The percentage of women employed in different subject areas varies from a high in such areas as education (12 percent) to a low (one percent) in physical and biological sciences. In the field of research, women represent 23 percent of researchers. Thus, few women hold full professional staff positions even though they are well represented in the lower ranks, and are making great contributions to their fields at the lower levels. Reasons for their failure to advance need more investigation. Survey questionnaires and supplementary correspondence supplied the data.

125

Powers, Lee; Wiesenfelder, Harry, and Parmelee, Rexford. PRACTICE PATTERNS OF WOMEN AND MEN PHYSICIANS. Preliminary report to the American Association of Medical Colleges, October 1966. 41 pages.

Career Patterns. Medicine. Family Responsibilities. Career Achievement.

A study of the patterns of practice of male and female graduates of U.S. medical schools from 1931 to 1956 showed that nearly 55 percent of female physician graduates for the entire sample were engaged in full-time medical activity; 31 percent were practicing part time. Eighty-six percent of single women were in full-time practice. Family responsibility was the determining factor for most women who chose not to work or to work part time, though 39 percent of married women with three or more children were in full-time practice. The annual median income for full-time work for women was $16,132, as compared to $25,879 for men. The part-time figures for annual median income were $8,635 and $19,791, respectively. Thirty percent of the female graduates of 1931 married before completion of training; 25 years later, in 1956, the figure had increased to 63 percent.

All female graduates (2,078) and a random sample of male (2,580) graduates from seven graduating classes separated by five-year intervals during this period completed a three-page confidential information form. The response rate for women was 78 percent, slightly higher than the 76 percent rate for men. Cooperating agencies included the American Medical Association, Association of American Medical Colleges, and American Women's Medical Association.

126

Renshaw, Josephine E. and Pennell, Maryland T. DISTRIBUTION OF WOMEN PHYSICIANS, 1969. *The Women Physician*, 1971, 26(4), 187-195.

Medicine. Career Achievement.

A survey of 24,000 female physicians living in the United States and possessions, completed in December 1969, indicates that 84.3 percent of these women were professionally active. The majority (17,400) were involved in direct care of patients, and 2,900, in other activities related to medicine such as teaching, administration, research. Female physicians comprise 6.7 percent of all active physicians in the country. The majority specialize in pediatrics, psychiatry, general practice, and internal medicine, in that order. They comprise 20.3 percent of all pediatricians and 18.5 percent of all public health physicians. Almost 1,200 of the women physicians are federal employees, or four percent of all federal physicians. Data were drawn from the American Medical Association "physician master file."

127

Rossi, Alice S. WOMEN IN SCIENCE: WHY SO FEW? *Science,* 1965, 148 (No. 3674), 1196-1202.

Science. Minority Status. Engineering. Career Patterns. Medicine.

Women who are appointed, elected or promoted to professional positions of high status and large responsibility are usually unmarried or widows. No real solution to the problem of women's status in America will be found until all women are able to benefit from the full range of society's professional opportunities. According to the 1960 census, only nine percent of the employed natural scientists and less than one percent of the engineers were women. In the 1950s, the rate of increase in scientific professional employment was much greater for men than women. In 1960, female scientists and engineers were less likely than men to have advanced degrees, to be employed in industry or to be married. They earned less money at each level of education and worked fewer hours per week. Female physicians have very low withdrawal rates, whereas, female scientists withdraw at a higher rate than teachers—51 percent as against 34 percent. Upper-middle-class values, in particular, give women status on the basis of their husbands' occupations and the bearing of children. Men are more conservative than women on the issue of women's careers.

128

Sassower, Doris L. WOMEN IN LAW. A report to the Conference of Professional and Academic Women, Professional Women's Caucus, June 1970, Washington, D.C. Mimeo. 4 pages.

Law. Discrimination. Career Barriers.

One in every forty lawyers in the U.S. today is a woman. The proportionate number of female lawyers is decreasing; in 1950, one in every 28 lawyers was a woman. During this same period, the number of practicing female lawyers in other countries has more than doubled. Subtle prejudices still exist in jobs, salaries and advancement opportunities for female lawyers, although the barriers to entrance in law schools, including the most prestigious (Harvard and Yale), have been eliminated somewhat, and admittance to bar associations is more open. Trends and cases of job discrimination, including professorships in law schools, judgeships, and salaries, are discussed, and recommendations made for changes that will help women advance in the legal profession.

129

Schuck, Victoria. WOMEN IN POLITICAL SCIENCE: SOME PRELIMINARY OBSERVATIONS. *Newsletter of the American Political Science Association,* 1969, 2(4), 642-653.

Political Science. Higher Education. Graduate Education.

Women are most likely to be political science faculty members in colleges and universities with small political science departments and in institutions offering undergraduate work only. Most women in all types of colleges and universities are concentrated in the lower ranks of the faculty. Of the institutions surveyed, over half reported having no women on the political science faculty at all. While 23.2 percent undergraduate political science majors are women, only 17.5 percent of graduate school students in political science are women. There are factors such as the recency of the women's appointment to the faculty that mitigate against the seeming suggestion of discrimination, but more study is needed. The responses of 473 chairmen of political science departments and graduate schools to a four-item questionnaire were analyzed to provide the data.

130

Sharp, Laure M. EDUCATION AND EMPLOYMENT: THE EARLY CAREERS OF COLLEGE GRADUATES. Baltimore: The Johns Hopkins University Press, 1970. 162 pages.

Career Patterns. Graduate Education. Higher Education. Career Achievement. Educational Counseling.

An examination of the early careers of women college graduates reveals that more women terminate their education with a B.A. degree than men. However, more women take graduate courses for academic and intellectual reasons, while most men continue their education to achieve the goal of broadened job opportunities. Although about a third of all graduate students study part time during their academic career, more women than men find themselves in this position because of financial and family obligations. The majority of women in this study who held masters degrees had majored in education, and most were teaching on the secondary or college level.

Advanced degrees apparently provide considerable professional pay-off to women in all occupations. However, only in the field of education are women fully satisfied with their status and chances for advancement. Teaching represented the highest proportion (67 percent) of the women's occupations in the survey and the teachers exhibited a firm commitment to their occupation as a career, with 80 percent of the B.A. graduates and 90 percent of the M.A. graduates remaining in the field. Although 75 percent of both men and women are employed three years after graduation, only 56 percent of the women are still working five years after graduation. It is clear from the data that colleges and universities must develop new and innovative programs specifically for women so as to prevent talent loss promoted by current collegiate practices.

The book is a report of a comprehensive, nationwide set of studies conducted from 1959 through 1969. It examines the educational and occupational development of a cohort in relation to graduate study, employment, military service, and the nature and importance of undergraduate institutions and education. Data for this study were gathered by the Bureau of Social Science Research under the sponsorship of the National Science Foundation.

131

Simon, Rita James and Rosenthal, Evelyn. PROFILE OF THE WOMAN PH.D. IN ECONOMICS, HISTORY, AND SOCIOLOGY. *Journal of the American Association of University Women,* 1967, 60(3), 127-129.

Graduate Education. Career Barriers. Marital Status. Discrimination.

Women with doctoral degrees earn about $700 less annually than men with doctoral degrees and generally have less access to colleagues and research possibilities. Fifteen percent of married women with Ph.D. degrees reported that their careers had been affected by nepotism rules and that they were not able to hold the position they desired at the salary level desired, even though they appeared to be professionally competent. The women reporting discrimination based on nepotism had published more than the men in the sample and the rest of women with Ph.D's in the sample (both married and unmarried). When professional ranks were compared in history, economics and sociology, women were overrepresented in the lower ranks. This study compared the professional characteristics and productivity of women who had recently received their doctoral degrees by marital status. They were also compared to the men who had recently received doctoral degrees. The sample consisted of

5,370 women and 1,787 men with doctoral degrees. A nationwide mail survey was completed and returned by 60 percent of the women, with a comparable rate of return for the men.

132

Simon, Rita James; Clark, Shirley Merritt, and Galway, Kathleen. THE WOMAN PH.D.: A RECENT PROFILE. *Social Problems,* 1967, 15(Fall), 221-236.

Higher Education. Discrimination.

In terms of "formal rights" and objective measures of equality, the woman with a doctoral degree, regardless of marital status, seems to be an accepted professional colleague of men. Although there are differences between male and female Ph.D.'s, they are small enough to be negligible. The woman publishes as much as the man (the married women, slightly more); is involved in the activities of her professional organization; does consulting work, and is more likely to be awarded fellowships and accepted in honorary societies. However, women may suffer discrimination such as denial of many informal signs of belonging and recognition—not being able to find someone with whom to share a research project or with whom to talk professionally. To find out if women Ph.D.'s are as productive as male Ph.D.'s and if married women Ph.D.'s are as productive as unmarried women Ph.D.'s, the researchers examined the responses of 1,764 women Ph.D.'s in the sciences, social sciences, humanities, and education who received their doctoral degrees between 1958 and 1963 to a mail questionnaire. The responses of a smaller male sample were also examined.

133

The National Council of Administrative Women in Education, National Education Association. WANTED—MORE WOMEN IN EDUCATIONAL LEADERSHIP. 1965. 28 pages.

Higher Education. Discrimination.

A review of research on the status of women in elementary, secondary, and higher education shows a loss in status and number over the last 20 years. Cultural mores and discrimination against women have caused this. Moves to correct such inequities must be undertaken by concerned organizations and individuals.

134

Thomas, Martha J. B. ENGINEERING. *A Woman's Work.* New York, N.Y.: Barnard College, 1967. Pages 10-11.

Engineering.

The female engineer in this country is a rarity, comprising only about one percent of our total engineering force, compared to 30 percent in the Soviet Union. The average female engineer is 37 years old, has three children, and earns over $10,000 a year.

135

Torpey, W. G. A MORE SIGNIFICANT ROLE FOR WOMEN ENGINEERS. *Journal of the American Association of University Women,* 1964, 57(2), 59-61.

Engineering. Educational Facilitators.

Educators, employers, and professional associations of engineers must accept the challenge of stimulating maximum development and utilization of the engineering abilities of men *and* women. Although women have demonstrated their abilities in all areas of engineering and the number of female engineers has constantly risen from 750 in 1940 to 7,404 in 1960, women still represent only one-half of one percent of all engineers working for the federal government, the single largest employer of engineers. Supply and demand prognostications indicate a continual shortage of engineers unless steps are taken to increase manpower supplies. Thus, more qualified women should be encouraged to enter the engineering field. Although opportunities for part-time education and employment are increasing, more are needed. Recent research into the employability of women refutes widely-held notions that women are too emotional and unreliable to hold responsible positions in industry. Counseling and training must be provided to upgrade women in technical jobs to high-level positions. The author, a manpower specialist in the Office of Emergency Planning, Executive Office of the President, draws on data provided by OEP, the Bureau of Labor Statistics, the U.S. Civil Service Commission, and recommendations from the Commission on the Status of Women and the Science Advisory Committee, Executive Office of the President.

136

U.S. Department of Labor, Women's Bureau. FIRST JOBS OF COLLEGE WOMEN, REPORT ON WOMEN GRADUATES, CLASS OF 1957. Bulletin No. 268, 1959. 4 pages.

Career Expectations. Employment.

Most of the women college graduates entering the labor market in the second half of 1957 found jobs related to their fields of study. Eighty-three percent of them were able to obtain professional positions. Seventy-six percent of the graduates surveyed were working full time; three percent were looking for work; nine percent were attending school full time; five percent were working and/or attending school part time; and seven percent were not looking for work. Almost three-fourths of the married graduates (38 percent) were working. Fifty-nine percent of the employed graduates were teachers; 6.9 percent were nurses, 6.7 percent were secretaries and stenographers; three percent were biological technicians, and two percent were social and welfare workers. The remaining 22 percent were employed in jobs ranging from stock-and-bond portfolio analyst to probation officer. Approximately 88,000 women were represented in these findings, which were obtained through analysis of the responses of about 4,400 women graduates of 150 colleges and universities to a mail questionnaire survey. The survey was conducted by the National Vocational Guidance Association in cooperation with the Women's Bureau, U.S. Department of Labor.

137

Walt, Dorothy E. THE MOTIVATION FOR WOMEN TO WORK IN HIGH-LEVEL PROFESSIONAL POSITIONS. Doctoral Dissertation (American U.), 1962.

Career Achievement.

The motivation to work of high-level professional women is related to job events and psychological need satisfaction. If job events provide interesting work, responsibility, and recognition, women can be expected to achieve optimal levels of efficiency. It is also suggested that for the woman who lives alone, a job provides a means for belonging and identification. Negative factors or occurrences vis-a-vis work generally centered around poor interpersonal or group feelings. Fifty women employed by the government in high-level professional positions were interviewed with a semistructured interview schedule about various aspects that motivate or hinder performance and advancement in the work world.

138

Weinberg, Ethel. PART-TIME RESIDENCY TRAINING. *Journal of the American Medical Association*, 1969, **210**(8), 1435-1438.

Medicine. Educational Facilitators.

Although the majority of specialty certifying boards (anesthesiology, dermatology, internal medicine, etc.) report sympathy with the concept of part-time residency training and would consider it on an individual basis, only the field of psychiatry offers part-time training opportunities on a regular basis. Growing numbers of women are entering the field of medicine and there is a real need for more doctors. Examination of the arguments most frequently used against part-time training—patient care problems, institutional inconvenience, program inadequacies for trainees—reveals that more study and testing of the real effects of such training is needed before either accepting or rejecting it. The author conducted a survey of the attitudes of the certifying boards toward part-time training to find out whether they would accept such training as sufficient for certification. The AMA's recently-adopted favorable position on the subject may increase the acceptability of part-time training.

139

Wetherby, Phyllis. LIBRARIANSHIP: OPPORTUNITY FOR WOMEN? A report to the Conference of Professional and Academic Women, Professional Women's Caucus, June 1970, Washington, D.C. Mimeo. 4 pages.

Librarianship. Income.

Librarianship is an open field for men and a "dead end" for women. There are more female librarians than male librarians and the field is dominated by women, but few women are employed in administrative posts. Salaries for men in library science are generally a third greater than salaries for women. A comparison of the membership in the American Library Association (1965), of which three-fourths are women, and the Special Libraries Association, of which three-fourths are women, supports this conclusion. A table of comparative data is included in the report.

140

White, James J. WOMEN IN THE LAW. *Michigan Law Review*, 1967, 65(6), 1051-1122.

Law. Income. Career Advancement. Discrimination.

Male lawyers make approximately $1,500 more than female lawyers in their first positions and the difference in income increases over time. At the end of ten years of legal experience, nine percent of the men earn $20,000, as compared to the one percent of women earning similar income. Men far outnumber women in their first job placement in large firms, but this difference equalizes itself over time with equal proportions of male and female lawyers employed in large and small firms, but more males than females employed in medium-sized firms. Men often use the federal government and state and local government as stepping stones into the field of law, while more women (about one-third) find long-term employment in government.

In terms of work tasks, more women than men are involved in trusts and estates, domestic relations and tax work. Full-time married female lawyers earn more than full-time unmarried female lawyers. Fifty percent of the women lawyers in this study stated they had experienced discrimination because of sex. The income difference between men and women (the major factor surveyed in this study) cannot be traced to the class rank or Law Review representation, school attended, type of employer, type of work, or rate of job turnover. From this, it is clear that female lawyers are discriminated against. Recommendations to eliminate such discrimination include: initiation of more thorough and sophisticated studies of the effectiveness of women lawyers; increase in corrective action on the part of American law schools by hiring more women faculty and by combating discriminatory hiring practices through placement facilities; increased collective action on the part of women lawyers themselves. These findings were based on a mailed questionnaire from 1,298 female and 1,329 male lawyers who graduated from law school between 1956 and 1965.

141

White, Kinnard. SOCIAL BACKGROUND VARIABLES RELATED TO CAREER COMMITMENT OF WOMEN TEACHERS. *Personnel and Guidance Journal*, 1967, 45(7), 648-652.

Career Commitment. Education.

Social background experiences appear to affect the level of career commitment in young women employed as elementary school teachers. Married women from working-class backgrounds who financed their own college education and who had working mothers are likely to have a strong commitment to a teaching career. In comparison, single women from middle- or upper-class backgrounds who had nonworking mothers and whose parents financed their education exhibit less career commitment to teaching. The type of college attended is not a significant factor in career commitment. However, further research on the effect that social class and mobility have on career commitment is needed. The sample was 143 female elementary school teachers employed in their first teaching position. Career commitment was measured by a preference scale developed by the investigator and a questionnaire concerning the socioeconomic background, mothers' work histories, source of financial support through college, type of college attended, and marital status of the subjects.

142

Bayer, Alan E. and Astin, Helen S. SEX DIFFERENCES IN ACADEMIC RANK AND SALARY AMONG SCIENCE DOCTRATES IN TEACHING. *The Journal of Human Resources*, 1968, 3(2), 191-199.

Career Advancement. Income. Higher Education. Science.

The beginning academic rank of new scientists in college and university teaching positions is unrelated to sex. Over time, women in the natural sciences continue to receive promotions comparable to those of men. However, women in the social sciences tend to be promoted less rapidly than men. Salary differentials exist in beginning and later academic positions, regardless of major field specialty, work setting, or academic rank. These data support the contentions of women that salary discrimination is practiced more severely than discrimination in relation to tenure or promotions. Data were derived from employment information provided by 2,074 scientists with Ph.D.s for the 1964 National Register of Scientific and Technical Personnel.

143

Bernard, Jessie. ACADEMIC WOMEN. University Park, Pennsylvania: The Pennsylvania State University Press, 1964. 331 pages.

Higher Education. Academic Reform.

In this study of the sociology of academic women, the author reveals the low status of such women and the need for institutions of higher education to eliminate institutional barriers that prevent women from full participation in academic life. Women are concentrated in the low-prestige positions of teaching (principally in undergraduate departments), and few are in high academic or administrative positions. It often appears that women prefer to be teachers, while men prefer to be "men of knowledge." Also, in campus social life, women faculty members achieve status on the basis of their sex, rather than academic profession or achievements. Thus, they are treated and are expected to behave like faculty wives at social gatherings.

An examination of the lives of several early academic women—Maria Sanford, Ellen Swallow Richards, Florence Sabin, Alice Freeman Palmer, M. Carey Thomas, Vida Scudder, Ruth Fulton Benedict—shows the strengths of their belief in reform and their idealism. Today, although many women are brighter than their male peers, their devotion to reform is somewhat less than, or different from, that exhibited by academic women earlier. Although academic women generally do not achieve the same status and prestige as academic men, there is little support or evidence that it is the result of discrimination. Their lower status is probably due to the lowered supply of qualified academic women. The author draws on autobiographical accounts of academic women, interviews, existing literature, and the results of the Pennsylvania State University Studies on academic performance, the Matched Scientists Study, and the Biological Sciences Communication Project Study of Laboratory Bioscientists to develop her discussion.

144

Bynum, Caroline Walker and Martin, Janet M. THE SAD STATUS OF WOMEN TEACHING AT HARVARD OR "FROM WHAT YOU SAID I WOULD NEVER HAVE KNOWN YOU WERE A WOMAN." *Radcliffe Quarterly*, 1970, 54(2), 12-15.

Higher Education. Harvard. Discrimination.

Women have low status at Harvard and are virtually excluded from regular academic positions. In the 1960s, the number of women in regular tenured appointments—full and associate professorships—decreased from 12 to 11, while the total number of such appointments rose from 550 to 731. Most of the women on the faculty of arts and sciences are concentrated in the irregular categories of lecturer and researcher.

145

Committee on University Women. WOMEN IN THE UNIVERSITY OF CHICAGO: REPORT OF THE COMMITTEE ON

UNIVERSITY WOMEN. Prepared for the Committee of the Council of the University Senate, University of Chicago, 1970. 122 pages.

Higher Education. Discrimination. University of Chicago.

Discrimination against women at the University of Chicago may not be overt, but of the 1,189 members of the regular teaching faculty in 1969, only 87 (seven percent) were women. This figure is considerably below the average for all universities in the country, but is about the same as at other "elite" universities. Many procedures for hiring and retaining faculty are flexible, but faculty members are often unaware of them. Problems cited by nontenured faculty and student women generally related to issues affecting both men and women and were the result of lack of awareness by high administrative and academic personnel. Undertaken to examine the status and opportunities open to academic women, the study includes data and opinions gathered from various questionnaires. The scope of the investigation was limited by lack of information and record-keeping in various academic departments which operate somewhat independently of university administration.

146

Graham, Patricia A. WOMEN IN ACADEME. *Science*, 1970, 169(3952), 1284-1290.

Higher Education. Educational Facilitators. Graduate Education.

The lack of widespread feminine militancy on college campuses gives administrators opportunity to move to correct the demonstrated lack of status for women on campus. Possible corrective measures include: • appointing more qualified women to positions in administration and teaching, • increasing the availability of part-time teaching and other professional positions, • instituting more realistic maternity leave policies, • making rigid tenure procedures more flexible, • abandoning nepotism rules so that both husband and wife can work at the same institution, • developing day care centers, and • instituting curriculum changes to show contributions women have made in history.

The need for these changes is shown by recent research findings. Women represented 47 percent of the undergraduate population in 1920, and 15 percent of them earned Ph.D. degrees. Today, only 40 percent of the undergraduate population is women, and only ten percent of them earn the Ph.D. Among persons qualified to be college students who do not enter college, 75 to 90 percent are women. Women represent only 18 percent of college and university faculties, and most of them teach in female-oriented subjects such as education, social science, and home economics.

Single women Ph.D. holders achieve professional status and high salary on college campuses faster than married Ph.D. holders, although consistently less often than men with Ph.D. degrees. Possible explanations for the low proportion of women employed in higher education include the discriminatory factors inherent in "equal" recruitment and employment procedures, the internal ambivalence experienced by many women about career versus home, and the cultural attitude against women taking on the responsibilities of a career. The scarcity of adequate household help and lack of day-care centers are also influencing factors. The author surveyed recent research on the status of women in higher education, discussed the history of higher education for women, and used personal observation and experiences to support arguments presented.

147

Harris, Ann Sutherland. THE SECOND SEX IN ACADEME. *American Association of University Professors Bulletin,* 1970, Fall, 283-295.

Higher Education. Discrimination. Graduate Education.

Discrimination against women at all levels of higher education is widespread. Men continue to discourage women from intellectual pursuits in spite of evidence of ability and low attrition among female graduate students and the high career commitment demonstrated by women earning Ph.D. degrees. Male faculty members persistently express attitudes showing they doubt women's capabilities. Common discriminatory practices include: low salaries for women, rigid antinepotism rules, and exploitation of part-time women faculty members. Discrimination against women may be even greater in relation to administrative positions than in relation to faculty appointments. Women must work to promote changes in attitudes, for, as women come to be seen as human beings with ability and potential—rather than as quota requirements—higher education will benefit. Women must work to secure services such as day-care centers to help bring about change. Anecdotes, quotes, and empirical data are used to support theses of discrimination against women in higher education.

148

Harvard University. PRELIMINARY REPORT ON THE STATUS OF WOMEN AT HARVARD. Cambridge: Harvard University, 1970 (March 9), 16 pages.

Harvard. Higher Education. Graduate Education..

Prepared by a women's faculty group at Harvard, this report demonstrates the need for an in-depth study of the status of women at that institution and poses a number of policy questions that need investigation. Overall employment figures on women in academic and administrative positions showed that women held only 13 percent of all academic and administrative positions. These were concentrated mainly at lower levels outside the regular rank and promotion system for faculty; the women held posts as teaching fellows, lecturers, and instructors. No woman held an associate or full professorship. Although women held about one-fourth of the university's administrative positions, only nine of them had high-level posts. Graduate enrollment figures showed that roughly equal percentages of men and women applicants were accepted into the Graduate School of Arts and Sciences. Data were not available, however, on several important issues bearing on equal treatment. For example, there were no data on whether women were given equal financial aid and assistantship opportunities or whether women applicants in general have better academic qualifications than men. Data accompanying this report provide the basis for an outline of issues and policy questions that need further study. The appendix includes limited data on female attrition rates in the graduate school.

149

Kaufman, Helen. THE STATUS OF WOMEN IN ADMINISTRATION IN SELECTED INSTITUTIONS OF HIGHER EDUCATION IN THE UNITED STATES. Doctoral Dissertation (New York University), 1961.

Educational Administration.

There is a discrepancy between theory and action in the hiring of women for administrative posts in institutions of higher education. Data supplied by college presidents and women in executive positions in colleges and universities indicated that 43 percent of the respondents preferred male administrators. A tendency was noted to hire women administrators only in fields such as nursing. Education and experience were reported as the major considerations in hiring, and respondents said that few women were qualified for administrative positions. The sample included 355 presidents and 156 women executives; a review of literature was also conducted.

150

Mooney, Joseph D. ATTRITION AMONG Ph.D. CANDIDATES: AN ANALYSIS OF A COHORT OF RECENT WOODROW WILSON FELLOWS. *The Journal of Human Resources*, 1968, 3(1), 47-62.

Graduate Education. Educational Attrition.

Knowledge of the educational, social, and economic factors associated with attrition among graduate students has been limited to date. This author attempts to isolate systematically the quantitative importance of a number of explanatory variables in the attrition of doctoral degree candidates. Sex, field of study, size of graduate school, and academic achievement (but not socioeconomic status of parents) all seemed to have a significant impact on the success or failure of the graduate students in this sample. "Failure" was defined as attendance in graduate school for six to eight years without acquiring the Ph.D. Attempts to increase the number of Ph.D.s simply by providing more fellowship money will be hampered by social and educational barriers. Since the size of the graduate school is inversely related to the percentage of graduate students acquiring a Ph.D., graduate schools should make a more intensive effort to see that more students get the degree. This makes better sense than simply expanding enrollment in an attempt to satisfy the demand for more Ph.D.s.

151

Oltman, Ruth M. CAMPUS 1970—WHERE DO WOMEN STAND? RESEARCH REPORT OF A SURVEY ON WOMEN IN ACADEME. Washington, D.C.: American Association of University Women, 1970. 25 pages.

Income. Educational Administration. Higher Education.

Women are underrepresented at every level in institutions of higher education, particularly in large public institutions. Representation is more equitable in smaller women's colleges. Ninety percent of the 450 schools surveyed indicated that promotional policies are the same for men and women faculty, but the mean percentage of female heads of departments was less than three percent per school. A similar absence of women administrators exists. Of all the schools surveyed, 43 percent indicated that women students are represented in proportionately smaller numbers than men on student/faculty committees, and 46 percent indicated that no on-campus programs meeting the special educational needs of women had been held during the year preceding the survey. To obtain these findings, the AAUW sent questionnaires to 750 institutional members of the AAUW.

152

Robinson, Lora H. THE STATUS OF ACADEMIC WOMEN. Washington, D.C.: ERIC Clearinghouse on Higher Education, The George Washington University, 1971. 26 pages.

Higher Education. Discrimination.

An examination of the research on the status of women in academe reveals their low status. Specific studies of women doctoral degree holders—such as *Academic Women*, Jesse Bernard; *The Woman Doctorate*, Helen Astin; *Women and the Doctorate*, Susan Mitchell—provide a comprehensive picture of such women and the obstacles they encounter in the pursuit of careers. Examination of recent studies by colleges and universities also confirms the existence of sex discrimination against women in colleges and universities. An annotated listing of 54 such studies of 65 institutions of higher education is included along with a description of 23 projects underway to define the issue in greater detail and to develop strategies for improving the status of academic women.

153

Roby, Pamela. STRUCTURAL AND INTERNALIZED BARRIERS TO WOMEN IN HIGHER EDUCATION. In Rothschild, Constantina S. (Ed.) *Sociology of Women*. Boston: Ginn-Blaisdell, 1971. In press.

Higher Education. Discrimination. Educational Facilitators. Educational Attrition.

Barriers to women in higher education are described and documented. Discrimination in admissions is based on the often mistaken belief that women will have a high rate of attrition. Financial aid is often limited to male full-time students, and married female students subordinate their interests to "putting hubby through." College counselors often advise women not to pursue "masculine" interests and fail to provide encouragement in intellectual development. In course work, the traditional role of women is reinforced, and career development of women is neglected in most curricula. Potential women faculty members are discouraged due to antinepotism rules, low salaries, and lack of arrangements to facilitate combining marriage and career. The low representation of women faculty in turn discourages students who lack role models. Internalized barriers result from the socialization process which reinforces the culturally defined role expectations, and actually creates in women a need to fail, a lack of confidence in other women, and a fear of acting aggressively. Among the suggestions for change are provisions for transfer of credits, part-time study, lifting of age limits, curriculum changes, better counseling, more female faculty, and enforcement of laws barring discrimination. Literature surveys are used to document the arguments.

154

Rossi, Alice S. STATUS OF WOMEN IN GRADUATE DEPARTMENTS OF SOCIOLOGY, 1968-1969. *The American Sociologist*, 1970, 5(1), 1-12.

Sociology. Educational Attrition.

Undertaken to ascertain the status of women students, faculty, and research personnel in 188 graduate departments of sociology, the survey reveals that the more prestigious the department, the lower the representation of women among top faculty. The status of women in the field is evident in these statistics: 43 percent of women college seniors plan graduate work in sociology, but none of the 44 full professors at five elite departments—Berkeley, Chicago, Columbia, Harvard, Michigan—are women. High attrition rates and low career achievement cannot be attributed to lack of ability. Women planning graduate work in sociology often have better academic records than men. One factor contributing to the attrition rates is the absence of female models or colleagues in the field who can provide support and advice. The survey was based in part on data collected previously by the ASA and the results of a questionnaire designed by the author.

155

Simon, Rita James; Clark, Shirley Merrit, and Tifft, Larry L. OF NEPOTISM, MARRIAGE, AND THE PURSUIT OF AN ACADEMIC CAREER. *Sociology of Education*, 1966, 39(4), 344-358.

Higher Education. Discrimination. Antinepotism.

Married women with Ph.D.'s who complain that antinepotism rules hinder their pursuit of careers in higher education are no worse off than women who do not complain of such restrictions. Women who complain, however, are much more productive professionally than other women, married or single, and as productive as men. A change in antinepotism rules will not solve the problems of married women Ph.D.'s as long as de facto discrimination continues. The study of antinepotism regulations in institutions of higher education and their effect on the careers of married women with Ph.D.'s was part of a larger study of their social and professional characteristics. Questionnaires were completed by 2,500 women in four major fields of study. Of these women, 325 had husbands in administrative or teaching posts with colleges or universities, and 192 were affected by antinepotism rules.

156

Simpson, Lawrence Alan. A STUDY OF EMPLOYING AGENTS' ATTITUDES TOWARD ACADEMIC WOMEN IN HIGHER EDUCATION. Doctoral Dissertation (Penn State University), 1968.

Higher Education. Discrimination.

Employing agents at colleges and universities discriminate against academic women when they choose between equally qualified candidates for faculty posts. However, they select a statistically significant number of superior women in preference to less well qualified men. There is no significant difference among deans, departmental chairmen or faculty in their discriminatory attitudes toward equally qualified male and female candidates or in their selection of superior female candidates over less qualified males. Age and experience had an influence on the employment prospects of females while degree and rank did not. Generally, those who discriminate against academic women also exhibit negative attitudes toward women in general. Employing agents were asked to choose between paired resumes to fill hypothetical vacancies. The resumes were paired in three ways: equally qualified man and woman, superior qualified woman over man, and equally qualified candidates with no reference to sex. The employing agents were also administered employment rating scales and the Likert-type Open Subordination of Woman Attitude Scale. The sample consisted of employing agents from six fields of humanities and social sciences in six institutions of higher education.

See also: Simpson, Lawrence. SEX DISCRIMINATION IN THE ACADEMIC WORLD, A SUMMARY OF RESEARCH. Business and Professional Women's Foundation, 2012 Massachusetts Ave., N.W., Washington, D.C. 20036.

157

Beck, Esther Lily. AN ANALYSIS OF SELECTED FACTORS RELEVANT TO THE EMPLOYMENT STATUS IN BUSINESS OFFICES OF MARRIED WOMEN COLLEGE GRADUATES. Doctoral Dissertation (Indiana University), 1963.

Business. Employment. Management. Higher Education.

Education beyond an undergraduate degree appears to be the most important factor in the employment status of women. To attain employment at a managerial level, a woman must generally have supplementary training beyond the bachelor's degree, remain with one firm for an extended period of time, and be of high socioeconomic level. These factors suggest that a woman works because she *wants* to, not because she has to. The smaller the firm, the better the chances for advancement. Interviews with 62 employed women and 37 company representatives of 27 firms with at least 100 employees each supplied the data for the survey. Twelve of the firms were in manufacturing and 15 in service areas such as banking.

158

Burns, Dorothy M. WOMEN IN EDUCATIONAL ADMINISTRATION: A STUDY OF LEADERSHIP IN CALIFORNIA PUBLIC SCHOOLS. Doctoral Dissertation (University of Oregon), 1964.

Educational Administration. Higher Education. Employment Trends. Career Advancement.

Between 1952 and 1962, the proportion of women in administrative positions in California schools declined, while the number of women in supervisory or coordinating positions increased. The lower the job level, the higher the proportion of women employees. Elementary school districts employ more women than high school districts. All women assigned to high-level positions had advanced degrees and credited either their immediate supervisor or themselves for their advancement. All had worked in the field for an extended period. They suggested that women themselves have the responsibility to attain graduate degrees and advance themselves by accepting responsibility. One hundred women holding leadership positions in selected California school districts were administered a questionnaire designed to obtain information on present position and on personal, educational, and work experience background. A review of trends of female employment over the ten-year period was also compiled.

159

Gehlen, Frieda L. WOMEN IN CONGRESS: THEIR POWER AND INFLUENCE IN A MAN'S WORLD. *Trans-action*, 1969, 6(11), 36-40.

Politics. Career Patterns.

A study of the activities of 11 Congresswomen of the 88th Congress showed that they were neither typical housewives nor typical feminists. Four were married, four were widows of former Congressmen, two were widows, one was divorced. Their average age was 58, six years above the average age of Congressmen. Because they were women, potential restraints on their activities existed, such as lack of access to "informal" working associations and policy-making bodies. But most had developed ways to gain insight into situations that male legislators get from "gym room" confabs. Acceptance of a Congresswoman by Congressmen depends on whether the men view her as rational rather than emotional. The Congresswomen did not specialize in service fields such as education and health but they did introduce more bills on cultural matters than men did. All the women liked responding to requests from constituents but none of the men did. The author interviewed Congressmen and Congresswomen to obtain these findings.

160

Kay, Jane J. WHAT DO WOMEN IN PERSONNEL DO? *Personnel Journal*, 1969, 48(10), 810-812.

Personnel. Management.

Women are well represented in the field of personnel management, probably because they are thought to have a greater facility than men for working with people. But they have not been extensively involved in all areas of personnel management. They are most likely to be responsible for limited aspects of employment and are not adequately represented in personnel administration, especially in companies with over 5,000 employees. The most frequently reported job title is Personnel Assistant, followed by Employment Interviewer, Job Analyst, and Training Coordinator. These findings are based on a survey of all 1,000 members of the International Association of Personnel Women.

161

Maule, Frances. EXECUTIVE CAREERS FOR WOMEN. New York: Harper, 1961. 240 pages.

Employment. Business. Career Planning. Executive Careers.

Good opportunities exist for interested women to advance in executive positions. There are more executive positions than there are men to fill them, and attitudes in many fields about women as executives are changing in favor of women. In addition, the number of educated women is increasing. Interested women should become aware of procedures and methods that can help them prepare to assume executive responsibilities. Required education, training and personality characteristics for major business fields are described. The conflict between work and homemaking and the role of the woman as boss are discussed, along with procedures for finding the appropriate career. The last chapter includes soul-searching questions for women such as: Are you really willing to accept the responsibility of an executive position?

162

News Front, THE MANAGEMENT MYSTIQUE. 1964, 8(9), 18-21.

Executive Careers. Dual-Career Families. The Working Wife.

Businessmen react ambivalently to executive women associates and to their own wives' efforts to find careers. Forty-eight percent of 300 business men surveyed had women associates, and half claimed they would not hesitate to hire women for top-level positions. Some men feel that women have advantages and assets as executives and that they tend to evoke loyalty in their subordinates through a personalized approach. Others feel that this personalized approach reduces the woman executive's necessary authority. Men also have ambivalent feelings toward working wives, and neither the men nor their wives have a clear definition of woman's role in marriage and career. Fifty-seven percent of the men said they would not object to their wives working, but 67 percent of the women showed no interest in working. Dual-career families can experience problems, but the more secure the husband is, the less likely the couple is to experience such problems. The article is based on the responses of 300 *News Front* readers to a questionnaire.

163

Parrish, John B. OCCUPATIONS FOR WOMEN: THE COMING REVOLUTION. *Journal of the American Association of University Women*, 1964, 57(3), 132-135.

Employment. Employment Trends. College Teaching. Family Responsibilities.

A revolution in education and employment for women started in the 1950s. Before that time, most women workers became employed for economic reasons and were from middle or lower classes, single, and working in clerical positions. Gradually, more middle- and upper-class, married, and educated women entered the labor force, demanding greater recognition of their education and experience and placement in professional positions. Several factors helped bring about the influx of women. The number of jobs in upper occupational levels had surpassed the number of qualified men, opening the door to qualified, motivated women. Other changing trends in employment included the eager recruitment of women for short-term entry-level technological positions such as key punch and other computer-related jobs, the change from long-term output to short-run specialty items, and the acceptance of women in previously male-dominated occupations such as engineering. Social changes also contributed. More college-educated women married college-educated men who were less opposed to working wives, and these couples increasingly settled in urban areas where there was increased opportunity for employment. College teaching is one successful means of employment for women who want to work part-time since it often requires spending only a small amount of time in the classroom and many hours in class preparation and research at home. Better educated women will continue to enter the labor force and more women will seek a "second career" when their family responsibilities allow it.

164

Pressman, Sonia. THE STATUS OF WOMEN IN THE FEDERAL GOVERNMENT. Paper presented at the Conference of Professional and Academic Women, Professional Women's Caucus, June, 1970, Washington, D.C. Mimeo. 4 pages.

Federal Employment. Discrimination. Feminism.

Women comprise about one third of the full-time white-collar work force of the federal government, but most of them are employed in the four lowest grades of government service. Only about two percent of all professionals employed at government service grade levels of 16 to 18 are women. The history of women government workers is traced from 1787 to the present, along with a discussion of legislation leading to Civil Service Commission laws banning sex discrimination in employment. The objectives and accomplishments of two organizations dedicated to the advancement of women workers within the government are discussed—Federal Women's Award Study Group and Federally Employed Women. Women government workers are urged to express their views and put pressure on agencies for equal rights and equal pay.

165

Women's Equity Action League. SEX DISCRIMINATION AT THE UNIVERSITY OF MARYLAND. Fall, 1969. Mimeo. 10 pages.

College teaching. Discrimination. University of Maryland.

Most women faculty members are at the bottom of the academic hierarchy and excluded from the power structure of the University of Maryland. For example, nine of the 15 departments surveyed had no women with full professorships. Percentage distributions by sex for all rank positions are also included in this report.

166

Bennett, Walter Wilson. INSTITUTIONAL BARRIERS TO THE UTILIZATION OF WOMEN IN TOP MANAGEMENT. Doctoral Dissertation (University of Florida), 1964.

Business. Discrimination. Executive Careers. Career Barriers.

There are three million more women than men in the total population, yet only one-third of the women in the labor force are in managerial positions. They earn lower salaries than men in similar positions. Prejudice against women managers derives from attitudes related to marriage, education, and religion. As long as top-level executives believe that woman's role is defined by family, church, and school, potential women executives will not have equal opportunity. The data for these conclusions came from attitude questionnaires sent to 500 presidents of large corporations.

167

Bowman, G. W.; Worthy, N. B., and Greyser, S. A. PROBLEMS IN REVIEW: ARE WOMEN EXECUTIVES PEOPLE? Reprinted from *Harvard Business Review*, 1965, 43(4), 17 pages.

Business. Executive Careers. Advancement Barriers.

Thirty-five percent of male executives who responded to a questionnaire favored the assumption of executive roles by women, but 41 percent had reservations about it. Male and female executives both believed that women have only moderate opportunity to become executives and that women have to be exceptionally good executives to succeed at all. Older men who had worked with women executives were more likely than younger men to accept women in this role.

Very few men and women felt that Title VII of the Civil Rights Act, 1964, will have any impact unless its provisions are enforced, but they believed that laws have served to make the public aware of the status of women. Respondents suggested specific actions to be taken by business, by women, and by individual executives to further equal opportunity for women. The sample was 2,000 executives, half male and half female, drawn from a sample of subscribers to the *Harvard Business Review* and to professional and trade directories.

168

Bryce, Rose Ann. CHARACTERISTICS OF WOMEN HOLDING EXECUTIVE, MANAGERIAL, AND OTHER HIGH-LEVEL POSITIONS IN FOUR AREAS OF BUSINESS. Doctoral Dissertation (Colorado State College), 1969.

Business Administration. Business. Radio-TV. Banking. Discrimination. Manufacturing.

Qualified women entering the fields of radio-TV or retailing advance more rapidly than those entering banking or manufacturing. Over time, however, women in manufacturing can expect the highest salaries. Lack of education and career orientation and the discriminatory practices of management are the greatest deterrents to executive careers for women. Vocational counselors should make women aware that above-average intelligence, self-assurance, decisiveness, and the ability to supervise others are necessary characteristics for executive careers. The sample was

226 women in high-level positions in Denver, Colorado. Instruments included a demographic questionnaire and Ghiselli's Self-Description Inventory, which is designed to measure 13 personality traits.

169

Cussler, Margaret. THE WOMAN EXECUTIVE. New York: Harcourt, Brace, and World, Inc., 1958. 165 pages.

Management. Business. Career Patterns.

The result of six years of research by the author and a survey of similar research and data, this book focuses on women in middle management rather than in high-level executive posts. The executive is defined as a woman with three or four people under her supervision and earning more than $14,000 annually (1956-57). Executive women were represented in occupations ranging from banking to retailing in five Eastern metropolitan areas. The report is divided according to specific factors or aspects of the life and work of an executive woman, such as occupational history, marital status, work with men as supervisors or subordinates, and outside activities. The 52 women in the sample were observed at work and at home and interviewed by a research staff. The project was funded by the National Federation of Business and Professional Women's Foundation, Inc.

170

Dawkins, Lola Beasley. WOMEN EXECUTIVES IN BUSINESS, INDUSTRY AND THE PROFESSIONS. Doctoral Dissertation (University of Texas), 1962.

Executive Careers. Career Planning. Business.

A woman aspiring to an executive position should seek guidance during high school and college, find out which professions and firms practice equal opportunity, plan to remain with one firm permanently in order to advance to a managerial position, and complete at least a bachelor's degree with courses in communications and problem-solving techniques. Generally, women should be encouraged to start at a younger age than most do now to attain executive positions. The sample was 523 women employed in diverse areas such as research, education, social work and government, 251 of which held executive positions. Three kinds of data were obtained: educational background, personal characteristics of the women, and data on personnel policies and practices of firms.

171

Dewey, Lucretia M. WOMEN IN LABOR UNIONS. *Monthly Labor Review*, 1970, 94(2), 42-48.

Labor Unions.

Although the number of women union members has increased, the number has not kept pace with the overall increase in the number of women entering the labor force. The proportion of union members among employed women dropped from 13.8 percent in 1958 to 12.5 percent in 1968. Women have not achieved a level of representation as union officials that reflects their union membership. However, women in several unions are taking steps to correct this situation and are beginning to deal with such issues as equal opportunity for entering jobs, seniority rights, pay, promotional opportunities, and the need for day-care services. These findings were based on data provided by the Bureau of Labor Statistics, national and international unions, the Equal Employment Opportunity Commission, and other organizations.

172

Dolson, Miriam Terry. WHERE WOMEN STAND IN ADMINISTRATION. *The Modern Hospital*, 1967, 108(5), 100-105.

Hospital Administration. Career Patterns.

Women constitute the majority of the labor force in hospitals but only 21 percent are in administrative positions. Promotion to an administrative position takes longer for women than men, and women are generally paid less for the same work. More women hold administrative positions in hospitals in the Middle Atlantic and the North Central states than in the South or West. Most women administrators are older than men administrators and they work in smaller hospitals. Women administrators identified 33 characteristics for effective administration including ability to inspire loyalty toward the hospital, ability to work under pressure, and willingness to delegate authority and to give credit to others. Possible reasons for the low percentage of women in hospital administration include their lack of technical knowledge and the demands of travel and entertaining. Findings are based on the Cornell Study of Hospital Administrators. The sample included 4,038 replies from top administrators of U.S. hospitals, including 817 women.

173

Foster, Ann. EXECUTIVE POTENTIAL ON THE DISTAFF SIDE. *Banking*, 1969, 61, 47-49.

Banking. Advanced Training.

In the past, few women have taken advantage of American Institute of Banking (AIB) advanced training opportunities even though they have expressed interest in further education. Most candidates have been selected from among women officers who have achieved their positions through experience and seniority. Many of these women are satisfied with their current posts. Now that candidates are selected increasingly on the basis of potential, rather than seniority, greater opportunity exists for career-oriented women. The AIB, the National Association of Business Women, and individual banks should encourage young women to enroll in educational programs.

174

Gardner, Helen Rogers. WOMEN ADMINISTRATORS IN HIGHER EDUCATION IN ILLINOIS: A STUDY OF CURRENT CAREER PATTERNS. Doctoral Dissertation (Indiana University), 1966.

Educational Administration. Career Patterns.

The majority of women in college administrative positions come from small families, are single, and hold either a master's or a Ph.D. degree. They began their careers as teachers or office workers and held positions subsidiary to the administrative positions they now occupy. Generally, they support professional organizations. The personal characteristics found necessary for attainment of an executive position in higher education include ability to understand people, ability to organize, and a willingness to accept responsibility. Most of these administrators reached their present status through their own initiative.

175

Livingston, Omeda Frances. A STUDY OF WOMEN EXECUTIVES IN LIFE INSURANCE COMPANIES OWNED AND OPERATED BY NEGROES WITH IMPLICATIONS FOR BUSINESS EDUCATION. Doctoral Dissertation (New York University), 1964.

Life Insurance. Business Education. Executive Careers. Career Patterns.

Most women executives in selected black insurance firms began work as secretaries. Most developed specialized clerical and correspondence skills, and then moved up to become executives in personnel, advertising, or public relations. The implication is that business training institutions should prepare women for high-level positions through sound programs that provide business understanding and professional training. The sample consisted of 108 black women executives at 49 black-owned life insurance firms who completed questionnaires on employment history, duties, education, salary and personal characteristics. Selected interviews were also conducted.

176

Merritt, Doris H. DISCRIMINATION AND THE WOMAN EXECUTIVE. *Business Horizons*, 1969, 12(6), 15-22.

Executive Careers. Business. Medicine. Discrimination. Career Barriers.

It remains to be seen whether American industry will use the human resource of able intelligent women as executives to their fullest potential. Doing so will require making work schedules less rigid, providing day-care facilities, and paying equal salaries for equal work. Discrimination against women executives is more visceral than objective and based on the belief that men are physically stronger and superior. Understanding the myths that derive from this belief can help women turn the myths from liabilities into assets. Such myths are "woman's place is in the home," "career women are unfeminine," and "women don't understand business." When young men share business and educational experiences and opportunities with women, the myths begin to fall away. This has begun to happen in medicine. But there is still "visceral response" discrimination against women doctors. To enter medical school, women have to have higher grade point averages than men. Inflexible training schedules make the drop-out rate for women two to three percent higher than the rate for men. Of 1,060 department chairmanships in the nation's medical schools, 13 are held by women and 1,047 by men. The author, a pediatrician and medical educator, draws on personal experience to support her analysis of problems.

177

Shearer, Lloyd and Dunlap, Carol. THE FIRST WOMAN PRESIDENT OF THE U.S.—WHY NOT AND WHEN? *Parade Magazine*, February 7, 1971, 4-6.

Politics. Behavioral Motivation.

The argument that women are unqualified for the presidency because of hormonal changes is refuted. Women's high estrogen level acts as a deterrent to heart attacks. Women are also less likely to fall ill or to commit suicide or violent crime, and they live longer than men. The three women prime ministers—Gandhi, Meir, and Bandaranaike—are all heads of state in countries with monumental problems that require strong, creative, and pragmatic leadership. These women are described as highly talented in effecting compromise.

178

Warner, W.L.; Van Riper, Paul P.; Martin, Norman H., Collins, Orvis F. WOMEN EXECUTIVES IN THE FEDERAL GOVERNMENT. *Public Personnel Review*, 1962, 23(4), 227-234.

Federal Employment. Executive Careers. Higher Education. Career Patterns.

Over one-fourth of all government employees are women, but only two percent of them hold administrative posts with government service ratings of 14 or over. Women in executive positions are most heavily represented in departments and agencies concerned with traditionally feminine pursuits such as the Department of Health, Education, and Welfare. Sixty percent of federal women executives are directors, 16 percent are assistants to heads of units, and the remainder are attorneys, advisors, and staff officers. Like their male counterparts, many had fathers in professional careers, and most are college educated. More women executives than men hold advanced degrees. Forty-one percent of the women and 27 percent of the men in federal executive positions have master's degrees; and 15 percent of the women and 10 percent of the men have doctoral degrees. Most female executives entered federal service from a profession such as teaching; only about one-fourth entered as white-collar workers. Two-thirds of the women surveyed were not married. It appears that women are underrepresented in high-level positions and that it takes them longer to get as far as their male co-workers. The sample for this survey consisted of 145 women with ratings of GS 14 or higher working for the federal government in 1959. Questionnaires were filled out to provide the data.

179

Breytspraak, Charlotte Helfand. THE RELATIONSHIP OF PARENTAL IDENTIFICATION TO SEX-ROLE ACCEPTANCE IN MARRIED, SINGLE, CAREER AND NONCAREER WOMEN. Doctoral Dissertation (Columbia University), 1964.

Sex Role Identification. Sex Role Acceptance.

In general, women who accept the female sex role identify with their mothers. It was hypothesized that married women would exhibit more sex role acceptance than single women, that identification with her father is important to the development of the woman's personality, and that distinct groups based on career and marital status would exhibit differing degrees of sex role acceptance. Evidence was not found to support these hypotheses. Four groups of women college graduates aged 25-35 were divided into two groups representing married or single noncareer women. All groups were administered two questionnaires to obtain biographical and attitudinal information and to test the hypotheses. The author suggests that further research on the process and structure of the sex-role identification process is needed.

180

Epstein, Cynthia Fuchs. WOMAN'S PLACE: OPTIONS AND LIMITS IN PROFESSIONAL CAREERS. Berkeley: University of California Press, 1970. 221 pages.

Career Barriers. Role/Sex Conflict.

A study of labor-force participation rates for women and social attitudes toward woman's role reveals that American women who become professionals must frequently overcome tremendous odds against them. The spread of the ideology of equality, the lifting of legal restrictions concerning women at work, the rise of industrialization and professionalization, and the increasing importance of higher education have all helped to raise women's status. Yet cultural factors and social images, which are often contradictory, effectively inhibit women from pursuing high-status careers. The socialization process undergone by most young girls can also inhibit their pursuit of careers by limiting their horizons. Women who do pursue careers have to reconcile various roles assigned them by society. Once in a profession considered atypical for women, the woman must either accept or learn to circumvent informal exclusionary practices upheld by established colleagues and must develop ways to reconcile her uniqueness in that setting so she can function effectively. A re-evaluation of woman's place in society and the increase of actual numbers of women in male-dominated occupations will greatly increase women's equal access to work. The author draws on existing theory and research and government statistics to develop her argument.

181

Eyde, Lorraine D. ELIMINATING BARRIERS TO CAREER DEVELOPMENT OF WOMEN. *Personnel and Guidance Journal*, 1970, 49(1), 24-29.

Vocational Counseling. Career Barriers. Discrimination.

The counselor's bias against women, possibly based on misconceptions regarding women's commitment to jobs, may prevent some women from entering such traditionally "unfeminine" fields as engineering. Vocational counselors need to consider women's life styles as well as subtle changes occurring in occupations opening to women. The author reviews recent research on the effects of sex-role bias in vocational counselors (Pietrofesa and Schlossberg, 1969) and clinicians (Broverman et al., 1970) and studies of women's life styles.

182

Fidell, L.S. EMPIRICAL VERIFICATION OF SEX DISCRIMINATION IN HIRING PRACTICES IN PSYCHOLOGY. *American Psychologist*, 1970, 25(12), 1094-1098.

Psychology. Hiring Practices. Discrimination.

Academic departments of psychology appear to discriminate on the basis of sex in hiring academic and research personnel. Males with the Ph.D. receive more offers for associate professorships and full professorships, but females with the Ph.D. generally are offered assistant professorships or lower-status positions. Apparently, the level of academic position and the rank offered depend on sex as well as on the applicants' personal and academic credentials. These results are derived from a survey of 155 college and university graduate psychology departments. Responses to forms describing 10 young Ph.D. holders as potential faculty supplied the data. Four descriptions were of women, two were of men, and four were not descriptive of sex. Department chairmen were instructed to judge the chances of offering each potential candidate a full-time position on a scale of 1 to 7

(7 highest), to indicate the level of the position offered (full professorship to lecturer), and to rank the 10 people from 1 to 10 (1 highest) on desirability.

183

Hahn, Marilyn C. EQUAL RIGHTS FOR WOMEN IN CAREER DEVELOPMENT. *Personnel*, 1970, 47(4), 55-59.

Employment. Employment Trends. The Working Wife. Maternal Employment.

Thirty million or 43 percent of all women in the United States are now part of the labor force, and the number is increasing. Acceptance by women of less than equal rights in career development will disappear. In 1968, 60 percent of working women earned less than $5,000 as compared to 28 percent of men; 20 percent of the men earned $10,000 as compared to only 3 percent of the women. However, more women are now acquiring college education in preparation for careers, and women are becoming more aware of the need to handle the dual role of mother and professional. Changing attitudes toward working women on the part of colleges and private businesses, enforcement of equal rights legislation, and emergence of technological advances will enable women to forge forward to new career development opportunities. The author cites Department of Labor statistics and describes new career development programs for women in business.

184

Hyatt, Jim. WOMEN AT WORK: PRESSURE IS MOUNTING ON CONCERNS TO END SEX BIAS ON THE JOB. *Wall Street Journal*, 1970, September 21.

Discrimination. Employment Trends. Maternal Employment. Employment Legislation.

This article traces one woman machinist's efforts to be promoted into a formerly male position and her fight with the union, her employer, and the courts. Law suits are now being filed all over the country against employers who have been practicing sex discrimination in job placement and advancement. Some of these suits are outgrowths of the new guidelines for federal government and federal contractors set in recent years. With the changing trend of women working not specifically for economic reasons but also for fulfillment, the emphasis is on more professional jobs at equal salaries. The type of working women has shifted from single, lower class to mostly married, middle- and upper-class women who are better educated and more articulate in their demands. Recent government guidelines on the employment of women with provisions for working mothers are expected to increase the pressure on many employers to treat women equally.

185

Issues in Industrial Society. WOMAN'S PLACE IN THE WORK FORCE. 1971, 2(1). 76 pages.

Employment. Familial Roles. Employment Legislation. Discrimination. Career Barriers.

This is a collection of articles that touch on many aspects of women in the world of work—changing family life styles within the framework of role theory (Jessie Bernard); the recent history of women in the world of work (Elizabeth Duncan Koontz); the status of legislation concerning working women (Ann Scot); the move to professionalize and upgrade household employment (Ethlyn Christensen); the relationship between state protective legislation and Title VII of the Civil Rights Act of 1964 (Barbara and Byron Yaffe); the damaging effect of sex discrimination on women's aspirations (Marcia Greenbaum); psychological barriers to universal employment of women (Ellen Bay Schwartz); and a list of recommended readings.

186

Katz, Joseph; Comstock, Peggy, and Lozoff, Marjorie M. EDUCATIONAL AND OCCUPATIONAL ASPIRATIONS OF ADULT WOMEN: REPORT TO THE COLLEGE ENTRANCE EXAMINATION BOARD. Institute for the Study of Human Problems, Stanford, California: Stanford University, 1970. 261 pages.

Career Motivation. Women's Magazines. Life Style Aspirations.

More than half of the married women in this study felt that having a career and being a housewife are both important. A fifth had no feelings on the matter, and the rest felt the issue was unimportant. Many indicated that financial considerations figured in their decisions to work outside the home, but they also indicated that personal development was an important factor. Many felt that their educational and occupational needs had not been met, although they were relatively content with their lives. To meet the needs of women with this "double picture," social and educational planners should recognize that middle-class women have a wide range of needs.

A review of women's magazines, conducted in conjunction with the study, showed that topics covered extensively were clothing, personal appearance, and health and medicine. Fashion magazines feature fashion; homemaker's magazines, family and child-rearing matters; and young and singles' magazines, psychological self-analysis and relations with other people. Although such magazines are beginning to highlight women's potential outside the home and family, they still remain unattentive to the larger world. Findings of the 1968 study are based on the questionnaire responses of 494 alumnae of Stanford University and 91 alumnae of Santa Rosa Junior College, ranging in age from 26 to 50 years. For the purposes of comparison, the results of previous research on the career and autonomy of college women (Katz, Joseph, 1969), in which women students at both colleges participated, are also included in the report. A selected bibliography on women is included.

187

Klein, Viola. WOMEN WORKERS. Paris: Organization for Economic Cooperation and Development, 1965. 100 pages.

Employment Facilitators. Employment.

A survey of the employment practices for women workers in 21 countries and the services provided for them, this report outlines the special needs of such workers. Compiled with the view of facilitating the employment of women, the report analyzes existing practices and includes recommendations on the provision of child care and home help services and adult training programs, the increase in availability of part-time work, and the improvement of service and work schedules. Data were collected from questionnaires sent to the 20 member countries of the Organization for Economic Cooperation and Development and Yugoslavia.

188

Kresge, Pat. THE HUMAN DIMENSIONS OF SEX DISCRIMINATION. *Journal of the American Association of University Women*, 1970, 64(2), 6-9.

Discrimination. Employment Legislation. Advancement Barriers.

Of nearly 8,000 women responding to an AAUW opinion survey on the status of women, 1,000 wrote case histories of sex discrimination. Inequities were cited in state and federal laws; in hiring, promotion, and pay practices in business, industry, and higher education; and in the abuse of administrative policy to discriminate against women.

189

Maslow, Albert P. JOB FACTORS, ATTITUDES, AND PREFERENCES AFFECTING THE RELATIVE ADVANCEMENT AND TURNOVER OF MEN AND WOMEN IN FEDERAL CAREERS. American Psychological Association, Washington, D.C. Paper presented at the APA convention in Miami, 1970. 11 pages.

Federal Employment. Work Values. Career Patterns. Career Aspirations.

A comparison of men and women in the same federal service salary grades showed that men were younger, had less time in service, and a lower level of education than women. The women participated as much or more in professional societies, published as much or more, and undertook more job-related training than men. Most women and men indicated preference for working under male supervisors. As a group, women had lower aspirations than men. In an examination of the turn-over rates of federal career employees, sex differences were found to be negligible, but the turn-over rate for middle-aged women was lower than for younger men. The work attitudes and expectations were the same among young men and women entering federal service in professional, technical, and managerial careers. Both men and women stated that the most significant aspects of a job are the work itself, personal work accomplishments, and salary. The findings are derived from the responses of approximately 38,000 federal workers.

190

McCune, Shirley. THOUSANDS REPLY TO OPINIONNAIRE; MANY DOCUMENT CASES OF SEX DISCRIMINATION. *Journal of the American Association of University Women*, 1970, May, 202-206.

Discrimination. Career Barriers. Role/Sex Conflict.

Among the 4,065 women and 2,940 men who completed an AAUW "opinionnaire," one-fourth of the women reported personally experiencing sex discrimination and one-fourth of the

men had observed discrimination against females. A majority of the entire sample agreed on the following generalizations:
• Women experience discrimination in the working world.
• Women do not want full job equality if it means loss of femininity. • Women successfully compete with men. • Women prefer working for men and men resent having a female boss.
• Women are not paid the same salary as men doing the same job. • Women tend to think of employment as a job rather than a long-term career. • Women are held back professionally because of the lack of adequate day-care facilities. A majority of females indicated that female intellectual achievement is viewed as competitively aggressive behavior; the males did not agree. The subjects thought that women who work are just as likely to have successful marriages as those who don't, that abortion should be universally available, that families should have no more than two children, and that husbands and wives should share equally in family decision-making and in child care. In general, women reported significantly stronger responses in support of women's equality than the men. A five-point Likert Scale was used.

191

McKiever, M.F. THE HEALTH OF WOMEN WHO WORK. Public Health Service Publication No. 1314. Washington, D.C.: U.S. Department of Health, Education, and Welfare, 1965. 62 pages.

Health Patterns. Pregnancy. Employment Legislation.

Women have strikingly greater resistance than men to heart attacks, the chief killer in contemporary society; they also have longer life expectancies and slight superiority in disease resistance. A three-year study indicated that males average 5.5 sick days per year while females average 5.7, but these rates varied greatly according to the level of occupation, region, and age. Acute conditions due to injuries occurred more frequently among men, although when pregnancy is included, women average slightly more. For chronic conditions, men lose more days of work than women. This booklet also provides information on the standards and laws governing employment, health services provided by industries and the effects of pregnancy on women's work habits and employers' policies.

192

Mitchell, Susan B. WOMEN DOCTORAL RECIPIENTS EVALUATE THEIR TRAINING. *The Educational Forum*, 1970, 34(4), 533-539.

Higher Education. Doctoral Degrees. Career Barriers. Educational Patterns. Career Satisfaction. Educational Barriers.

The investment that society and the women themselves make in producing women doctoral recipients is well worth the effort because 99 percent of these women enter and remain in the work force and are satisfied with their positions. Lack of guidance and counseling, financial problems, and cultural expectations are the greatest obstacles to women's achievement. Most of the women in this study were housewives, most had been encouraged by their mothers to pursue higher education, and most had an Ed.D. degree rather than a Ph.D. They averaged 17 years between receipt of the B.A. and the doctorate, over half were married before completing their doctoral work, and over half of their husbands had advanced degrees. Sources of encouragement for these women included professors and family; sources of discouragement were colleagues. Over 80 percent of these women are employed in higher education, with most holding high-level and administrative positions in colleges rather than universities. Most reported satisfaction with their decisions to obtain the doctoral degree despite the sacrifices required in terms of loss of income while studying and the disruption of family life. The sample included 208 women doctoral degree recipients from three Oklahoma institutions of higher education from 1929-1967. Each subject filled out a four-page questionnaire.

193

Myers, George C. LABOR FORCE PARTICIPATION OF SUBURBAN MOTHERS. *Journal of Marriage and the Family*, 1964, 26(3), 306-311.

Maternal Employment.

Mothers living in suburban communities with diverse social characteristics are more likely to work than mothers in suburban communities with homogenous characteristics. The immediate availability of employment is not an important factor, but economic necessity and the number of children are factors in a mother's decision to work. Questionnaire responses of 941 junior and senior high school students from three suburban communities—one upper class, one middle class and one lower class—were examined. More than one third of their mothers worked either full or part time.

194

Roe, Ann. SATISFACTION IN WORK. *Journal of the American Association of University Women*, 1962, 55(January), 230-232.

Occupational Choice. Career Planning.

Whether one works primarily for financial reasons or for personal fulfillment, an occupation is more than just a job. Since a person spends about half his time at work and half at home, personal needs must be fulfilled at work as well as at home. A good occupation makes demands that stretch a person's capabilities but not beyond one's reach. Personal needs of recognition, coherency, curiosity and aesthetics, though existing in differing degrees within each individual, are discussed in terms of the working environment. The article concludes with a discussion on career planning that emphasizes the need for women to plan or seek occupations that will best fit into their lives and fulfill their personal needs.

195

Rossman, Jack E. and Campbell, David P. WHY COLLEGE-TRAINED MOTHERS WORK. *Personnel and Guidance Journal*, 1965, 43(June), 986-992.

Maternal Employment. Marital Satisfaction. Employment Motivation.

Marital and life satisfaction, spouse's educational level, and family income all affect a mother's decision to work outside the home. In this comparison of working and nonworking mothers, women who were employed full time had higher MSAT scores and were less satisfied with their marriages and life in general. They were likely to have more education than their husbands. Families with working mothers had lower family incomes, and the women were more likely to have received vocational counseling in college. To obtain these findings, the authors analyzed the responses of 238 women to mailed questionnaires, their SVIB-W and MSAT scores, and data from personal interviews. Enabling, facilitating and precipitating conditions that led to the decision to work were measured. The study was based on Sohol's 1963 "theory of commitment to work."

196

U.S. Department of Labor, Women's Bureau. COLLEGE WOMEN SEVEN YEARS AFTER GRADUATION. (RESURVEY OF WOMEN GRADUATES—CLASS OF 1957). Bulletin 292, 1966. 54 pages.

Employment. Employment Motivation. Educational Motivation. Graduate Education. Educational Barriers.

Women seven years out of college are generally interested in some form of paid employment outside the home. Fifty-one percent of the women in this study had joined the work force, most for financial reasons. The women in this survey had put in an average of 5.5 years' paid employment between graduation and the resurvey seven years later. Most wanted to continue their educations through university work, either for career purposes or for purposes of personal development. Almost half of the women had taken at least one graduate course since leaving college, but only 15 percent had earned the master's degree and only one percent had earned the doctor's degree. The women with doctoral degrees were concentrated in the fields of medicine, chemistry or physical sciences, journalism, or social sciences. Those with master's degrees were concentrated in the fields of education, English, and sociology. Many of those women involved in graduate study reported encountering such obstacles as age requirements, financial aid restrictions, and limited course offerings.

The great majority of the women were or had been married, and over half had children under 18 years of age. The majority with children under six years of age were not working at the time of the resurvey. More than half the married graduates described their husbands' attitudes toward their working as favorable. More than four-fifths of the employed graduates had the kind of jobs they wanted. Over three-fourths of the women were active members of one or more voluntary organizations. To obtain these findings, the researchers used questionnaires to resurvey 5,846 women originally surveyed in 1957. The sample represented almost 88,000 women who were graduated in June 1957 from colleges and universities granting bachelor's degrees.

197

U.S. Department of Labor, Manpower Administration, Bureau of Employment Security. COUNSELING GIRLS AND WOMEN: AWARENESS, ANALYSIS, ACTION. 1966. 71 pages.

Vocational Counseling. Employment.

Prepared by staff of the University of Missouri at Kansas City for use in counselor inservice training programs in state employment service agencies, the book is designed to bring counselors up to date on the results of new research on women in the world of work. Calling on the counselor to help change the misguided attitudes of women and of the communities they live in concerning women in the labor force, the book refutes myths about the working wife and mother and strongly supports the view that women must prepare for productive work during their various life cycles. Data for the book were drawn from various private research and government reports. An annotated reading list is also included.

198

U.S. Department of Labor, Women's Bureau. ECONOMIC INDICATORS RELATING TO EQUAL PAY, 1963. Pamphlet 9, 1963. 21 pages.

Discrimination. Employment. Hiring Practices.

Most women workers receive lower salaries than men for similar work. In job hiring orders in public employment offices in nine cities, 91 examples of wage differentials in favor of men were found. Over half of the examples were for clerical, service, or sales personnel. The majority of labor-management contracts studied guaranteed equal pay, however. Of more than 1,900 employers in the United States and Canada questioned in another survey, 33 percent admitted to a double-standard pay scale in favor of men. Women earned, on the average, less than two-thirds as much as men from 1955 to 1961. As white-collar workers, service workers, and plant workers, women generally earn less than men in similar positions. Women teachers in many public school districts earn less than men. Wage differentials in salaries for recent college graduates also exist in favor of men. Although no wage differentials exist for federal workers, the great majority of female federal employees hold jobs in government service grades one through five, while most men hold middle-level jobs. Source material for this pamphlet included statistics and figures prepared by the Women's Bureau; several private researchers; the U.S. Department of Commerce, Bureau of the Census; the U.S. Department of Labor, Bureau of Labor Statistics; the National Educational Association; Bureau of Social Science Research, Inc., and the U.S. Civil Service Commission.

199

U.S. Department of Labor, Women's Bureau. FACT SHEET ON THE EARNINGS GAP. 1970. 5 pages.

Discrimination. Income.

The median wage of women who work full time year round is less than that of men, and the difference in wages has increased in recent years. In 1955, women's median wage was 64 percent of the men's median wage; in 1968, it was 58 percent. The gap varies among occupational groups—women sales workers earn 40 percent of the amount earned by men, and women professional and technical workers earn 66 percent of what men earn. Also, 20 percent of women, but only eight percent of men, earned less than $3,000 in 1968, and 60 percent of women, but only 20 percent of the men, earned less than $5,000. Only 3.9 percent of the women, but 28 percent of the men, earned $10,000 or more. Based on data prepared by the National Education Association, private researchers, the National Science Foundation, and the U.S. Department of Commerce, Bureau of the Census, the fact sheet also includes figures on the earnings gap in several specific occupational fields.

200

U.S. Department of Labor, Wage and Labor Standards Administration, Women's Bureau. FACTS ABOUT WOMEN'S ABSENTEEISM AND LABOR TURNOVER. 1969. 9 pages.

Employment. Job Performance.

Impartial analysis of the skill level of a job, the age of the worker, the worker's length of service with one employer, and the worker's record of job stability all provide better bases than sex for understanding differences in workers' performance. This is true despite the widespread belief that men make better workers than women. To obtain these findings, up-to-date statistics and the results of recent research efforts were analyzed in terms of absenteeism, labor turnover, job tenure, and labor mobility.

201

U.S. Department of Labor, Women's Bureau. JOB HORIZONS FOR COLLEGE WOMEN. Bulletin 288 (revised), 1967. 83 pages.

Higher Education. Career Opportunities.

Intended for the woman college student, the book describes positions in 32 occupational fields open to women and discusses such considerations as the job market and salaries, the accessibility of graduate study, and the steady increases in professional employment of women over recent years.

202
U.S. Department of Labor, Women's Bureau. 1969 HANDBOOK ON WOMEN WORKERS. Bulletin 294, 1969. 384 pages.

Employment Patterns. Employment Legislation.

Published periodically, the handbook contains up-to-date information on the participation and characteristics of women in the labor force, their employment patterns, their occupations, their income, their education and training, the federal and state laws concerning the employment and civil and political status of women, and a bibliography on American women workers.

203
U.S. Department of Labor, Wage and Labor Standards Administration, Women's Bureau. PROFILE OF THE WOMAN WORKER: 50 YEARS OF PROGRESS. April 1970.

Clerical Work. Employment Patterns. Employment.

The woman worker of 1970, in comparison to the woman worker of 1920, is an older, married woman living with her husband, who has had high school and some post-secondary school education. Even though she has about 500 occupational options, she is most likely to be a clerical worker, and she will probably remain in the labor force longer than she would have in 1920. The statistical source for this one-page fact sheet is not cited.

204
U.S. Department of Labor, Wage and Labor Standards Administration, Women's Bureau. WOMEN AND TEENAGE WORKERS IN SELECTED STATES AND METROPOLITAN AREAS, 1969. 1970. 4 pages.

Employment. Adolescent Employment. Employment Patterns.

More than half of the 27.4 million American women workers aged 20 or older live in the nation's 10 largest states. Labor force participation rates for teenagers (both sexes) in these 10 states were higher than those of all women in the states. That is, more teenagers are employed than women in the same states. About three out of five of all working women live in six of the 20 largest Standard Metropolitan Statistical Areas (SMSA). The same figure holds for teenagers. Data and tables for the brief were supplied by the U.S. Department of Labor, Bureau of Labor Statistics.

205

U.S. Department of Labor, Women's Bureau. WOMEN IN THE WORLD OF TODAY: NOTES ON WOMEN'S EMPLOYMENT IN THE UNITED STATES AND NINE EUROPEAN COUNTRIES. International Report 7, 1963. 5 pages.

Employment Trends. Employment.

Social and economic changes of the last 50 years have led to expanded employment of women in highly industrialized nations including Belgium, Denmark, France, Germany, Great Britain, Italy, The Netherlands, Norway, Sweden, and the United States. In the U.S., Great Britain, France, and Germany, one-third of the total labor force is made up of women; in Denmark, the proportion of women is higher. In Belgium, Norway, Sweden, The Netherlands, and Italy, women number about one-fourth of the total labor force. Other information concerning marital status, occupational breakdown, etc., is also included in the report. The source material for this pamphlet was the *1960 Handbook on Women Workers* (U.S. Department of Labor, Women's Bureau) and the *Labour Gazette, 1961* (Department of Labour of Canada, Women's Bureau).

206

U.S. Department of Labor, Wage and Labor Standards Administration, Women's Bureau. WOMEN PRIVATE HOUSEHOLD WORKERS FACT SHEET. May 1970. 6 pages.

Household Employment. Career Patterns. Employment Legislation. Income.

In 1969, about 1.6 million women were employed as private household workers and babysitters, and women constituted 98 percent of all workers in private household employment. Annual wages in this occupation, however, are very low and employment is generally intermittent. Many private household workers are heads of families. Over half lived in the South, and about three-fourths in urban areas. The average age of women in this occupation was about six years older than the average age for women in the rest of the labor force. Less than three of every 10 household workers were single. The average years of school completed was 8.8. Household workers are not covered by the federal minimum wage and hour law, and they receive credits toward social security benefits only if they earn $50 from any one employer in a calendar quarter. Wisconsin is the only state with a minimum wage order that covers domestic workers without numerical or hourly exclusions. Few states provide household workers with such coverage as unemployment compensation and workmen's compensation. The statistical data in this report are from the U.S. Department of Commerce, Bureau of the Census and the U.S. Department of Labor, Bureau of Labor Statistics.

207

U.S. Department of Labor, Wage and Labor Standards Administration, Women's Bureau. WOMEN WORKERS TODAY. June 1970. 7 pages.

Employment. Marital Status. Employment Motivation.

The likelihood that a woman will work varies according to age, marital and family status, education, race, and, if the woman is married, her husband's income. A woman is most likely to work if she is young and has finished her schooling or if she is mature and has no young children. Married women are more likely than widows to work but they are less likely to be in the labor force than divorced, separated, or single women. Among married women, 30 percent with children under six and 50 percent with school-age children are workers. Generally, the more education a woman has, the more likely she is to be in the labor force. Labor force participation rates for nonwhite women are generally higher than those for white women. A married woman is most apt to be working if her husband's income is between $5,000 and $7,000 and least apt to be working if her husband's income is either below $3,000 or over $10,000. Married women with family responsibilities, students, and women 65 years of age and over prefer part-time employment, and only 40 percent of all women workers have full-time jobs year round. Women are more apt to be white-collar workers, but generally earn less than men in similar job categories. Figures for this pamphlet were from statistics and charts prepared by the U.S. Department of Commerce, Bureau of the Census, the U.S. Department of Labor, Bureau of Labor Statistics, and the Westinghouse Electric Corporation.

208

U.S. News and World Report. REBELLING WOMEN—THE REASON. 1970, April 13, 35-37.

Employment. Discrimination. Family Responsibilities. College Teaching. Employment Patterns.

A news magazine survey indicates that men earn considerably more than women, and the gap in recent years has been widening. In 1955, women who worked full time earned $63.90 for each $100 earned by men, but by 1960, women were earning only $60.80, and by 1968, only $58.20. Over half of the 31.1 million women in the labor force are employed as subprofessionals in low-paying jobs, but 70 percent of the men are professional and technical workers. Men traditionally hold jobs in which paid overtime work is available. A high degree of education and training does not necessarily bring the average woman a salary comparable to a man's. Women are more vulnerable to unemployment. As the result of family responsibilities, women often bring less experience to the labor market. Few women have been able to enter the professions; even in the teaching field, only 19 percent of college faculties are made up of women. Of the female labor force, 60 percent are married and living with their husbands and over 50 percent have children under 18, contradicting prevailing beliefs that the moment a woman marries, she quits work.

209

Whitehurst, Robert Noel. EMPLOYED MOTHERS' INFLUENCES ON WORKING-CLASS FAMILY STRUCTURE. Doctoral Dissertation (Purdue University), 1963.

Maternal Employment. Familial Roles.

Mothers who value economic security are more likely to work than mothers who value motherhood and children in marriage. In this comparison of working and nonworking mothers in low-income areas, husbands generally disapproved of their wives' working. No differences regarding authority of wives or the amount of shared decision-making were found between the working and nonworking mothers. One suggested difference was that working families value more companionship, a higher standard of living, and fewer children while the nonworking families seem to have a traditional, family-oriented value system. The sample consisted of 45 lower-class working mothers and 38 lower-class nonworking mothers. All were interviewed.

210

Williamson, Thomas R. and Karras, Edward J. JOB SATISFACTION VARIABLES AMONG FEMALE CLERICAL WORKERS. *Journal of Applied Psychology,* 1970, 54(4), 343-346.

Clerical Work. Career Expectations. Work Values.

Female clerical workers tend to value factors associated with job environment ("hygienes") within the job context over factors associated with an individual's need for self-actualization ("motivators"). This finding is in conflict with previous research (Burke, 1966) which indicated that female and male college students valued "motivators" (which lead to job satisfaction) over "hygienes" (which lead to job dissatisfaction). The difference in job satisfaction preferences between female college students and female clerical workers may reflect the differences in career development expectations. That is, clerical workers do not anticipate promotion and increase in responsibilities, while college students do. To obtain this finding, the authors asked 34 female clerical workers to rank ten job characteristics (developed by Herzberg, Mausner, and Snyderman, 1959) which consisted of five motivators and five hygienes in terms of how important each was to them, to another woman, and to a man.

211

Wolfe, Helen Bickel. WOMEN IN THE WORLD OF WORK. University of the State of New York, The State Education Department, Division of Research, 1969. 65 pages.

Employment Motivation. Work Values. Vocational Counseling.

The reasons women work and the satisfactions they seek from working are related to such demographic factors as age, marital status, socioeconomic status, career patterns, and education. The implication of these findings for counselors and educators is that since most women entering the labor force in the future will hold low-paying, low-status jobs, the preparation given these women should be reexamined to bring it into line with realistic job aspirations and opportunities. For example, all women in this study ranked the need to use their training and education and gain a sense of accomplishment and satisfaction (mastery-achievement) as primary reasons for work. Motivation to fulfill social needs—avoiding loneliness, boredom, stagnation—ranked second in importance. After this, the women ranked the needs to vary their experiences and to demonstrate independence as important. The least important work values were the need to supervise, control, and lead. The need for economic reward ranked low. To obtain these findings, the author analyzed the responses of 1,871 women in New York State to the Work Values Questionnaire (Eyde, 1962). Of the women, seven percent were single, 83 percent were married and living with their husbands and ten percent were divorced, separated, and widowed.

212

Zytowski, Donald G. TOWARD A THEORY OF CAREER DEVELOPMENT FOR WOMEN. *The Personnel and Guidance Journal*, 1969, 47(7), 660-664.

Vocational Theory. Vocational Counseling.

In an effort to describe and characterize the differences in the life work of men and women and the patterns or stages of women's vocational participation and home life, nine postulates were developed. These included: the modal life role for women is that of a homemaker; a woman's life is orderly and developmental; a woman's vocational patterns may be distinguished in terms of entry age, span, and degree of participation. The implication to counselors is that additional research is needed to verify these postulates, describe their processes, or produce innovations which ultimately would prove them invalid. The author draws on existing research and theory and personal observation to develop the postulates.

Developmental Studies

213

Bayer, Alan E. EARLY DATING AND EARLY MARRIAGE. *Journal of Marriage and the Family,* 1968, 30(4), 628-632.

Early Dating. Marriage Stability.

Young people in all socioeconomic groups who begin dating early (before 15 years of age) are more likely to marry earlier (before 23 for men and 21 for women) than those who begin dating at a later age. Early dating may have little to do with marriage stability—as many in the field believe—but the duration of dating experience before marriage does. Since these findings partially contradict existing theory on the relationship of early marriage and marriage instability, we should delay the formulation of conclusions on early dating as a predictor of marital success. But since the duration of premarital dating experience seems to be a crucial variable, dating can be viewed as an educational experience. To obtain these findings, the author analyzed data obtained through Project TALENT, a nationwide longitudinal study of 32,833 American youths begun in 1960, with one-year and five-year follow-ups completed, and 10-year and 20-year follow-ups planned.

214

Broverman, Inge K.; Broverman, Donald M.; Clarkson, Frank E.; Rosenkrantz, Paul S.; and Vogel, Susan R. SEX-ROLE STEREOTYPES AND CLINICAL JUDGMENTS OF MENTAL HEALTH. *Journal of Consulting and Clinical Psychology,* 1970, 34(1), 1-7.

Psychological Health Patterns. Sex Role Perceptions. Sex Role Stereotypes.

An examination of the concepts of practicing mental health clinicians concerning healthy, mature men, women, and adults (sex unspecified) reveals that men and women clinicians agree on particular attributes of health for each category and hold different concepts of health for men and women that parallel current sex-role stereotypes. By adult standards of health, women are perceived as less healthy than men. This "double standard" probably stems from the widely-held belief that health requires adjustment to environment, which revolves on differential norms of behavior for men and women. The researchers administered a questionnaire of their design (Sex-role Stereotype Questionnaire) to 46 men and 33 women, all of whom were clinically trained psychologists, psychiatrists, or social workers. The questionnaire, which consists of 122 bipolar items, each of which describes a given behavior trait (i.e., very aggressive/not at all aggressive) measured the extent to which the subjects' concepts of sex role corresponded to conventional wisdom.

215
Brown, D. G. SEX-ROLE DEVELOPMENT IN A CHANGING CULTURE. *Psychological Bulletin*, 1958, 55(4), 232-243.

Sex Roles. Sex Role Perceptions. Sex Role Development.

A survey of the literature provides evidence that masculine and feminine sex roles are converging in our society. As the distinctions between activities and beliefs considered masculine and feminine become diffuse, interfamily relationships become more culturally diverse. More research is needed to determine the effects of these changes on the process of sex-role development in light of the present knowledge of the process. The changes in feminine sex-role that have occurred in Japan, Germany, and the United States over the last ten years should be studied continuously to measure the effect. The author also discusses the various theories of sex-role development and cites the implications of change on individual, group, and institutional behavior.

216
Dornbush, Sanford. AFTERWORD, in *The Development of Sex Differences*. Maccoby, Eleanor E., ed. Stanford, California: Stanford University Press, 1966. Pages 205-216.

Sex Differences. Sex Roles. Research Needs.

Detailed examination of research on the development of sex differences shows that sex differences and roles in industrialized societies have become elaborate cultural products, so that it is very difficult to separate biological facts and forces from cultural "realities." Also, hard data on several crucial matters are nonexistent. For example, we lack understanding of the consequences of hormonal fluctuation on behavior. There is little detailed data based on observation on the interaction between parents and children. Research must be undertaken to fill the gaps in our knowledge of sex differences so that we can better understand the forces that shape men and women.

The book is the result of discussions on sex differences of a work group at Stanford University conducted between 1962 and

1964. The Committee on Socialization and Social Structure of the Social Science Research Council sponsored the discussions. A lengthy, annotated bibliography is included in the book, as is a "Classified Summary of Research in Sex Differences" compiled from the Bibliography. Contributing authors are: David Hamburg and Donald Lunde, "Sex Hormones in the Development of Sex Differences in Human Behavior"; Eleanor Maccoby, "Sex Differences in Intellectual Functioning"; Walter Mischel, "A Social-learning View of Sex Differences in Behavior"; Lawrence Kohlberg, "A Cognitive-developmental Analysis of Children's Sex-role Concepts and Attitudes"; Roy G. D'Andrade, "Sex Differences and Cultural Institutions"; Roberta M. Oetzel, "Annotated Bibliography," and "Classified Summary of Research in Sex Differences."

217

Erikson, Erik H. INNER AND OUTER SPACE: REFLECTIONS ON WOMANHOOD, in Lifton, Robert J., ed. *The Woman in America*. Boston: Houghton Mifflin, 1965. Pages 1-26.

Sex Differences. Sex Role Development.

As technology brings mankind to the brink of nuclear threat and to a new awareness of the world through global communication, our images of the two sexes must be redefined. Awareness of the threat to the species has increased the need to examine, after long neglect, the nature of woman. Historically, though privately, she has stood for "realism of householding, responsibility of upbringing, resourcefulness in peacekeeping, devotion to healing." Thus, she might infuse technological society with species-saving restraint. While post-Freudian practitioners have discarded original psychoanalytic theory that defined woman in terms of the lack of male characteristics, we should not deny the biological reality of the "nature and nurture" of woman. Observation of healthy children in play activity revealed sex-differences in use of space. The girls designed constructions emphasizing inner space; the boys designed constructions emphasizing outer space. Ascribing this difference to aculturation is not sufficient. The correspondence to bodily structures was strikingly consistent. Observation of other mammals supports the theory of inner and outer space. Anatomy does affect personality. This theory of woman's and man's nature does not condemn either sex to each sexually-determined spatial mode. Rather, it can help explain distress within "cultural space-time." Observation of the Carribean matriarchal society supports the theory's validity within a historical frame. Any consideration of the nature of man and woman should be based on soma, psyche, and polis, which reveals man to be an individual, biological being within a social order. Women should be permitted to bring their uniqueness to the imaginative invention of much-needed, new social orders.

218

Freedman, Mervin B. SOME THEORETICAL AND PRACTICAL IMPLICATIONS OF A LONGITUDINAL STUDY OF COLLEGE WOMEN. *Journal for the Study of Interpersonal Processes,* 1963, 26(2), 1-21.

Adolescence. Individual Growth and Development. Educational Theory. Higher Education.

The widely-held belief that adolescence is a period of turmoil may apply in some cases, but not in the majority. The theory of adolescent turmoil was derived from clinical observation rather than empirical data. Unfortunately, the widespread impact of dynamic psychology on higher education has dictated an approach to higher education based on the promotion of stability and the reduction of stress-producing situations among adolescents. This approach probably helps those experiencing a turbulent adolescence but produces apathy and shallow personality development in the great majority of students who are free of neurotic distress. Rather than promoting just stability, educators should view education as a "process of challenge and response" so that young students able to grow naturally will be encouraged to do so, rather than having to remain at the level of development of those in adolescent turmoil. To support his argument, the author draws on existing research and the research he conducted at Vassar College in the late 1950s. In the Vassar study, which caused the author to question the notion that adolescence is a painful time, few of the college-age subjects interviewed recalled problems or fears associated with pubertal changes and few engaged in or expressed strong need for sexual relations. Although conflict with parents increased during the college years, it was experienced by less than one-fourth of the girls. From a mental hygiene point of view, the subjects were healthy, but the lack of challenge and response caused them to develop stable but shallow personalities. The Vassar survey was based on unstructured interviews over four years, with 80 members of the class of 1958.

219

Gallup, George. POLLING WOMAN ON HER ROLE. Princeton, N.J.: American Institute of Public Opinion, 1970.

Discrimination. Career Opportunities.

Two-thirds of American women believe they get as good a break in employment opportunity as men do. However, among those who have attended college, many do not believe they get as good a break, and the majority feel that women have greater difficulty in reaching the upper echelons of business because of their sex. The majority of women with only a grade-school education believe employment opportunities are equal. Most of the two-thirds of American women presently not working in jobs outside the home prefer not to work. Most of those among this group who wish to work outside the home would choose a part-time job over a full-time position, either because they "need the money" or are bored. To obtain these findings, 778 women were interviewed in more than 300 different locations throughout the country.

220

Goldberg, Philip. ARE WOMEN PREJUDICED AGAINST WOMEN? *Trans-Action*, 1968, April, 28-30.

Prejudice. Intellectual Attainment. Higher Education.

This study indicates that women are prejudiced negatively against the intellectual attainment of women and that they accept the dominant social view of higher education as a masculine preserve. The specific question for this study was whether or not women would evaluate a professional article more negatively if they thought it was authored by a woman. The subjects were 140 randomly selected college girls. Six articles from different fields were prepared. Two copies of each article were made— one bearing a woman's name as the author and the other, a man's. Nine questions asked for ratings in terms of value, persuasiveness and profundity of the article and the writing style of the author. The results showed that women consider themselves inferior to men, even in traditionally female professions. When the author was presented as a man, the women consistently rated the article as more valuable and the author as more competent.

221

Helson, Ravenna. GENERALITY OF SEX DIFFERENCES IN CREATIVE STYLE. *Journal of Personality*, 1968, 36(1), 33-48.

Creativity. Sex Differences.

There are sex differences in creative style, regardless of field of specialization. Creative women have an "inner orientation," a defensive attitude toward their environment, and narrow interests. Creative men exhibit opposite characteristics (Neumann, 1954). To obtain these findings and extend previous research (Helson, 1957), the author conducted an analysis of variance on the SVIB data from 56 male mathematicians (27 creative), 41 female mathematicians (15 creative), 83 architects (40 creative), and 51 Mills College seniors (22 creative).

222

Helson, Ravenna. SEX DIFFERENCES IN CREATIVE STYLE. *Journal of Personality*, 1967, 35(2), 214-233.

Creativity. Mathematics. Sex Differences.

An examination of sex differences in creative style isolated matriarchal and patriarchal consciousness patterns like those described by Eric Neumann (1954) in creative female and male mathematicians. The same patterns were not found in comparison groups of mathematicians not judged as creative. Creative male mathematicians had high organizing control, integrative mastery, and enjoyed achievement-oriented symbolic manipulation. They were more effective than the women as researchers, leaders, and evaluators. The creative female mathematicians had low active and high passive direction, less flexibility and confidence, and tended to internalize. Although the findings do not demonstrate a relationship between an individual's "procreative image" and research style, the relationship could probably be demonstrated directly, especially in light of Erikson's findings (1964). A total of 109 subjects were administered a test on research habits and attitudes and the CPI.

223

Kalka, Beatrice Symbol. A COMPARATIVE STUDY OF FEMININE ROLE CONCEPTS OF A SELECTED GROUP OF COLLEGE WOMEN. Doctoral Dissertation (Oklahoma State University), 1967.

Role Perceptions. Man's "Ideal" Woman.

Comparison of freshmen and senior women majoring in home economics or arts and science revealed no significant differences in perceptions of "own self" or "average woman." However, freshmen and seniors did differ significantly in their perceptions of "man's ideal woman." Generally, the less achievement-oriented, more traditional women drop out of college, leaving the more aggressive and achievement-oriented women to comprise the senior group. Thus, those who complete college are likely to have similar attitudes toward the feminine role. A random sample of 200 women, freshmen and seniors, from the college of arts and sciences and home economics was administered the Fand Role Inventory. The inventory was used to explore overt attitudes toward the feminine sex role, on a continuum from other-oriented to self-oriented. Home economics majors were more "other-oriented" than the arts and science majors.

224

Kammeyer, Kenneth. THE FEMININE ROLE: AN ANALYSIS OF ATTITUDE CONSISTENCY. *Journal of Marriage and the Family*, 1964, 23(3), 295-305.

Consistency of Feminine Self-Image. Higher Education. Role Influences.

The level of interaction between the American college girl and others in the college setting and, to a limited extent, her parents, is related to the consistency of her attitudes about the feminine role. The more friends a college girl has, the more dates she has and the more she sees her parents, the more likely she is to hold consistent views of "feminine role behavior" and "female personality traits" (the two dimensions of feminine sex role explored). This study was formulated on the basis of the results of previous research (Komarovsky, 1953), and the hypothesis that the two dimensions of feminine sex role would be highly related was partially confirmed. The author developed ordinal scales to measure the two dimensions of feminine sex role, which he used to examine the responses of 209 unmarried girls on the same campus to a questionnaire. Further analysis of the data revealed the effect of interaction on internal attitude consistency.

225

Kuvlesky, William P.; Obordo, Angelita S., and Preston, James D. RACIAL DIFFERENCES IN TEEN-AGE GIRLS' ORIENTATIONS TOWARD MARRIAGE: A STUDY OF YOUTH LIVING IN AN ECONOMICALLY DEPRESSED AREA OF THE SOUTH. Paper presented at the annual meeting of the Southern Sociological Society, 1969. 40 pages.

Career Expectations. Racial Differences. Life Style Aspirations. Life Style Expectations.

Little empirical evidence exists on the expectations of adolescent girls about marital status and procreation. Racial comparison of a set of aspirations and expectations held toward marriage by a sample of adolescent girls from three East Texas counties indicated that except for number of children desired and expected, statistically significant racial differences existed. Both black and white girls desired and expected to have families and children. Black girls desired marriage significantly later than white girls. A large majority of both racial groups desired and expected to work after marriage. Racial differences persisted even when socioeconomic status was controlled.

226

Lynn, David B. SEX-ROLE AND PARENTAL IDENTIFICATION. *Child Development*, 1962, 33, 555-564.

Sex Roles. Parental Identification. Sex Role Development. Sex Role Identification.

Women's personality and behavior have been attributed to many factors ranging from genetics and physiology to cultural conditioning. To accommodate apparent inconsistencies in previous research findings, this author developed several broad hypotheses supported by his own research and the work of other researchers. He postulated that differences in male and female sex roles can be attributed to the child's parental identification. Thus, women learn to behave the way they do through a socialization process in which they identify with and copy their mothers' behavior. Men behave the way they do because they tend to identify with a cultural stereotype of the masculine role. To determine the effect of parental identification on the development of behavior, these hypotheses about the behavior of women and men should be tested: • Females evidence greater need for affiliation than males. • Females are more dependent on the external context of a situation and more reluctant than males to deviate from the given. • Females tend to be more receptive than males to standards held by other people. • Males tend to develop better problem-solving skills than females. • Males tend to place higher value on the internalization of moral standards.

227

Maccoby, Eleanor E. SEX DIFFERENCES IN INTELLECTUAL FUNCTIONING, in *The Development of Sex Differences.* Stanford, California: Stanford University Press, 1966. Pages 25-55.

Sex Differences. Intellectual Functioning. Intellectual Development.

Despite limitations in various research methods and findings about sex differences in intellectual functioning, evidence suggests that substantial differences do exist. From early childhood on, males appear to be superior to females in spatial and analytic ability. Differences in verbal ability are less substantive but females demonstrate superiority. Evidence also indicates substantial sex differences in the relationship between intellectual performance and other personality characteristics of individuals. For example, impulsiveness seems to be a negative factor in the intellectual development of boys, but less negative in girls. Aggressiveness seems to inhibit intellectual development in boys more than in girls. Evidence on the relationship between anxiety and intellectual development in boys and girls is inconclusive, as is evidence concerning the relationship between level of aspiration and achievement motivation on intellectual development in both sexes. Dependency may be one reason for such differences, i.e., boys are more independent and more active than girls, and girls are more passive-dependent than boys. Evidence also suggests that family socialization practices affect intellectual development in boys and girls, and that such practices affect each person differently. Thus, males and females appear to have different intellectual strengths and weaknesses, but the complex interaction of influences can counteract weaknesses and heighten strengths.

228

McClelland, David C. WANTED: A NEW SELF-IMAGE FOR WOMEN. In Lifton, Robert J., Ed., *The Woman in America.* Boston: Houghton Mifflin, 1965. Pages 173-192.

Sex Differences. Life Styles. Occupational Choice. Feminine Self-Image.

The characteristics used to define women have historically centered around woman in terms of men, not in terms of herself. Any attempts to establish a new self-image for woman should be based not on how she should behave, but on how she does behave. A comparison of boys and girls reveals that girls excell in tasks involving rapid and fine-motor adjustments and that they are more observant and see things in their entirety more than boys do. Generally, the life styles of males can be characterized as analytic and manipulative, and the life styles of women as contextual and interdependent. Women are more concerned with issues regarding people, as reflected in their common choice of occupations which deal with people. Even within the sciences, women show a preference for biology and biochemistry, sciences which deal with human beings and animals. Sex differences are a combination of biological and social factors. Rather than being concerned that "women's work" is held in low esteem, women should take more pride in the work they do (such as teaching or nursing) which utilizes their interest in people, and their ability to perform many tasks simultaneously. They should also continue to develop new skills, and accept part-time employment opportunities to realize their full potential.

229

Rappaport, Alan F.; Payne, David, and Steinmann, Anne. PERCEPTUAL DIFFERENCES BETWEEN MARRIED AND SINGLE COLLEGE WOMEN FOR THE CONCEPTS OF SELF, IDEAL WOMAN, AND MAN'S IDEAL WOMAN. *Journal of Marriage and the Family,* 1970, 32(3), 441-442.

Man's "Ideal" Woman. The "Ideal" Woman. Feminine Self-Image. Sex Role Perceptions. Marital Status.

Married and single college women differ in their perceptions of self and ideal woman, but not in their perception of man's ideal woman. Married women see themselves and this ideal woman as more self-achieving than single women do, and single women see the ideal woman as more family-oriented than their own self perceptions. Both groups, however, see man's ideal woman as being more family-oriented than their own perception of the ideal woman or themselves. The perceptions of these women are shaped by cultural stereotypes of the female sex role. Further research for the purposes of validating the general applicability of the findings is planned. The sample consisted of 45 married and 45 single women enrolled at the University of Connecticut. The instrument used to measure sex role perceptions—the Inventory of Female Values (Botwin)—was modified by Steinmann and Fox (1966) and consists of 34 items, each of which describes a value or judgment related to women's activities and satisfactions.

230

Sandis, Eva E. THE TRANSMISSION OF MOTHERS' EDUCATIONAL AMBITIONS, AS RELATED TO SPECIFIC SOCIALIZATION TECHNIQUES. *Journal of Marriage and the Family*, 1970, 32(2), 204-211.

Educational Motivation. Parental Ambitions for Children. Socialization Practices.

A mother's own educational plans for her children appear to have greater effect than parent-initiated activities to promote high educational planning by the children themselves (concert-going, music lessons, etc.). This finding conflicts in part with current notions regarding the transmission of parental educational ambitions through specific socialization practices such as cultural activities. Children appear to develop their educational plans on the basis of many cues, rather than on the basis of specific activities. To obtain this finding, the author conducted semistructured interviews with 524 tenth graders and their mothers in eight New Jersey communities. Half the students were in above-average groups, and half, in below-average groups.

231

Searls, Laura G. LEISURE ROLE EMPHASIS OF COLLEGE GRADUATE HOMEMAKERS. *Journal of Marriage and the Family*, 1966, 28(1), 77-82.

Leisure Activity. Life Style Satisfaction.

The more active a college graduate woman homemaker is in leisure pursuits, the more likely she is to be basically satisfied with her role of homemaker. Older homemakers are more active in community welfare activities, although they may not necessarily be more involved than younger homemakers in total leisure pursuits. While social class level has little bearing on a homemaker's pursuit of leisure, her orientation to her family governs her level of participation in community welfare activity. Homemakers married at least 11 years are highly involved in total leisure and community welfare activities, while homemakers married from six to 10 years display a low level of involvement. Homemakers who were high academic achievers in college are more active in total leisure pursuits than others, but college achievement is not related to level of participation in self-enrichment and recreational activity. Homemakers with steady household and childcare help are more involved in total leisure activity than homemakers with little or no help. College major and place of residence have no bearing on a homemaker's pursuit of leisure. The researchers examined the responses to a mail questionnaire of 181 homemakers (married, living with husband, with one or more children, not presently employed) from four alumnae classes (1949, 1950, 1959, 1960) of the women's college of a coeducational university.

232

Steinmann, Anne. THE VOCATIONAL ROLES OF OLDER MARRIED WOMEN. *Journal of Social Psychology,* 1961, 54, 93-101.

Role Perceptions. Feminine Self-Image. Life Styles.

Married women between the ages of 40 and 50 demonstrated an orientation to the feminine role that was balanced between self-realization through the family (other-oriented) and self-realization through the fulfillment of individual potential (self-oriented). They did not, however, see vocational interests as integral to their life styles and, in many cases, they oriented themselves away from such activities. Most thought it unpractical, in terms of family relationships, to seek employment outside the home in an effort to change their status of homemaker, which they seem to have accepted. The author administered the Fand Inventory to 51 college girls to measure the level of other- and self-orientation. Of the 51 daughters, nine were other-oriented, seven were self-oriented, and 35 were balanced. Of the mothers, eight were other-oriented, five were self-oriented, and 38 were balanced.

233

Steinmann, Anne. FEMALE-ROLE PERCEPTION AS A FACTOR IN COUNSELING. *Journal of the National Association of Women Deans and Counselors,* 1970, Fall, 27-32.

The "Ideal" Woman. Sex Role Perceptions. Parental Influences. Educational Counseling.

The views of young women concerning work and family seem to reflect those of their parents. Most young women in this study felt they were capable of handling both work and family, which seems to derive from the mothers' unfulfilled wishes. On the other hand, most felt that working was not an important part of their lives, which may stem from the difficulties their mothers had in handling both family and work. The fact that most of the subjects stated that their "ideal woman" should be home-oriented indicates they were probably voicing their fathers' views. Most of the subjects felt children suffer if the mother works. Because most young women are unaware of the problems they will encounter in terms of work and family and the influences on their outlook, counselors need to help them make informed decisions and plans. In addition, counselors must promote the establishment of free day care, since this will enable women to choose freely. To obtain these findings, the author administered the 34-item Inventory of Feminine Values to 51 undergraduate women enrolled in sociology courses at a liberal arts college. The parents of the subjects were interviewed also.

234

Steinmann, Anne. WOMEN'S ATTITUDES TOWARDS CAREERS. *Vocational Guidance Quarterly,* 1959, **Autumn,** 15-18.

Parental Attitudes. The Working Wife. Career Barriers. Sex Role Perceptions.

An examination of young women's attitudes toward careers should take into consideration the attitudes of their parents toward careers for women. In this study, it appears that the daughters and mothers are inhibited in pursuit of work interests because they are convinced that men prefer women who are traditional homemakers. Interviews with the principal men in these women's lives (fathers and husbands) reveals acceptance of the working wife on an intellectual level but apparent rejection on an emotional level. Such ambivalence hinders decisive action on the part of the women. To obtain these findings, the author administered inventories on attitudes toward the role of women in society to 51 middle-class women college students and their parents. Eleven families were also interviewed. All the students planned careers after college and almost all of them planned to leave their work upon marriage. All parents supported their plans.

235

Steinmann, Anne and Doherty, Sister Mary Austin. PERCEPTIONS OF WOMEN RELIGIOUS REGARDING THE FEMALE ROLE. *National Catholic Guidance Conference Journal*, 1970, 15(1), 43-54.

Nuns. Sex Role Perceptions.

Nuns perceive the female role differently than other women do. Beginning nuns have a passive orientation which decreases with time. Generally, nuns seem to express their feelings as women and as individuals. To obtain these findings, the authors administered the Maferr Inventory of Female Values to 176 nuns who were students or faculty members at Alverno College, Milwaukee, Wisconsin. Comparative data were drawn for 75 women enrolled in a comparable public college and 53 business women.

236

Steinmann, Anne and Fox, David J. ATTITUDES TOWARD WOMEN'S FAMILY ROLE AMONG BLACK AND WHITE UNDERGRADUATES. *The Family Coordinator*, 1970, October, 363-368.

Man's "Ideal" Woman. The "Ideal" Woman. Marriage Counseling. Racial Differences.

Do black women believe, like women studied in England, France, Greece, Japan, Turkey and elsewhere, that man's ideal woman is more passive and family-oriented than women themselves perceive their ideal women and themselves to be? This study suggests that black women undergraduates believe that men want women to have both self-actualizing and family-oriented goals. In contrast, white women undergraduates think man's ideal woman is strongly family-oriented. But both black and white male undergraduates share the perception of black college-age women of the ideal woman. The reasons for the discrepancy between white and black women's perceptions of man's ideal woman, and the similarity of the perception of black men and women, may be the result of the greater exposure of black men to working women, and to increased communication between the sexes among blacks because of the mutual problems they share in white society. The implication of this study for marriage counselors is that black couples will not have fewer conflicts than white students in marriage, but that they will have different ones. The findings of this study may forecast a new level of understanding between the sexes. The authors administered the Maferr Inventory of Female Values of 100 female and 100 male black undergraduates in the South in 1967 and 1968. Comparative data for 126 female and 82 male white undergraduates were collected in 1963 and 1964 in the North. Male subjects only took the Man's Ideal Woman scale of the inventory.

237

Steinmann, Anne; Fox, David J., and Levi, Joseph. CROSS-CULTURAL STUDY OF MALE-FEMALE PERCEPTIONS OF THE FEMALE ROLE—A PILOT STUDY IN GREECE. Paper presented at a seminar of the Society for Psychoanalytic Study and Research, Inc., New York City, 1965. Mimeo. 8 pages.

Man's "Ideal" Woman. Feminine Self-Image. Psychological Counseling.

A comparison of the sex role perceptions of Greek, North American and South American women reveals the self perceptions of each are similarly balanced between active and passive. Women in different cultures share values with respect to the female role and perceive man's ideal woman as more passive than they perceived themselves or their ideal woman. Their perceptions of ideal women are also similarly balanced. Their perceptions of man's ideal woman are similar in that they all believe men want women to be highly passive and family-oriented. Greek and North American men, however, see their ideal woman as active. The potential for conflict between self-effacement and self-realization in these women is obvious, as is the need for better communication between the sexes. Psychologists and educators should encourage the self-actualization of women and the acceptance by men, if their liberal perceptions prove to be a facade, of active women so as to diminish conflict and promote growth and development. The authors administered the Inventory of Feminine Values to 24 Greek women and the Man's Ideal Woman measure of the inventory to 43 Greek men as part of a larger study of men and women throughout the world. The Greek subjects were all professionals. Scores on composite samples for 336 South American women and 837 North American women were used for purposes of comparison. A similar cross-cultural comparison of scores for men was included in the study.

238

Steinmann, Anne; Levi, Joseph; and Fox, David J. A CROSS-CULTURAL STUDY: WOMEN'S ATTITUDES TOWARDS CAREER AND FAMILY ROLES. *International Journal of Health Education,* 1963, 8(4), 1-8.

Man's "Ideal" Woman. The "Ideal" Woman. Sex Role Perceptions. Feminine Self Image. Employment. Career-Marriage Conflict.

A comparison of women's perceptions of the female role in the United States, Peru, Argentina, and Mexico reveals that all see their role as balanced between passive and active. They also believe that men prefer women who are extremely passive and who place more importance on the duties of wife and family than on their own personal growth and development. The discrepancy between self-perception and man's ideal woman is most striking in women in the United States. Studies underway, however, reveal that men do not seem to hold the passive ideal as highly as women believe they do. The implications of these findings, which were predicted as reasons for the conflict women often experience in seeking careers outside the home, are that government and industry must seek ways to diminish the ambivalent feelings in women regarding home and career that can endanger mental health over time, rather than concentrate only on finding ways to recruit women into the labor force. The authors administered the Inventory of Feminine Values to four groups of women—150 North American women, 153 Peruvian women, 29 Mexican women, and 157 Argentinean women—in 1963 as part of a larger, cross-cultural study of both sexes' perceptions of the female role. Each sample consisted of students, housewives, and working women.

239

Steinmann, Anne; Levi, Joseph; and Fox, David J. SELF-CONCEPT OF COLLEGE WOMEN COMPARED WITH THEIR CONCEPT OF IDEAL WOMAN AND MEN'S IDEAL WOMAN. *Journal of Counseling Psychology,* 1964, 11(4), 370-374.

Man's "Ideal" Woman. The "Ideal" Woman. Feminine Self Image. Higher Education. Educational Counseling. Psychological Counseling.

A study of college girls reveals that they see themselves as balanced between active and passive orientations, and that they see their ideal woman as being slightly more active. An examination of what they think men's ideal woman is reveals a belief that men prefer women who are extremely passive and who put family considerations before personal growth and development. Further analysis shows evidence of some inner conflict in these women in that their self concept agrees neither with what they think they should be nor with what they believe that men want women to be. Counselors should be aware of this conflict so that they can encourage women to integrate vocational and professional activities into their lives, particularly if further research shows that men do accept the active aspects of women's needs. To obtain these findings, the authors administered the Inventory of Feminine Values to 75 undergraduate women. The 34-item Inventory measures perceptions of woman's activities and satisfactions in terms of self and in terms of perceptions of woman's ideal woman and man's ideal woman.

History and Economics of Women at Work

240

Baker, Elizabeth F. TECHNOLOGY AND WOMAN'S WORK. New York and London: Columbia University Press, 1964. 460 pages.

Occupations. Technology. Employment Legislation. Employment Trends.

A presentation of the history of the changes in women's occupations through 160 years of technological growth in America, the book includes discussions of the obstacles to women's progress. Social, economic, physical, cultural and psychological obstacles are discussed and a review is provided of legislation on women workers, including minimum wage, equal pay, etc. The shift from traditional occupations for women such as secretary and teacher to more executive positions is explained and discussed. Specific occupational areas are described such as factory work, office, computer, sales, education and nursing.

241

Bass, Ann T. THE DEVELOPMENT OF HIGHER EDUCATION FOR WOMEN IN THIS COUNTRY. *Contemporary Education*, 1970, 41(6), 285-288.

Higher Education. Educational Barriers. History of Women's Education.

Higher education for American women has changed—from colonial times when women were considered inferior and education the prerogative of the leisure class to today when women are acknowledged to have the same academic ability as men. A review of the history of women's education points up the acrimonious debate that accompanied women's educational progress and leads one to question whether "avenues of eminence" are really open to women. Especially in the face of Castle's *Statistical Study of Eminent Women,* which indicates that only 891 women were mentioned in three out of six standard reference works. Several factors have affected women's educational development. As the notion of equality for all began to spread, early 19th century theorists contested the colonial view that women were inferior and started to promote the cultural value of educated women. As the public education system grew, women were used in great numbers as teachers. At all times, women's educational progress was wedded to the concept that it would not raise her above the "duties of her station." The author draws on Thomas Woody's *History of Women's Education in the United States*, (1929) and Thorstein Veblen's *The Higher Education in America*, (1957) to develop her discussion.

242

Berry, Jane; McCarty, Edward R.; Bates, Jean M. and Terrill, Hazel J. GUIDE FOR DEVELOPMENT OF PERMANENT AND PART-TIME EMPLOYMENT OPPORTUNITIES FOR GIRLS AND WOMEN. Kansas City: University of Missouri-Kansas City, 1969. 76 pages.

Part-time Employment. Employment facilitators.

The opportunities for permanent part-time employment (usually under 35 hours a week) are increasing as the need for the creative use of resources throughout the nation becomes more urgent. It is up to educators, counselors, and manpower specialists to promote the use of part-time employees in all occupational fields. Prepared for the Missouri Department of Labor and Industrial Relations, the book traces the history of part-time employment and describes what various private organizations and several state Employment Service agencies are doing to promote part-time employment. Profiles of several successful part-time employees are included, accompanied by predictions of the future of part-time employment and day-care. Data from a national survey of U.S. Employment Service offices are used to demonstrate the changing attitudes toward, and realities of, permanent part-time employment.

243

Cain, Glen George. MARRIED WOMEN IN THE LABOR FORCE: AN ECONOMIC ANALYSIS. Chicago: University of Chicago Press, 1966. 159 pages.

Employment. Racial Differences. Marital Status. Employment Trends.

A comparison of labor force participation rates reveals that nonwhite wives have a higher participation rate in the labor force than white wives at any given time. However, they have had a slower rate of increase in labor force participation over time. More nonwhite wives work because they find it necessary to supplement family income and their husbands generally earn lower salaries than white men. Day care for their children is readily available (that is, two families frequently live in one apartment, making it possible for one of the mothers to work outside the home). And they are more frequently widowed, divorced, or separated. Over time, however, the rate of entry into the labor force by nonwhite women has dropped because of increasing pressure on younger women to continue their education and increasing numbers of older nonwhite women drawing welfare payments. The general rise in employment of both white and nonwhite wives can be attributed to the increase in wages for women, the continued education of women, and the growing belief that women do not have to stay at home with their children. The results of a study of the economic determinants of labor force participation of married women for 1962 and 1963, the book includes tables that describe trends and factors affecting labor force participation of women from 1950 to 1960. An extensive appendix of specific statistical analyses of such factors as education, attitudes, labor supply and demand as they relate to the employment of married women is included.

244

Conway, Jill. JANE ADDAMS: AN AMERICAN HEROINE. In Lifton, Robert J.., Ed., *The Woman in America.* Boston: Houghton Mifflin, 1965. Pages 247-266.

Higher Education. Sex Role Perceptions. Career Achievement. History of Feminism.

A review of the accomplishments in public life of educated women such as Jane Addams, Lillian Wald and Eleanor Roosevelt reveals three major bases for their success. These are 1) a sense of mission among the first American women to receive graduate education, 2) their desire to use education and training to open up new roles for women, and 3) their recognition of the lack of life models other than the typical passive feminine model or the masculine model. Their philosophies, particularly Jane Addams', emphasized extreme individualism and the belief that many problems associated with urbanization could be solved by using women's intellects and wills along with men's.

245

Degler, Carl N. REVOLUTION WITHOUT IDEOLOGY: THE CHANGING PLACE OF WOMEN IN AMERICA. In Lifton, Robert J., Ed., *The Woman in America.* Boston: Houghton Mifflin, 1965. Pages 193-210.

Employment. Career Opportunities. Employment Trends. Higher Education.

Several historical developments have affected the drive for equality of opportunity for women. These include expanded employment opportunities during and after World Wars I and II, the increased number of women earning college and advanced degrees, and changing relationships between the sexes resulting from egalitarian concepts of marriage. Yet, the majority of employed women are still in fields traditionally open to women such as teaching, nursing and clerking. Moreover, the actual number of women enrolled in and completing college and advanced degrees has decreased somewhat since the 1930s. In addition, the extent of American women's participation in government is far below that of European countries, 11 being the highest number of women in Congress so far (1951), compared to 17 women in the British House of Commons (1951) and 41 in the German Reichstag (1922). Although the number of women seeking work outside the home has increased, equality of the sexes will not be achieved until women overcome the American tendency to emphasize individuality and to reject support of an ideology of equality.

246

Erikson, Joan M. NOTHING TO FEAR: NOTES ON THE LIFE OF ELEANOR ROOSEVELT. In Lifton, Robert J., Ed. *The Woman in America.* Boston: Houghton Mifflin, 1965. Pages 267-287.

Historical Biography. Career Achievement.

During the 1930s, Eleanor Roosevelt was prominent in the press as a butt of jokes and anecdotes aimed at her personal appearance as well as her phenomenal energy and involvement in the improvement of conditions for the underprivileged. Early childhood deprivation helps explain her adult development and accomplishments. She was driven to help others overcome their deprived states; her sensitivity to her own failures made her reach out to help others achieve success. Her development as an individual throughout her marriage and her life is marked by her refusal to let illness or domination by others prevent her from fulfilling personal needs or public aspirations.

247

Falk, Ruth; Maraventano, Frances, and Ralph, Diane. A WOMAN'S PLACE, AN UPDATING OF WOMEN'S

LIBERATION. National Institute of Mental Health, Office of Youth and Study Affairs, 1970. 18 pages.

Women's Organizations. Educational Facilitators. Federal Employment.

Major trends in the women's liberation movement are summarized, including the work of professional women's caucuses and federal women's programs. Such programs include the Federal Women's Program, the Professional Women's Corps Career Service Boards of the Department of Health, Education and Welfare, Interdepartmental Committee and Citizen's Advisory Council on the Status of Women, the Presidential Task Force on Women's Rights and Responsibilities, and Federally Employed Women, Inc. (FEW). Day-care centers are seen as a benefit to women and children, and as a vehicle to assist in training professionals for new careers. Thorough investigations regarding abortions and alternative contraception devices are urged. Stereotyped sex roles in public school education should be overcome. Other inequalities are found in jobs and education and in manpower training programs.

248

Farber, Seymour M. and Wilson, Roger M. L., Eds. THE POTENTIAL OF WOMEN. San Francisco: McGraw-Hill, 1963. 328 pages.

Women's Potential.

The basic potential of woman is to be a free and independent human being. Changes in social and environmental systems can facilitate the fulfillment of this potential. The record of one in a series of symposiums on "Man and Civilization" held at the University of California San Francisco Medical Center, the book includes papers presented and transcripts of panel discussions on the study of the female, the spectrum of femininity, the roles of woman, the consequences of equality, the male revolt, and the ideal man and woman. Participants included Phyllis Jay, Eleanor Maccoby, Marya Mannes, Mark Harris, John Money, and others.

249

Folger, John K.; Astin, Helen S., and Bayer, Alan E. HUMAN RESOURCES AND HIGHER EDUCATION. Staff Report of the Commission on Human Resources and Advanced Education.

New York: Russell Sage Foundation, 1969. 475 pages. (Chapter 9: THE EDUCATIONAL AND VOCATIONAL DEVELOPMENT OF WOMEN, 280-304.)

Employment. Employment Facilitators. Educational Facilitators. Employment Trends.

The lower educational and career attainment of women as compared with men indicates that attitudes and values operating at present in the occupational world prevent equal participation of women. However, there are evidences of change in the labor force participation of women that have occurred along with changes in the economy and needs for highly-trained manpower. To realize the contributions of increasing numbers of women in the labor force, society must recognize the discontinuity of a woman's career by providing greater opportunities for continuing education, retraining, and counseling for adult women returning to the labor force. There must be an increase in the availability and acceptability of part-time employment and child-care facilities. Young girls and women must receive more encouragement from teachers, parents, and counselors if they are to develop the self-image and self-esteem required for high-level career commitment. Information on the goals and career aspirations of different groups of women must be studied in relation to changes in professions to assess the likelihood of a greater proportion of women entering particular career fields.

250

Freedman, Mervin B. CHANGES IN SIX DECADES OF SOME ATTITUDES AND VALUES HELD BY EDUCATED WOMEN. *Journal of Social Issues*, 1961, 18, 19-28.

Value Changes. Higher Education.

Comparison of the general outlook of Vassar alumnae (from 1904 to 1956) reveals a close parallel between social change and psychological change processes. Older alumnae scored higher than younger alumnae on tests of authoritarianism and ethnocentrism, and 1956 graduates scored higher than 1940 graduates on the same measures. Perhaps "the tenor of the times" is a greater factor in the formation of outlook in college than simple differences in age of the subjects. The importance of the college years as a time of change in attitudes is indicated by the finding that freshmen classes were more authoritarian than senior classes over time, but that no significant changes were apparent following graduation. The sample included 85 members of the class of 1904, 43 members of the class of 1914, 73 members of the classes of 1921-1924, 50 members of the classes of 1929-35, 77 members of the classes of 1940-43, and 200 members of the class of 1956. The F and E Scales of the California Public Opinion Survey, a 60-item questionnaire for measuring kinds of changes in students, were used to measure changes in outlook.

251

Ginzberg, Eli, and Associates. LIFE STYLES OF EDUCATED WOMEN. New York: Columbia University Press, 1966. 224 pages.

Educational Facilitators. Career Patterns. Life Styles. Employment Facilitators. Career Barriers.

Women have a more complex career and life pattern than men. They face a larger number of significant options and conflicts inherent in the dual role of worker and mother. The major change in a woman's life pattern began after the Civil War, with the industrial and urban revolutions, and continued with the broadened work opportunities resulting from World Wars I and II. The data suggest that the more education a woman has, the more likely she is to be in the labor force. The ability to control the size of one's family, the invention of labor-saving devices, the increase of premarital work experiences, and the broadened opportunities for education have all served as a stimulus to women's increasing involvement in the world of work. Recommendations for the effective utilization of educated women include: • further research into the socialization processes of women; • change in tax laws to include deductions for household workers; • increase in child-care facilities and trained child care workers; • elimination of discrimination against women in business and higher education; • increase in the quality and quantity of counseling and placement services for mature women; • increase in the acceptability and availability of part-time work. The authors used a questionnaire to gather information on 311 educated women who had pursued graduate education at Columbia University between 1945 and 1951.

252

Gordon, Michael, and Bernstein, M. Charles. MATE CHOICE AND DOMESTIC LIFE IN THE NINETEENTH-CENTURY MARRIAGE MANUAL. *Journal of Marriage and the Family,* 1970, 32(4), 665-674.

Nineteenth-century Marriage Manuals.

Marriage manuals of the 19th century were conservative in outlook but surprisingly diversified in perspective. As factors in the choice of a mate, consideration of religion, constitution and physical health, morality, and character were frequently mentioned. Marriage for love was not. A rational outlook on marriage and home management was characteristic of these books. The marriage guides made it clear that the husband was superior to the wife in all circumstances. A shift in attitude toward conjugal sex was evident by the end of the century. Couples were advised that sex by itself, rather than only for procreation, is beneficial to the marriage. The authors examined 63 marriage manuals published between 1830 and 1900 in the United States to develop their discussion.

253

Hughes, Marija Matich. THE SEXUAL BARRIER: LEGAL AND ECONOMIC ASPECTS OF EMPLOYMENT. California: University of California Hastings College of the Law, 1970. 35 pages.

Employment Legislation. Career Barriers.

A bibliography covering the laws and conditions governing the employment of women, the book includes the "most authoritative" books, articles, pamphlets, and government documents on the topic published since 1959. It is intended for use by lawyers, legislators, educators, researchers, and the general public. Straightforward bibliographic citations are provided in five categories: legal aspects, discrimination in employment, difference in pay, professional opportunities, and general.

254

Kanowitz, Leo. WOMEN AND THE LAW: THE UNFINISHED REVOLUTION. Albuquerque: University of New Mexico Press, 1969. 312 pages.

Employment Legislation. Discrimination. Status.

Although women's legal status is closer today than ever before to being equal to that of men, women still suffer discrimination which stunts personal development and promotes undesirable personal development. An essay on women's status under state and federal law and the Constitution, the book represents an objective analysis of the matter. The author describes legally-sanctioned discrimination on the basis of sex as represented in all laws—civil, criminal, political—relating to single adult women, women as minors, married adult women. He also evaluates the origin and impact of such laws and attempts to alter them; the scope of, and relationship between, Title VII of the 1964 Civil Rights Act and the Equal Pay Act of 1963; and "constitutional aspects of sex-based discrimination in American law." Heavily footnoted throughout, the book includes the texts of Title VII, Executive Order 11246 (promoting equal employment opportunity under federal contracting), and two important District Court Opinions relating to women's equal rights (*White v. Crook; U.S. ex rel. Robinson v. York*).

255

Keniston, Ellen, and Keniston, Kenneth. AN AMERICAN ANACHRONISM—THE IMAGE OF WOMEN AND WORK. *American Scholar*, 1964, 33(3), 355-375.

Sex Role Perceptions. Feminine Self-image. Sex Role Stereotypes.

This is a discussion of the historical, anthropological, social, and psychological bases for present attitudes regarding women. Today's American woman suffers from a "cultural lag" which persists as a result of the "transmission of images of feminity and masculinity from generation to generation within the family." The mothers of young women today are likely to have felt resentment toward the domestic role or guilt about their career aspirations. Traditional models of femininity are reinforced by the mass media, the educational system, and the social system. The authors suggest that because women must either work or spend most of their adulthood with "nothing to do," educational systems and mass media must strive to present an image of the working woman as feminine and fulfilled. More challenging work should be available to men so that husbands will suffer less resentment of their wives' work satisfaction.

256

Komarovsky, Mirra. WOMEN IN THE MODERN WORLD—THEIR EDUCATION AND THEIR DILEMMAS. Boston: Little, Brown and Company, 1953. 319 pages.

Career-marriage Conflict. Education. Sex Role Stereotypes.

Education for women is failing today. The fault is not in women, however, but in education and society. Women are schooled in the tradition of personal achievement and academic excellence but they also are pressured and conditioned to aspire to marriage, homemaking, and motherhood. They are forced to choose, in 19th century fashion, between marriage and career. They fall prey to the "romantic" view of life, and the gap between reality and romance becomes every wider and more difficult to overcome. Men are similarly confronted with fulfilling ancient and worn-out traditions that hamper the realization of a full, rewarding life. Women's education should endeavor to prepare women for the world of work and the role of citizen, as well as for the roles of wife and mother. The author bases her analysis on existing literature and on her own research on the educated woman.

257

Knudsen, Dean D. THE DECLINING STATUS OF WOMEN: POPULAR MYTHS AND THE FAILURE OF FUNCTIONALIST THOUGHT. *Social Forces*, 1969, 48(2), 183-193.

Discrimination. Status. Effect of Functionalism.

American women have suffered a gradual but persistent loss of status rather than a gain over the last 25 years in occupation, income, and education. The causes for the loss are institutionalized discrimination and diminished efforts by women, both of which result primarily from the dominance of functionalist interpretations concerning the family and sex roles in modern social science. To obtain this finding, the author compared U.S. census and other government data for education, occupation, and income of women and men over the last 25 years.

258

McGuigan, Dorothy Gies. A DANGEROUS EXPERIMENT—100 YEARS OF WOMEN AT THE UNIVERSITY OF MICHIGAN. Ann Arbor, Michigan: The University of Michigan, Center for Continuing Education of Women, 1970. 136 pages.

Higher Education. History of Women's Education.

A history of women at the University of Michigan since 1870, this report includes descriptions of the controversy surrounding the admission of women to the University, the problems encountered by early women students, the careers of early graduates, and the status of women as students, teachers, and administrators in the University today.

259

Millet, Kate. SEXUAL POLITICS. Garden City, New York: Doubleday & Company, Inc., 1970. 393 pages.

Oppression of Women. Patriarchy. History of Feminism.

The author demonstrates that patriarchy is a political institution that requires the oppression of women. The family, as the basic institution of patriarchy, insures women's oppression. The relationship of the sexes as a political one is demonstrated in a critical analysis of history and contemporary literature of three authors—Norman Mailer, D.H. Lawrence, Jean Genet. She also examines biases against women reported in writings of Freud about human behavior and how such writings operated to counteract (from 1930 to 1960) the feminist movement of the last century. She draws on existing theory, research, and criticism to develop her discussion.

260

Mueller, Kate H. EDUCATING WOMEN FOR A CHANGING WORLD. Minneapolis: University of Minnesota Press, 1954. 302 pages.

Education. Higher Education.

The book is a review of a ten-year study of women's strengths and weaknesses, their struggles and successes in modern society in light of the excellences and deficiencies of men. The author raises questions such as: should the education of women be different from that of men? If so, how and why? Is education today relevant to the demands of our changing world? College programs for women and methods of evaluating these programs are presented. The author concludes that because modern society emphasizes development of the individual's fullest potential and recognizes that women do not differ from men in intellectual ability, education in most colleges is outdated for all students, especially for women. Women teachers, counselors, and mothers need to reexamine their attitudes toward woman's education and development. An index of suggested readings follows each chapter. The data are based on questionnaire responses of male and female graduate students.

261

Newcomer, Mabel. A CENTURY OF HIGHER EDUCATION FOR AMERICAN WOMEN. New York: Harper and Brothers, 1959. 266 pages.

Higher Education. History of Women's Education.

Over one million women were enrolled in American colleges in 1957, just 120 years after Oberlin admitted the first female students. Today, it is acknowledged that women have an equal right to education. A review of the development of women's higher education in the United States shows that a college education was primarily professional education until 1870, when colleges were opened to women. Although major arguments for higher education of women centered on human rights, social good was also emphasized. Many factors contributed to the increases in women attending college during the 19th century, including the need for teachers in the growing public school system and the industrialization of the economy. As the right to higher education for women spread, more women's and co-educational colleges opened, and gave rise to the development of modern curriculum, the elective system of course selection, extra-curricular programs, etc. The history of women's education is marked by controversy, however, as shown by examination of financing procedures, teacher recruitment and student screening practices. Controversy persists even today. Educators are confronted with several decisions. Is higher education for women a privilege to be granted on an individual basis, or is it a right and a necessity that women be educated as highly as men for the maintenance and growth of society and the nation? Educators must act to promote the development of women as a valuable resource.

262

Oppenheimer, Valerie. THE SEX-LABELING OF JOBS. *Industrial Relations*, 1968, 7(3), 219-234.

Female-dominated Occupations. Sex Labeling of Jobs. Employment Trends. Employment Patterns.

There are many reasons for the development and continuation of female-dominated occupations and subsequent sex-labeling of jobs in the United States. In general, female occupations—teaching, nursing, clerical/secretarial work—require a fairly high level of education but little specific skill training. Career opportunity is not essential, and mobility for women workers is easily achieved because these jobs exist all over the country. Long-range commitments or extensive sacrifices of time and energy are not required. In spite of changes in trends of employment between 1900 and 1960, 70 percent of these occupations which employ mostly women today also did so in 1900. On the whole, these jobs exhibit characteristics which promote the attachment of the female sex label and lack characteristics which would favor the employment of male workers. It is remarkable that some individuals, male and female, have crossed over sex lines to seek employment. This survey was based on other papers by the author, 1960 Census data, and study of employment trends in female occupations.

263

Oppenheimer, Valerie K. THE INTERACTION OF DEMAND AND SUPPLY AND ITS EFFECT ON THE FEMALE LABOR FORCE IN THE UNITED STATES. *Population Studies*, 1967, 21(3), 239-259.

Employment. Mature Women Workers. Employment Trends.

Analysis of 20th century trends in patterns of female labor force participation in the U.S. reveals a definite trend in increased employment of older, married women, and a decline in the participation of younger, unmarried women. Reasons for the increase in the number of female workers include: 1) growth in demand for clerical and professional workers, 2) demand for more older women for second occupations, and, 3) more recently, emphasis on equal opportunity in jobs for women. The increase in entry into the labor force of more mature women has also created new practices and trends including a steady decline of discriminatory hiring policies and responsive shifts in positions according to the demands of labor. Data for this analysis included the writer's own research, U.S. Census Data (1960), and labor force statistics.

264

Oppenheimer, Valerie. DEMOGRAPHIC INFLUENCES ON FEMALE EMPLOYMENT AND THE STATUS OF WOMEN. Paper presented at the 137th Meeting, American Association for the Advancement of Science, December, 1970. 47 pages.

Employment. Employment Trends. History of Female Employment.

The extent of women's contribution to the national economy has increased over the past 70 years. In 1969, 50 percent of American women aged 18-64 years were in the labor force. In preindustrial times, most productive work was carried out within the family, and women were economically dependent on their husbands and families. With industrialization, productive labor moved outside the home. Because this trend posed a threat to the traditional family structure, the employment of women was sometimes limited to the unmarried to help preserve the family. With more women in all stages of family life entering and continuing in the labor force today, trends must evolve to produce a broader choice of occupations for women and entrance into previously male-dominated occupations. As women come to view work as an integral part of their lives, the traditionally low status women have had as a secondary manpower resource will change. Women will push for equality in the world of work.

265

Oppenheimer, Valerie. THE FEMALE LABOR FORCE IN THE UNITED STATES: DEMOGRAPHIC AND ECONOMIC FACTORS GOVERNING ITS GROWTH AND CHANGING COMPOSITION. Berkeley: Institute of International Studies, University of California. Population Monograph Series No. 5, 1970. 197 pages.

Employment Trends. Mature Women Workers.

The best explanation for the increase in labor force participation by older married women is that the demand for female labor has increased and the supply of the preferred female worker—young and unmarried—has decreased. Thus, the older married woman, who was previously excluded from the labor market, has had greater opportunities, and even invitations, to respond to the demand for female workers. The number of older, married women in the labor force has increased rapidly, but the number of women in the entire female labor force has increased only moderately since 1940. This report consists of detailed analysis of data on changing patterns of female labor force participation, supply factors that effect female employment, segregation of male and female labor markets, and the relationship of demographic and economic factors to the growth of a female labor force.

266

Peterson, Esther. ARE STANDARDS LOSING STATUS? *A Woman's Work*. New York, N.Y.: Barnard College, 1967. Page 15.

Employment Facilitators. Employment Legislation.

Labor laws establishing the 40-hour work week, minimum wages, and equal pay and the increase in educational opportunities for women have made it possible for increasing numbers of women to enter the labor market. Modern technology has opened many "men's" jobs to women and has made homemaking less time-consuming. However, some labor laws work against women—such as laws in many states limiting overtime work for women which may put them at a professional disadvantage and may seriously interfere with their earning power. Labor standards and practices should improve available maternity policies, child-care provisions, and opportunities for continuing education for women.

267

Peterson, Esther. WORKING WOMEN. In Lifton, Robert J., Ed. *The Woman in America.* Boston: Houghton Mifflin, 1965. Pages 144-172.

Employment. Education. Employment Facilitators.

At the turn of the century, a woman's life plan consisted of preparation for marriage, marriage itself, and devotion of her energies to the development and nurturing of her family. Today, however, an increasing number of women, particularly married women, enter the labor force and interest is increasing in equalizing occupational opportunities for women. Scientific and technological advances are providing women with more free time. Medical science has given women greater longevity. Husbands and fathers share more of the homemaking tasks. Moreover, the level of formal education for women has been raised. Nevertheless, the rate of college and graduate school degree attainment for women is still lower than the rate for men. Moreover, there have been changes in the dynamics of working women. For example, many women today work to pay for the educational expenses of their children rather than to earn some "pin money." Women are represented in almost every occupation, but they generally fill low-status, low-paid positions while men fill the high-status positions. Thus, although job opportunities have widened, opportunities for access to jobs have not. To achieve further equality between the sexes, there must be more child-care centers, continuing education, better counseling, and promotion of progressive attitudes toward woman's position in the world of work. The author cites U.S. Department of Labor, Bureau of Census statistics and other research findings.

268

Racz, Elizabeth. THE WOMEN'S RIGHTS MOVEMENT IN THE FRENCH REVOLUTION. *Science and Society*, 1952, 16(2), 151-174.

History of Women's Movement. The French Revolution.

This is a detailed account of the activities of French women's liberationists in the 1790s. In many parts of France, women led the struggle for human rights. Difficulties toward the end of the revolution undermined the women's movement so that the gains they had made previously were diminished. Similarly, failure of the revolution of 1848 and participation in Socialist programs discredited the women's struggle. The revolutionary activities of the 1870s and the Paris Commune of 1871 brought about a solid coalition of women liberationists and labor union activists, and their struggles achieved greater success.

269

Schwartz, Jane. PLANNING AHEAD. *A Woman's Work.* New York, N.Y.: Barnard College, 1967. Pages 38-39.

Career Opportunities. Career Planning. Employment Trends.

Young women can now expect to work a minimum of 25 years during their lifetimes and 40 years if they do not marry. Job opportunities for women have been steadily increasing, and training programs in government agencies and industries are now open to women. A great amount of useful information for vocational planning is provided by professional associations, the federal, state and local government, individual companies and professional schools as well as by career counseling services in institutions of higher education. However, in spite of the dramatic changes in women's lives and the broadening in educational and employment opportunities, the proportion of women in the professions is the same as it was 75 years ago and remains surprisingly low.

270

Scott, Anne Firor. AFTER SUFFRAGE: SOUTHERN WOMEN IN THE TWENTIES. *Journal of Southern History,* 1964, 30(3), 298-318.

History of Women's Movement. Political Activism. Social Welfare Activism.

This is a detailed account of the political and social welfare activities of women in the South in the 1920s. Many Southern women's organizations aligned themselves with labor unions and progressive politicians. The principal technique they used to effect reforms was education of the electorate. They contributed greatly to the institution of child labor laws, despite considerable resistance in all quarters of the South.

271

Smuts, Robert W. WOMEN AND WORK IN AMERICA. New York: Columbia University Press, 1959. 180 pages.

Employment. Employment Trends. Familial Roles. Changing Role of Women.

One of every three workers in America is a woman. The increase in labor force participation by women in the U.S. can be attributed to the improvement in communication and the rise of industrialization. As more family-centered activities—education, food and clothing production, etc.—are taken over by other institutions, the functional role of women is changing. The "cultural lag" resulting from this change, reflected in barriers to women's increased labor force participation, will disappear as interest in securing equal opportunity in the world of work for women spreads. Data for this analysis were drawn from research conducted under the Conservation of Human Resources Project at Columbia University.

272

Suelzle, Marijean. WOMEN IN LABOR. *Trans-action*, 1970, 8(1-2), 50-58.

Employment. Status. Barriers to Raising Status of Women.

An examination of labor force participation statistics and figures concerning women shows a loss in status for women in the last 50 years. This runs contrary to the popular belief that women have improved their status. For example, while the educational attainment of women has increased since 1920, the gap between earnings of women and men has been increasing, particularly in the last 15 years. And despite evidence to the contrary, myths and traditions that hinder improved status of women still prevail and will continue to do so unless recognized for what they are. For example, the belief that women "naturally" do not want careers and that they just want jobs is as erroneous as the belief that members of ethnic minorities "naturally" do not aspire to positions of leadership. The belief that women control most of the country's wealth is equally unfounded: of the total number of shares of public corporations owned by individuals, 18 percent are owned by women, 24 percent by men, and 58 percent by institutions, brokers, or dealers. Of the estimated market value of such stock, 18 percent of the total is held by women, 20 percent by men. Existing research and U.S. Department of Labor Statistics document these findings.

273

Thompson, Mary Lou, Ed. VOICES OF THE NEW FEMINISM. Boston, Massachusetts: Beacon Press, 1970. 246 pages.

Feminism. Women's Organizations. Women's Liberation.

This is an examination by the Unitarian-Universalist Women's Federation of the situation of women in the world today and of the various recommendations for change put forth by members of the National Organization for Women (NOW) and other new feminists. The contributors treat the many issues involved in women's liberation, some taking a rhetorical approach, others drawing on the research and literature to develop views of the movement. Articles cover the history of the movement, its ideology, problems and goals, emerging life styles and programs for the future. Contributors include Alice Rossi, Betty Friedan, Joyce Cowley, Martha Griffiths, Mary Daly, Caroline Bird, and Shirley Chisholm. A partially annotated bibliography on women by Lucinda Cisler is also included.

274

Time. WHO'S COME A LONG WAY, BABY?, 1970, 96(9), 16-21.

Employment Patterns. Income. Women's Liberation.

This article traces some of the reasons for the re-emergence of radical women's liberation groups. Economic statistics cited include: • Women constitute only nine percent of all professionals, seven percent of all doctors, three percent of all lawyers, one percent of engineers. • Although nine of ten elementary school teachers are women, eight of 10 school principals are men. • Harvard had two tenured women professors in 1970, but granted 15 percent of its graduate degrees to women. • Few women hold high office, often only because they succeeded their husbands in office. • Of the 8,750 judges in America, only 300 are women. • The median wage for full-time women workers is 58 percent of the median wage for men.

275

U.S. Department of Labor, Wage and Labor Standards Administration. Women's Bureau. AMERICAN WOMEN 1963-1968:

REPORT OF THE INTER-DEPARTMENTAL COMMITTEE ON THE STATUS OF WOMEN, 1968. 31 pages.

Employment Legislation. Status.

Legislation on the status of women passed between 1963 and 1968 greatly expanded women's rights, responsibilities and opportunities. Growing interest by private organizations, professional and volunteer, and all levels of government in correcting existing inequities reflects the progress witnessed in the same five years. A positive review of progress during President Johnson's administration, this report examines the status of women in terms of education and counseling, home and community, labor standards, and the security of basic income.

276

U.S. Department of Labor, Wage and Labor Standards Administration, Women's Bureau. AUTOMATION AND WOMEN WORKERS, 1970. 12 pages.

Career Opportunities. Technology. Employment Trends.

The employment opportunities and status of women workers improved considerably between 1958 and 1968, but the part played in the change by technological progress is difficult to determine. The general decline in low-skilled jobs, brought about by the increased use of computers and higher paying jobs, benefited women in general. It is probable that over the years women with technical, scientific, clerical, or other specialized skills will reap the benefits of progress, but that women with limited training and education will have difficulty remaining in the labor force. Undertaken to examine the effects of scientific and technological progress on the employment of women, the report also discusses trends in vocational guidance and training, training and retraining of older women, remuneration, hours of work and leisure, safety and health, and child care.

277

U.S. Department of Labor, Workplace Standards Administration, Women's Bureau. BACKGROUND FACTS ON WOMEN WORKERS IN THE UNITED STATES, 1970. 20 pages.

Employment. Status. Employment Patterns.

This is a short analysis of the status of American women workers. Statistics are provided on the number of workers, labor force reserve, age, marital and family status, female heads of families, educational attainment, occupations, industries, full-time and part-time job status, work experience, unemployment, earnings and reasons for nonparticipation of women in the labor force.

278

U.S. Department of Labor, Wage and Labor Standards Administration, Women's Bureau. EQUAL PAY FACTS. Leaflet 2, 1970. 7 pages.

Employment Legislation.

This leaflet lists the states in which equal pay legislation has been passed, the legislative history of equal pay, the scope of the various laws, and the organizations and commissions supporting equal pay.

279

U.S. Department of Labor, Wage and Labor Standards Administration, Women's Bureau. EXPANDING OPPORTUNITIES FOR GIRLS: THEIR SPECIAL COUNSELING NEEDS, 1970. 4 pages.

Career Aspirations. Educational Counseling.

The career goals of too many girls remain limited, traditional, and unrealistic despite the fact that nine out of every ten of them will work sometime during their lives, and about half of the women in this country between the ages of 18 and 65 are in the labor force today. Low career expectations help explain why women earn considerably less than men even though their educational attainment is quite similar to men's. Statistical data support the need for better counseling for girls.

280

U.S. Department of Labor, Wage and Labor Standards Administration, Women's Bureau. LABOR LEGISLATION FOR WOMEN WORKERS, 1970. 4 pages.

Employment Legislation.

Virtually all legislation concerning women workers and dealing with fair employment practices, age discrimination, equal pay, minimum wage and overtime, etc., has been passed since 1920.

Included in this leaflet are synopses of important federal and federal-state legislation for women workers such as the Federal Fair Labor Standards Act of 1938, Title VII of the Federal Civil Rights Act of 1964, and the Federal Social Security Act of 1935.

281

U.S. Department of Labor, Wage and Labor Standards Administration, Women's Bureau. LAWS ON SEX DISCRIMINATION IN EMPLOYMENT: FEDERAL CIVIL RIGHTS ACT, TITLE VII; STATE FAIR EMPLOYMENT PRACTICES LAWS; EXECUTIVE ORDERS, 1970. 20 pages.

Employment Legislation. Discrimination.

A survey of existing legislation concerning sex discrimination, the book describes the coverage and exceptions, unlawful employment practices, and major exceptions to prohibited employment practices of the Federal Civil Rights Act of 1964, Title VII. It also covers State Fair Employment Practice Laws and the relationship of these laws and Title VII of the Civil Rights Act to state protective labor legislation for women. Descriptions are provided of Executive Order 11246, as amended, which covers equal employment opportunity in federal contracting, and Executive Order 11478 which covers equal employment opportunity in the federal government.

282

U.S. Department of Labor. MANPOWER DEMAND AND SUPPLY IN PROFESSIONAL ORGANIZATIONS: A REPRINT FROM THE 1970 MANPOWER REPORT OF THE PRESIDENT. 1970. 29 pages.

Employment Trends. Career Opportunities.

Based on data prepared principally by the Departments of Labor and Health, Education, and Welfare, this pamphlet describes overall trends in the supply and demand of manpower, projected manpower needs in specific fields, and the improved access to professional education and employment that low-income youth, Negroes, and women will have during the decade of the seventies. Because of the anticipated decline in the need for teachers, women should seek employment in career fields other than those traditionally open to women.

283

U.S. Department of Labor, Women's Bureau. SEX DISCRIMINATION IN EMPLOYMENT PRACTICES, 1968. 43 pages.

Discrimination.

Despite the progress in recent years in correcting inequitable employment practices, discrimination against women is still widespread in government and private industry. This is a report of a conference sponsored jointly by the University Extension Service, University of California at Los Angeles, the Personnel and Industrial Relations Association, Inc., and the Women's Bureau, Wage and Labor Standards Administration, U.S. Department of Labor. It covers such issues as unlawful employment practices, consequences of proven charges of discrimination, pension and retirement plans, and so on.

284

U.S. Department of Labor, Wage and Labor Standards Administration, Women's Bureau. TRENDS IN EDUCATIONAL ATTAINMENT OF WOMEN, 1969. 19 pages.

Educational Patterns. Employment Patterns. Higher Education.

Since 1900, there has been a relatively steady increase in the number of girls graduating from high school in contrast to a less rapid increase in the number of boys. In October, 1968, first time college enrollees in degree and nondegree programs included nearly 819,000 women and over a million men. This represented an increase over the 1967 figures of 14 percent for women and 16 percent for men. The number of women earning bachelor's and first professional degrees also increased during the 70-year period from about 5,000 in 1900 to 279,000 in 1968. In 1900, women accounted for about 20 percent of all master's degree recipients; in 1930, they accounted for 40 percent. The greatest growth in the number of women earning doctor's degrees occurred between 1900 and 1930, a 15-fold increase from 23 to 353. Between 1960 and 1968, the numbers tripled. In terms of the relationship between the educational attainment of women and their labor force participation, the more education a woman receives, the greater the likelihood she will be engaged in paid employment. Source materials for this booklet included statistics and figures prepared by the U.S. Department of Health, Education, and Welfare, Office of Education, the U.S. Department of Commerce, Bureau of the Census and the U.S. Department of Labor, Bureau of Labor Statistics.

See also: FACT SHEET ON TRENDS IN EDUCATIONAL ATTAINMENT OF WOMEN, U.S. Department of Labor, Women's Bureau, 1969, for highlights of this report.

285

U.S. Department of Labor, Wage and Labor Standards Administration, Women's Bureau. WHY WOMEN WORK, 1970. 2 pages.

Employment Motivation. Employment.

Women usually work because of financial need, either to support their families and dependents or themselves. Based on figures from the U.S. Department of Commerce, Bureau of the Census, and the U.S. Department of Labor, Bureau of Labor Statistics, this leaflet briefly cites the most recent statistics concerning labor force participation of single, widowed, separated, divorced, and married women.

286

U.S. Department of Labor, Women's Bureau. WOMANPOWER—AN UNDER-UTILIZED RESOURCE?, 1968. 6 pages.

Employment Legislation.

Written by Mary Dublin Keyserling, Director of the Women's Bureau, this article discusses recent progress and the anticipated impact of legislation and programs on the status of American women workers.

287

Wilson, Kenneth M. SELECTED DATA PERTAINING TO THE HIGHER EDUCATION OF WOMEN. Paper prepared for the College Research Center, Vassar College, 1967. 15 pages.

Higher Education. Doctoral Degrees. Educational Patterns. Career Patterns.

The woman's share of doctoral degrees has declined from 18.4 percent in 1944 to 10.8 percent in 1964-65. The importance of this decline is magnified by the fact that 60 percent of the doctoral degrees earned during 1920-1962 were earned between 1950 and 1962. Even at highly selective women's colleges, relatively few graduates seek doctoral degrees. The woman's share of higher education positions has also declined from a high of 29.8 percent in 1946 to 22.2 percent in 1963. Tables and data were summarized to obtain findings on women's share of earned degrees (1895-1965); women's share of higher education positions (1930-1963); aspects of productivity of selected undergraduate institutions in turning out Ph.D. degree candidates; changing roles of women's colleges in producing doctoral degree recipients; and colleges and universities attractive to 11th graders of very high ability.

288

Zapoleon, Marguerite W. OCCUPATIONAL PLANNING FOR WOMEN. New York: Harper and Brothers, 1961. 276 pages.

Vocational Counseling. Career Planning.

The need for vocational guidance for the full realization of human resources is widely acknowledged today. Women, who for generations have limited their development in employment, especially need guidance. The author discusses the why, what, when, and where of vocational guidance for women. Presentations are included on: planning an occupation, guidance services, employment services and agencies, and state guidance facilities. The advice and guidelines presented in the book can be used readily by individuals and by counselors. An excellent resource, the book examines the relationship of individual interests, abilities and motivations to an infinite number of possible occupations. A 19-page bibliography on vocational guidance is also included.

Commentaries and Policy Papers

289

Alpenfels, Ethel J. THE WORLD OF IDEAS—DO WOMEN COUNT? *Educational Record*, 1963, 44(1), 40-44.

Status. Higher Education.

Women have low status in all levels of education today. Institutions of higher education should accept the responsibility of helping both men and women to become responsible, mature adults.

290

Bunting, J. Whitney. THE RELATION OF BUSINESS TO WOMEN'S HIGHER EDUCATION. *Educational Record*, 1961, 42(October), 287-295.

Women's Colleges. Business.

Contrary to general belief, women's colleges contribute significantly to business and industry by preparing women for careers and fulfilling important functions as wives, mothers, consumers, and citizens.

291

Bunting, Mary I. EDUCATION. *A Woman's Work.* New York, N.Y.: Barnard College, 1967. Page 9.

Educational Facilitators. Educational Policy. Women's Colleges.

New flexibility is needed in graduate and professional schools, including the establishment of financial aid policies that do not automatically disqualify part-time students. Women's colleges should seek funds to assist particularly promising alumnae who need financial assistance to continue their education. Schools should recognize that the young woman who has a family and still wants to pursue her studies is truly motivated.

292

Bunting, Mary; Graham, Patricia, and Wasserman, Elga. ACADEMIC FREEDOM AND INCENTIVE FOR WOMEN. *Educational Record*, 1970, 51(4), 386-391.

Educational Facilitators. Doctoral Degrees.

The proportion of women earning doctoral degrees has not risen significantly in the last 25 years even though approximately equal numbers of men and women finish high school and earn bachelor's degrees. There are several reasons for this lack of progress: 1) there are few women professors to provide role models for women students; 2) the views of many older men in positions of authority and influence are often limited with respect to women; and 3) institutional structures and procedures often constitute barriers to women (i.e., rules against part-time study, etc.). The significant steps being taken at selected institutions of higher education to improve the academic prospects of women include the elimination of nepotism rules; the inclusion of women on all slates of candidates for academic openings; increased flexibility in scheduling professional duties; increased integration of male and female students in all facets of campus living; and encouragement of women to express themselves intellectually to male students and professors.

293

Cassara, Beverly B., Ed. AMERICAN WOMEN: THE CHANGING IMAGE. Boston: Beacon Press, 1962. 141 pages.

Changing Role of Women.

This book is a product of the rapid social change in America and the effect of such change on the image and role of women. Pearl Buck and Agnes Meyer cite the need for women to accept the challenge of solving today's problems by throwing off stereotypic thinking and contributing their values and ideas more forcefully. Dorothy Hopper and Edith Hunter suggest that women need to value their age-old roles of homemaker and teacher as worthwhile and valid contributions to society. Chase Going Woodhouse argues for developing means for helping men and women of all ages contribute to the betterment of society as volunteers. Ethel Alpenfels calls on women to break down barriers to their full participation in the world of work and to repudiate the traditional image of woman that limits growth and development. Lillian Gilbreth, Bessie Hillman, and Vivian Mason discuss the career opportunities for women in business management, trade unions, and education. Agnes de Mille discusses one of the most important ingredients in combining marriage and career—cooperative, supportive husbands who take pride in their own and their wives' work.

294

Cless, Elizabeth L. A MODEST PROPOSAL FOR THE EDUCATING OF WOMEN. *The American Scholar*, 1969, 38(4), 618-627.

Educational Facilitators. Educational Policy. Higher Education.

The traditional approach to higher education of uninterrupted study suits the needs of upper- and middle-class men. American educators must develop educational programs that meet the needs of women and other disadvantaged groups. The lack of serious women students is just one of the many results of educators' failure to see how the present educational system keeps underprivileged young people—poor, black, Indian, Chicano—undereducated. The severe shortages in professional and managerial positions will persist if leaders in higher education fail to develop techniques and approaches that will permit able women to reach their full potential. Educators do not seem to understand that the majority of women entering the labor force today are over 35 and underemployed. Educational and institutional flexibility can be achieved by permitting the transfer of college credits between colleges, instituting many more part-time study programs, orienting women to home and careers, granting credit for life experience and nontraditional learning experiences, developing tests to measure knowledge gained in such fashion, and abandoning residency requirements for degrees. An advocate of long standing for more flexible approaches to education, the author draws on some of the literature to support her recommendations and describes some of the new programs being developed for women.

295

David, Opal D., Ed. THE EDUCATION OF WOMEN—SIGNS FOR THE FUTURE. Washington, D.C.: American Council on Education, 1959. 153 pages.

Higher Education.

This is a report of a conference on the status of women and the need for research in women's education held in 1957 by the American Council on Education. Five broad areas of women's education are treated in 12 papers and follow-up discussions: 1) traditional stereotypes as they limit women, 2) motivation of women for higher education, 3) current trends in the education of women, 4) research on women's education, and 5) pressures on women in education. Conference participants were leaders in women's education, including Robert L. Sutherland, Pauline Knapp, Kate Mueller, Harold Taylor, Mary Bunting, and William Fels. A 17-page bibliography of relevant literature is included.

296

Davis, Ann E. WOMEN AS A MINORITY GROUP IN HIGHER ACADEMICS. *American Sociologist,* 1969, 4(2), 95-98.

Sociology. Higher Education. Minority Status.

This is a brief overview of the literature and a description of a brief, loosely-structured survey of academicians' attitudes toward women in sociology. The article emphasizes the loss of the intellectual contributions of able young women and raises the question of whether young women are acquiescing to the perpetuation of a role for women that does not pertain to reality.

297

Eddy, Edward D. WHAT'S THE USE OF EDUCATING WOMEN? *Saturday Review,* 1963, May 18, 66-68.

Education. Women's Colleges.

In an argument for the maintenance of separate education in liberal arts for men and women, the author bemoans the tendency of women's colleges to copy men's colleges. He notes that women's colleges should let women be women, while requiring a high level of academic excellence so that educated women can develop an action orientation and social conscience that they can transmit to their families. Also, because no normal woman, according to Diana Trilling, wants to lead men, coeducational colleges hamper women's development due to men's domination of such institutions. Special education for women, because it is not geared to utility, awakens in the student a larger sense of value and results in a better person. Women, who are largely responsible for child rearing and who provide a valuable service as wives and mothers, must fight the self-pity that can overcome anyone who is not sufficiently recognized. Such activity, if done well, draws on every aspect of a woman's education. There are several other approaches to women's education, but women's colleges offer the best alternatives.

298

Featherstone, Joseph. THE DAY CARE PROBLEM: KENTUCKY FRIED CHILDREN. *The New Republic,* September 12, 1970, 12-16.

Day Care.

There are not enough adequate child-care facilities in the U.S., and very few successful attempts to provide care for the children of working parents. A nationwide network of franchised child care centers will not meet the needs of the estimated 5 million children under six years of age with working parents. Federal subsidy for good programs sponsored by labor and industry should help.

299
Greer, Germaine. THE FEMALE EUNUCH. New York: McGraw-Hill Book Company, 1970. 349 pages.

Oppression of Women. Patriarchy. Sex Role Stereotypes.

The total oppression of women—in the world of work, education, and the family—and the manifestations of oppression in individual behavior are discussed. Treated and considered as sexual objects, women have been denied their sexuality and their individuality. The glorification of the "eternal feminine" is in itself the effect of desexualization and oppression of all human beings in a capitalistic, patriarchal society. To throw off their oppressive mantle, women must come to understand their real condition and undertake to break away from the masculine-feminine polarity that perpetuates the myths that inhibit humanity. The author draws on observation, experience, and research to develop this argument.

300
Kelman, Steven. A NONCHALANT REVOLUTION: SWEDEN'S LIBERATED MEN AND WOMEN. *The New Republic*, 1971, March 13, 21-23.

Sex Roles. Equality Between the Sexes.

This article describes the "sex-role debate" and the quiet revolution that has occurred in Sweden under government auspices. Four years of national debate on sex roles preceded the official recognition in 1965 of the need for elimination of discrimination against women and men. Tax laws were changed, school textbooks revised, day-care centers built, part-time work opportunities for men and women established, and school reinforcement of sex stereotypes abolished.

301

Komisar, Lucy. THE NEW FEMINISM. *Saturday Review*, 1970, February 21, 27-30.

Discrimination. Women's Liberation.

This is a description of the various activities of the National Organization for Women (NOW), a left of center, action-oriented women's liberation organization founded in 1966 to eliminate institutional sex discrimination and sexist manifestations in the media.

302

Kruger, Daniel H. WOMEN AT WORK. *The Personnel Administrator*, 1964, 9(July-August), 7-15.

Employment. Employment Trends. Career Barriers.

Despite the steady increase in the number of women entering the labor force, it is unlikely that the utilization of womanpower will improve. Sex-labeling of jobs, woman's responsibility for children and family, prejudice against women in the world of work, and other cultural limitations hinder women's equal access to jobs. However, each woman should endeavor to live as an individual and as she sees fit. The reasons for the increase of female labor force participation include desire to work and financial necessity. Such factors as increased need for manpower, urbanization, and the rise in educational levels also affect the rise in female employment. A "two-phase" working cycle is common among women and affects the labor market. Smaller families and earlier marriages permit women to work before marriage and when children leave the home. U.S. Department of Labor and Bureau of the Census statistics document this discussion.

303

Lemberg Center for the Study of Violence. A QUESTION OF WOMAN'S STATUS. *Confrontation*. Waltham, Massachusetts: Brandeis University, April 1971. Pages 1-20.

Family Responsibilities. Technology. Status.

Prominent theories and research results on women's status are synthesized in this article which concludes that social orders are maintained through various means that reflect the level of education and enlightenment of the general population. Women's potential for fulfillment is tied to social systems, principally through the vehicle of the family. It is unlikely that the family will disappear from sight, whatever changes occur in the social system. However, the prospects look bright for women in the future because of the emergence of a technological society.

304
Lewis, Edwin C. CHOICE AND CONFLICT FOR THE COLLEGE WOMAN. *Educational Digest*, 1969, 35(3), 52-54. (Condensed from original publication in *Journal of the National Association of Women Deans and Counselors.*)

Career-marriage Conflict. Higher Education.

For a woman to combine the dual role of marriage and career, she must be motivated to face the responsibilities of each role and she must have a cooperative and supportive spouse. She will benefit if she has had close relationships with women who have successfully accomplished this dual role. It is shortsighted for college and high school counselors to encourage all academically bright women to enter the professions and for the feminist movement to demand that all capable women compete with all men on all professional levels. To make women carbon copies of men not only will deprive them of the fulfillment of many personal needs, but also will deprive society of the benefits of the many women who work without the pressure of having to support a family, have a strong concern for the welfare of others, and have lower achievement drives. Many factors are involved in women's present push for professional equality. For example, the pressure for advanced degrees for women may represent the desire for refuge in the university rather than commitment to a career. Women face identity crises caused by the conflict between career and family responsibility and the conflict between a profession or a traditional career. The role of women today involves conflict and confusion, and counselors and the new feminists must be more realistic in their demands on capable women.

305
Lifton, Robert J. WOMEN AS KNOWER: SOME PSYCHOHISTORICAL PERSPECTIVES. In Lifton, Robert J., Ed. *The Woman in America.* Boston: Houghton Mifflin, 1965. 27-51.

Three Aspects of Feminine Image.

Experiential patterns of cognition and feeling can be related to changing social forces. There are three aspects of womanhood: nurturer (wife and mother), temptress (sexual object), and knower (wise person). All women have some measure of all three within their psyches. They are unified within each woman by close identification with organic life and its perpetuation which provides a capacity to mediate between biology and history. All this can occur despite the turmoil of periods of rapid social change, when the three identities become unstable and confused, leading to psychological discomfort in men and women. Observation of the relationship between Japanese mothers and their radical sons reveals that this capacity holds in such troubled times and reveals the belief that women are conservative to be oversimplified. While their support is not for the militant activity, but a function of maternal efforts, it shows that it permits growth and establishes the importance of "connection" that is an element of feminine knowing.

306

Malcom, Janet. HOMEWORK FOR THE LIBERATED WOMAN: HELP! *The New Republic*, 1970, 163(15), 15-17.

Child Care. Feminism.

New feminists often fail to acknowledge the drawbacks that can derive from mother substitutes, institutional child care, and the working mother. Their claims that it is better for children to have working mothers than nonworking mothers obscures the fact that parental neglect can result in diminished affection in the child. By failing to accept such realities, the new feminism may cause even more unhappiness and discontent than the post-World War II drive for familial "togetherness."

307

Matthews, Esther. CAREER DEVELOPMENT OF GIRLS. Counseling and Guidance Training Institute, University of Maryland, 1964. Mimeo. 5 pages.

Educational Counseling. Career Opportunities. Research Needs.

Counselors should be aware that career development, like personality development, is a life-long process and that options open to women for careers today are greater than ever before. They should keep young women informed about career possibilities and help them make free and informed decisions concerning their futures. Women can combine career and marriage or they can opt for only a career or marriage without facing society's disapproval. Research is needed into career development for women. Counselors should avoid rigid classifications, especially when social attitudes are changing and evolving quickly.

308

Mercer, Marilyn. IS THERE ROOM AT THE TOP? *Saturday Evening Post*, 1968, July 27, 17-22.

Discrimination. Business. Sex Labeling of Jobs.

Actual cases of sex discrimination in business and industry as manifested in sex-labeling of executive positions, changing job titles, and unequal pay for equal work. Widespread sex discrimination is evident and shown by the fact that although almost half the women in the country work, less than one percent earn $10,000 a year or more in comparison to 13 percent of working men.

309

National Manpower Council. WOMANPOWER. New York: Columbia University Press, 1957. 371 pages.

Employment. Educational Policy. Career Facilitators. Educational Facilitators.

This book is the result of a two-year study of women's role in the labor force conducted by the National Manpower Council at Columbia University and sponsored by Ford Foundation. It demonstrates that women represent an essential part of our manpower resources and that effective use and understanding of womanpower is absolutely necessary. One-third of all women in the U.S. age 14 or over are in the labor force; three of every ten married women work, and nearly two of every five mothers work. To achieve the goal of integration of women into the labor force, professionals and lay persons concerned with womanpower should undertake several major activities, including: • The expansion and improvement of educational and vocational guidance for women of all ages. • Expansion of scholarship and fellowship programs and continuing education programs for women of all ages. • The institution and enforcement of the principle of equal pay for equal work. • Expansion of part-time and flexible work arrangements to meet the needs of the working wife and mother. • Expansion of research on the working woman. Discussion and analysis by staff members of the National Manpower Council outline the complexities of the issue of female labor force participation—number and types of positions, employers, expansion of employment opportunities; women in the armed services, changing patterns of women's lives, and public policy related to working women.

310

Neuman, Rebecca R. WHEN WILL THE EDUCATIONAL NEEDS OF WOMEN BE MET? SOME QUESTIONS FOR THE COUNSELOR. *Journal of Counseling Psychology,* 1963, 10(4), 378-383.

Educational Policy. Educational Counseling. Career Planning. Research Needs.

The educational needs of today's women are different from the needs of women of previous generations. Traditional educational and work patterns are designed to fit the needs of men. Counselors should be aware of the phases of a woman's life so that education can be planned to the best advantage of women of any age. The trend toward early marriage and employment is going to increase, and counselors and educators must not only help and encourage women to continue their education, but they must also follow the lead of several pioneering institutions (Harvard, Sarah Lawrence, Minnesota) to develop new educational programs for women. Counselors should also help women to realize the many lives they will lead—as homemaker, mother, wage earner, etc. More research is also needed to answer some universal questions. For example, are women to be viewed as individuals or primarily as mothers, wives, homemakers? Does the unmarried woman have neither status nor honor? Is there sufficient knowledge about women's needs, capacities, responsibilities? A survey of the literature provides the framework for the author's discussion.

311

Painter, Edith P.; Flemister, Ida, and Others. ON DOING HER OWN THING. *American Association of University Women Journal,* 1969, 62(4), 179-182.

Life Styles. Woman's Right to Choose.

Written in response to two articles on woman's role in the home and the world of work, letters to the editor focus on woman's right to choose to be either homemakers or professionals or both and on the need for appropriate services to facilitate such choices.

312

Parrish, John B. COMING CRISIS IN WOMEN'S HIGHER EDUCATION AND WORK. *American Association of University Women Journal*, 1970, 64(2), 17-19.

Higher Education. Educational Policy. Job Restructuring.

The outlook for professionally-employed and college-trained women is bleak. Higher education for women concentrates on "cultural" education with the result that 40 percent of the women college graduates in the 1970s will enter the labor force with no work training but with degrees in the humanities, social sciences, and psychology. Another 40 percent will enter teaching, a field that is becoming quickly overcrowded. Competition from men in fields traditionally open to women—teaching, library science, health service, etc.—is diminishing job options for women. And the need for college-educated workers is diminishing in the face of the increasing need for technically-trained personnel. To lessen the effects of these circumstances on women in the labor force, higher education for women should be more work-oriented. The traditional liberal arts requirement should be reduced. To achieve the goal of more women in higher places, jobs should be restructured; women should not have to adapt their lives to job requirements. "Women's work life centers," established in leading institutions, would concentrate on restructuring jobs for the new and old college graduate. AAUW and other organizations should help lead the difficult task of improving counseling services and occupational forecasting if the crisis in women's higher education is to be avoided.

313

Parrish, John B. WOMEN'S HIGH LEVEL TRAINING AND WORK: WHERE TO NOW? *Training and Development Journal*, 1970, 24(11), 20-23.

Higher Education. Job Restructuring.

The 1960s are cited as a period of "many breakthroughs for the few—few breakthroughs for the many" in the movement for women's rights in the world of work. But recent occurrences suggest better times for the movement in the 1970s. New educational technology (learning machines) and increased interest in developing new educational approaches will benefit women in higher education. The movement to "break up" professional jobs into levels and stages through job restructuring will also benefit women. Women's organizations should promote demonstration projects in education and business to show the positive effects of job restructuring.

314

Presidential Task Force on Women's Rights and Responsibilities. A MATTER OF SIMPLE JUSTICE: THE REPORT OF THE PRESIDENT'S TASK FORCE ON WOMEN'S RIGHTS AND RESPONSIBILITIES. Washington, D.C., April, 1970. 33 pages.

National Policy on Women's Rights.

Calling for a national commitment to basic changes that will bring women into the mainstream of American life, the Task Force makes recommendations to the President on: • Establishment of an Office of Women's Rights and Responsibilities to be under the direct supervision of the President. • A White House Conference on Women's Rights and Responsibilities. • A message to Congress calling for passage of a joint resolution proposing an equal rights amendment to the Constitution. • Amendment of existing legislation on women: Civil Rights Acts of 1957 and 1964, Social Security Act, Fair Labor Standards Act, Internal Revenue Code. • Enactment of legislation to guarantee to dependents of Federal women employees the same rights guaranteed to males. • Establishment of priorities by various executive department heads that are as sensitive to sex discrimination as to race discrimination. • The appointment of more women to positions of responsibility in all branches of the federal government by the President and the Cabinet and Agency heads.

315

President's Commission on the Status of Women. AMERICAN WOMEN. Washington, D.C. 1963. 86 pages.

Employment. Education. Status.

This is a presentation of data on education, counseling, women's life at home and in the community, private and federal employment, labor standards, legal status, women's voting, women in public office, women working for political parties, benefits to widows, dependents of single women, unemployment insurance and maternity benefits.

316

Reisman, David. TWO GENERATIONS. *Daedalus*, 1964, 93(2), 711-735.

Life Styles. Status.

A comparison of the life styles of the author's mother and daughter indicates general improvement in women's status over the years in education, marriage, occupations, interpersonal relations, etc. Women's new freedom has brought new, subtle restraints, but women of today suffer less inhibition and resignation than women of his mother's generation. They are free to lead full lives without the sense of urgency expressed by feminists.

317

Rossi, Alice. EQUALITY BETWEEN THE SEXES: AN IMMODEST PROPOSAL. In Lifton, Robert J., Ed., *The Woman in America.* Boston: Houghton Mifflin, 1965. Pages 98-143.

Feminism. Elimination of Sex Role Stereotypes. Equality Between the Sexes.

The movement in the U.S. for equality of the sexes started in 1869 with an appeal for equal political rights and culminated in the right to vote in 1920. It has been limited by the impact of psychoanalytic thinking. The conservative trend that took hold after the twenties is now seeing a slow reversal, with increased demand for occupational and social equality for the sexes. Today's movement is characterized not by the earlier feminist push for acceptance in the masculine world but by expansion of a common ground on which both sexes can function equally in politics, occupations, and family life. There is also a demand for recognition that characteristics and behaviors previously thought to be sex-linked be considered appropriate for both sexes. A review of research suggests that full-time motherhood is neither sufficiently absorbing for today's educated woman nor beneficial for her children. Occupational development of women should reduce women's dominance in marriage and parenthood, allowing equal participation for men in family life. Women's attitude toward education and work must change in order for women to reach a full realization of their abilities and to achieve higher levels in employment. There are several ways to achieve sex equality. For example, the development of a course of study in practical mothering and upgrading of child care centers would make it possible for women to remain in or reenter occupational fields with the satisfaction that their children were being cared for. A decentralization of business, educational institutions and industry would make them more accessible and thus afford both parents the advantages of working closer to home and thus spending more time with their family. A change in curriculum and staffing patterns in schools would encourage a more equal representation of both sexes and discourage stereotyping of women as homemakers and males as careerists. The author concludes with a hypothetical profile of a woman brought up under these suggested improvements in institutions, comparing her life style to that of her brother's. Extensive research and personal and professional observations are used to document this discussion.

318

Rossi, Alice. S. JOB DISCRIMINATION AND WHAT WOMEN CAN DO ABOUT IT. *Atlantic*, 1970, 225(3), 99-102.

Discrimination. Employment Legislation. Legislation Needs.

Discrimination against women in business and education is manifested in ridicule, social rejection, promotion of less competent men, etc. As women become more aware of this discrimination, they can begin to use new laws to combat it: Title VII of the Civil Rights Act of 1964 prohibits discrimination on the basis of sex as well as race. Passed with the support of Southern legislators in an attempt to divert attention from cases of racial discrimination, the law has been responsible for over a third of the complaints received by the Equal Employment Opportunity Commission having to do with sex discrimination. Such actions have proved effective in establishing equal opportunity and treatment of women in industry. Further change in the law at the national level is needed, however. Section 702 of Title VII should be amended to include the prohibition of discrimination against women in all educational institutions, in which many women are employed and in which they have lost ground since 1920. Prohibition against discrimination on the basis of marital status should also be included as an amendment to Title VII. Women's groups should concentrate on making sure these amendments are acted on. If they are not passed into law, we can expect increased militancy on the part of women in pursuit of their civil and human rights. As a veteran campaigner for women's rights, the author cites personal correspondence and government statistics to support her argument.

319

Rossi, Alice. STATEMENT AND RESOLUTIONS OF THE WOMEN'S CAUCUS TO THE GENERAL BUSINESS MEETING OF THE AMERICAN SOCIOLOGICAL ASSOCIATION. *American Sociologist*, 1970, 5(1).

Sociology. Higher Education.

The Women's Caucus seeks effective and dramatic action including an unbiased policy in the selection and stipend support of students. It also seeks a concerted commitment to the hiring and promotion of women sociologists to correct the present extreme imbalance in which 67 percent of women graduate sociology students in the U.S. never have a female sociology professor of rank during the course of their graduate training. Women participate in a national association of sociologists in which the 1970 Council has no women members. No woman is included among the Associate editors of the *American Sociological Review* or on the Advisory Board of the *American Journal of Sociology,* and the 13-member committees on publications and nominations have no women members.

320

Rostow, Edna G. CONFLICT AND ACCOMMODATION. In Lifton, Robert J., Ed. *The Woman in America.* Boston: Houghton Mifflin, 1965. Pages 211-235.

Career-marriage Conflict. Marriage Aspirations. Familial Roles.

Today's marriages are romantic in the sense that both partners exercise freedom in choosing each other, and both endeavor to experience a deep and intimate relationship within marriage. Both husbands and wives seek to accommodate the romantic notion of marriage with the traditional relationships assumed within marriage. Today, educated women expect to marry early, have children, and be involved in interesting work outside the home. They seek husbands who are sympathetic partners and not masters. Thus, with the emergence of emphasis on individual fulfillment for both partners, conflicts arise in the sharing of roles. Although most women today still feel that their greatest fulfillment is derived from the role of wife and mother, most educated women express a need for recognition and satisfaction afforded by a career or job outside the home. In addition to the problems and conflicts inherent in marriage under this new philosophy, i.e., sharing of home tasks, making arrangements for child care, etc., today's educated woman faces the question of finding a husband who is "strong" and "masculine" sexually and socially and yet sympathetic to her needs. Her major task is the attempt to achieve balance in her life between work and marriage.

321

Scully, Malcolm G. WOMEN IN HIGHER EDUCATION: CHALLENGING THE STATUS QUO. *The Chronicle of Higher Education,* 1970, IV(18), 2-5.

Higher Education. Women's Liberation. Discrimination.

The impact of the struggle for higher status in the academic world by women and the women's liberation movement in general is discussed. Discrimination in higher education against women is real, and the movement to correct injustices is far from over. Quotes from academic women—Rosemary Park, Anne Scott, Florence Howe, etc.—who have successfully climbed the academic ladder are included.

322

The Atlantic. WOMAN'S PLACE: A SPECIAL ISSUE, 1970, 225(3), 81-126.

Discrimination. Women's Liberation.

Ten short essays by nine women and a man are presented on sex discrimination and the Woman's Liberation Movement. Included are two documented treatises on legal discrimination and a "mod domestic story." Catherine Drinker Bowen writes of the joys of professional life and motherhood (the latter seen as particularly joyful when it is not the "be-all and end-all of existence"). Paula Stern cites some of the social commentators, statesmen, and psychologists whose ideas have contributed to perpetuating the myth that intellectual striving is masculine and unladylike. Diane Gerrity's essay describes the metamorphosis of an inhibited gentle woman to a more confident one through karate. Jane Harriman, an unwed mother, tells of her struggle to bear her child in peace and to overcome the stigma of her status, insensitive counseling, loss of job, and subsequent poverty. In separate essays, Alice Rossi and Diane Schulder discuss legal changes needed to advance the cause of equal opportunity for women such as amending Title VII to cover job discrimination based on marital status and revising laws governing the marital relationship, welfare law, criminal law and reproduction. Sandie North's essay focuses on the obstacles encountered in press coverage of the women's liberation movement. Essays by Anne Bernays, Benjamin DeMott, and Elizabeth Janeway all focus on marriage and childrearing in relation to work. Some of the themes include: the value of motherhood, the identity crisis faced by women, the freedom to choose domesticity, and the equilibrium of marriage based on satisfaction obtained through a more varied and less restricted life.

323

Trilling, Diana. THE IMAGE OF WOMEN IN CONTEMPORARY LITERATURE. In Lifton, Robert J., Ed. *The Woman in America*. Boston: Houghton Mifflin, 1965. Pages 52-70.

Women in Contemporary Literature.

Literature today mirrors the sickness of our world and does not provide or suggest solutions. Treatment of women by contemporary male authors such as Mailer no longer revolves around the shrew of two decades ago but as the embodiment of society asserting itself, mechanisms for sexual gratification, and the sex responsible for continuation of an unhappy humankind. Female writers generally echo the attitudes of male writers, consciously or unconsciously, in their treatment of women. Personal observations and analysis of contemporary literature and society are included.

324

Truex, Dorothy. FOCUS ON FEMININE FERMENT. *Journal of College Student Personnel*, 1970, 11(5), 323-331.

Discrimination. Educational Policy.

This is a sharp analysis of the female coed's experience in college as applicant, student and alumnae. The writer recommends that student personnel administrators take steps to eliminate discrimination against women. Recommendations include abolishing archaic and rigid regulations concerning nonacademic activities of women, sensitizing faculty and administrative personnel to their own biases against women, etc.

325

United States Department of Labor, Women's Bureau and the U.S. Office of Education. NEW APPROACHES TO COUNSELING GIRLS IN THE 1960s. A report of the Midwest Regional Pilot Conference, 1965. 88 pages.

Educational Counseling. Research Needs. Vocational Counseling.

Counselors and counselor educators should take an active role in helping educators and trainers to become more aware of the psychosexual differences between men and women and the special problems faced by women in society. Much more research into the effect of social class, socioeconomic level, and ethnic background on the growth and achievement of women is needed. Also included are speeches concerning the history of the women's movement in the American labor force, the need for a concerted effort to eradicate discrimination on the basis of sex and its implications for the future.

326

Westervelt, Esther M. ARE WE READY FOR EQUALITY? *American Association of University Women Journal*, 1970, 64(2), 20-23.

Role Theory. Role Perceptions. Equality Between the Sexes.

The inability of most educated women to redefine roles within the family so that husbands and wives share home maintenance and income production makes it appear that these women prefer privileges as wives to responsibilities as individuals. The author attributes the ambivalence characteristic of educated American housewives to widespread acceptance of role theory.

327

White, Sylvia. THE MODERN WOMAN'S DILEMMA. *American Association of University Women Journal*, 1964, 57(3), 125-126.

Career-marriage Conflict. Life Styles.

A wife's primary responsibility has been to provide a home life for her husband and security for her children, but without an identity and satisfaction for herself. Frustrations arising from unfulfilled interests or nonuse of skills learned in college can only be vented on her immediate environment—her family. To enrich the life of her husband and children, a woman must live an enriching, interesting, satisfying life herself. Thus, the author calls for social and attitudinal change toward women. Educated women must recognize their identity as individuals and contribute to society as well as to their home lives.

328

Whitney, Mary E. WOMEN STUDENT PERSONNEL ADMINISTRATORS: THE PAST AND FUTURE. *Journal of College Student Personnel*, 1971, 12(1), 7-10.

Student Personnel Administration. Higher Education.

In student personnel administration, women deans and administrators have lost status, and will continue to in the 1970s because the country is beginning a "conservative" cycle that could last ten years, if not longer. Aspiring women student administrators should be informed of this fact and advised to prepare for other, though related, employment in higher education.

329
Woodring, Paul. NEW HORIZONS FOR EDUCATED WOMEN. *Saturday Review*, 1969, July 19.

Part-time Employment.

Catalyst is the name of a national nonprofit organization established in 1962 to promote the part-time employment of educated mature women in occupational fields with shortages of manpower. The organization has coordinated its activities with colleges, public school systems, industry, and government agencies. Examples are given of women successfully combining teaching and family through part-time work. A study of five school systems employing part-time teachers for several years indicates that careful use of part-time teachers meets community and school approval.

Continuing Education of Women

330

Blackwell, Gordon W. THE COLLEGE AND THE CONTINUING EDUCATION OF WOMEN. *Educational Record*, 1963, 44(January), 33-39.

Continuing Education. Educational Policy.

New services and new programs of continuing education are needed to provide opportunities to adult women returning to education and the labor force after several years away from these fields.

331

Bunting, Mary I. THE RADCLIFFE INSTITUTE FOR INDEPENDENT STUDY. *The Educational Record*, 1961, 42(4), 279-286.

Continuing Education.

The Radcliffe Institute for Independent Study was established to enable the educated woman to fulfill her potential for achievement. An Associate Scholar Program is for gifted women who wish to conduct independent projects on a part-time basis. Women in this program generally hold advanced degrees or the equivalent and are provided physical and financial access to all the conveniences of the college. Women who have achieved fame in their fields of interest are invited to join the Institute each year as resident and research fellows to conduct studies and projects that regular commitments prevent them from doing. Vocational guidance and counseling services are also provided to women on request. Conferences on special topics of interest—urban planning, banking, finance—will be sponsored by the Institute for women working in these fields in relative isolation. The Institute will also sponsor research on the educated woman and related topics. It is hoped that the presence of Institute women will help Radcliffe undergraduate and graduate students become aware of their future and the need to plan for it.

332

Clarenbach, Kathryn F. CAN CONTINUING EDUCATION ADAPT? *American Association of University Women Journal*, 1970, 63(2), 62-65.

Continuing Education. Educational Policy.

Advances have been made in continuing education for women during the last decade. Several priorities should be established for continuing education for the next decade, including support of the movement to include educational institutions in the Civil Rights Act of 1964, encouragement of the employment of women as faculty and administrators, concentration on making institutions more flexible, etc.

333

Dennis, Lawrence E., Ed. EDUCATION AND A WOMAN'S LIFE. Washington, D.C.: American Council on Education, 1963. 153 pages.

Continuing Education. Educational Policy.

This report of the Itasca Conference on the Continuing Education of Women held in Minnesota in 1962 focuses on the need for continuing or "sustaining" educational facilities for women. Despite recent progress, resistance against continuing education persists, along with resistance against higher education for women in general and against the integration of women into the mainstream of intellectual, productive, economic activity. Papers and follow-up discussions cover pilot and experimental projects in continuing education for women, the environment of the educated woman, the need of society for educated women, the role of the college in continuing education, etc. Tables of female labor force participation rates are included.

334

Dolan, Eleanor F. WOMEN'S CONTINUING EDUCATION: SOME NATIONAL RESOURCES. *Journal of the National Association of Women Deans and Counselors*, 1965, 29(1), 34-58.

Continuing Education. Educational Policy.

The increase in the number of women seeking a "second career" after an extended period of unemployment has led to the development of continuing education programs. Several innovative programs for older or mature women are being developed at colleges and in private industry. Efforts of the American Association of University Women and the establishment of special programs at colleges are helping the move toward adequate continuing education programs. In addition to development of new programs, more financial aid resources are needed if women are to take advantage of new educational opportunities.

335

Letchworth, George E. WOMEN WHO RETURN TO COLLEGE: AN IDENTITY-INTEGRITY APPROACH. *Journal of College Student Personnel*, 1970, 11(2), 103-106.

Continuing Education. Educational Motivation.

Insights are provided to counselors and educators on the "identity-integrity model" of motivation that older women have in returning to college after many years away from the academic setting.

336

McGowan, Barbara and Liu, Phyllis Y.H. CREATIVITY AND MENTAL HEALTH OF SELF-RENEWING WOMEN. *Management and Evaluation in Guidance*, 1970, 3(3), 138-147.

Psychological Health Patterns. Continuing Education. Educational Motivation.

Middle-aged or self-renewing women who endeavor to develop serious commitments outside the home have several constant and unusual personality characteristics. They are highly intelligent, very creative, reserved, affected by feelings, relaxed, adventuresome, and assertive. They function within a creatively productive range of psychological health. The Cattell Personality Factors were administered to 168 women enrolled in a university extension class designed to help middle-aged women find satisfying educational, vocational, or volunteer involvements. The resulting group profile was compared to those of eminent researchers in biology, physics, and psychology (Cattell and Drevdahl, 1955), and to those of stable and unstable married women (Cattell and Nesselroade, 1967).

337

Randolph, Kathryn Scott. THE MATURE WOMAN IN DOCTORAL PROGRAMS. Doctoral Dissertation (Indiana University), 1965.

Discrimination. Educational Policy. Graduate Education.

In an effort to formulate recommendations for changes in policies and procedures to enable more mature women to participate in doctoral programs, literature written in the field since 1958 was reviewed. Discrimination toward women was found in admissions, financial aid, assistantships, attitudes, and guidance. Responsibility for these conditions stems from the archaic view of women held by administrators and graduate faculty and from the lack of capable women who are willing to work to surmount these practices. Conferences should be held with college administrators to discuss the higher educational needs of women, and financial aid for women should be increased for full-time and part-time work. Doctoral degree programs should be reviewed with emphasis on quality rather than on time requirements. Information concerning these changes should be made available to the public by organized groups such as the American Association of University Women, and universities.

338

Raushenbush, Esther. UNFINISHED BUSINESS: CONTINUING EDUCATION FOR WOMEN. *Educational Record*, 1961, 42(4), 261-269.

Continuing Education. Educational Policy.

There is a lack of continuing education for women, and womanpower is underutilized. Instead of discouraging young women from pursuing careers, institutions of higher education should develop mechanisms for helping women plan realistically for careers, marriage, child-rearing, and re-entry into the labor force.

339

Senders, Virginia L. THE MINNESOTA PLAN FOR WOMEN'S CONTINUING EDUCATION: A PROGRAM REPORT. *The Educational Record*, 1961, 42(4), 270-278.

Continuing Education. Career-marriage Conflict. Career Planning.

The Minnesota Plan, established in 1960, aims to return intelligent, educated women to the world of work—paid or volunteer—and to help women plan for the years that follow child-rearing. The plan is a facilitating agency, not a curriculum, college or super-institution, and is built into existing educational structures. The method of "challenge-and-response" group discussion with undergraduate women and men has proved successful in opening young people's eyes for the first time to the conflicts women experience between marriage and career. As a result of such discussions, the participants often "re-invent" the Minnesota Plan as a solution to intellectual deterioration before the discussion leader explains the plan. Individual counseling is available to interested undergraduates, along with a seminar on the educated woman in the United States. Senior women are encouraged to plan continuing "rust-proofing" coursework when they leave the work force to raise a family. Women who have been outside the mainstream for 20 years can avail themselves of vocational and personal counseling services under the plan. A special seminar course in the Extension Division of the University on a wide range of topics (New Worlds of Knowledge) has been widely acclaimed by such women seeking to "remove the rust" of years of intellectual inactivity. The author is the coordinator of the women's continuing education program at the University, a lecturer in psychology, and an architect of the Minnesota Plan.

340

U.S. Department of Labor, Women's Bureau. SELECTED LIST OF SPECIAL EDUCATIONAL SERVICES AND CONTINUING EDUCATION PROGRAMS FOR MATURE WOMEN, 1963. 2 pages.

Continuing Education.

This leaflet describes the educational services that 16 colleges and universities offer women. Included are programs at such institutions as Barnard College, Harvard Graduate School of Education, University of Minnesota, University of Oklahoma, and Pacific Oaks College.

341

University Extension Service, University of Wisconsin. A NEW DIRECTION FOR WISCONSIN INACTIVE HEALTH PERSONNEL. Madison, Wisconsin, 1969. 64 pages.

Nursing. Continuing Education. Employment Patterns.

A follow-up survey of inactive nurses who participated in refresher courses reveals that over half are now working. Of these, over three-fourths are employed on a part-time basis. The reasons nurses cited for remaining inactive included home and family responsibilities, health, unacceptable work schedules, etc. These findings are derived from the responses of 266 women who completed a six-week refresher course between September 1967 and December 1968. The follow-up survey was undertaken as part of a larger project designed to bring inactive health personnel back into practice.

342

Women's Service Committee, American Chemical Society. RETRAINING PROGRAMS FOR WOMEN CHEMISTS. Washington, D.C., 1970. 7 pages.

Chemistry. Continuing Education.

Information is provided on retraining programs for women in chemistry. Data are included on institutions that stress retraining for women. Included are 11 colleges and universities, with a brief description of programs offered, information on scheduling, costs, residence requirements, financial aid, and provision for part-time as well as full-time study.

Miscellaneous

343

Bird, Caroline. THE NEW WOMEN: OUT TO FINISH WHAT THE SUFFRAGETTE STARTED. *American Association of University Women Journal*, 1970, 64(2), 3-6.

Women's Liberation.

The emergence and impact of women's liberation movement is seen as a manifestation of revolutionary change in American society.

344

Carroll, Margaret S. THE WORKING WIFE AND HER FAMILY'S ECONOMIC POSITION. *Monthly Labor Review*, 1962, 85(4), 366-374.

Employment Motivation. The Working Wife.

This is an analysis of data obtained in 1950 by the Survey of Consumer Expenditures and City Worker's Family Budget. Financial need of new workers has some effect in increasing labor force participation, and such need tended to be greater in higher socioeconomic classes.

345

Crowley, Mary Mulvey. PSYCHOLOGICAL AND SOCIAL FACTORS IN PREDICTION OF CAREER PATTERNS OF WOMEN. *Genetic Psychological Monographs*, 1963, 68, 309-389.

Career Patterns. Career Prediction.

This study revealed 12 career patterns of middle-aged women based on combinations of work and marriage, continuity and interruption, entry and re-entry into job market, etc. The women in the study had a favorable attitude in general toward married women working in gainful employment. The study sample included 475 middle-aged women in Providence, Rhode Island, between the ages of 37 and 47.

346

Dudar, Helen. WOMEN'S LIB: THE WAR ON SEXISM. *Newsweek*, 1970, March 23, 71-78.

Women's Liberation.

This is a description of the women's liberation movement and the various factions, ideologies, and action programs of the many groups, including the Redstockings, The Feminists, The Radical Feminists, WITCH, National Organization for Women, etc. Brief biographies are included of four leaders—Leslye Russell, Ti-Grace Atkinson, Roxanne Dunbar, Jo Freeman—along with an overview of social scientists' response to the movement.

347
Gilman, Richard. THE FEMLIB CASE AGAINST SIGMUND FREUD. *The New York Times Magazine*, 1971, January 31. 10-11 and 42-47.

Freudian Theories on Women.

Arguments of feminists against Freud's theories concerning women are summarized. The writer generally supports their arguments and describes the reaction of followers of Freud to such assault.

348
Gottlieb, Annie. FEMALE HUMAN BEINGS. *The New York Times Book Review*. 1971, February 21. 1 and 26-27.

Women's Liberation.

This is an overview and analysis of writings, available in paperback, on women's liberation and activists in the movement. *Vindication of the Rights of Women*, Mary Wollstoncraft, 1971; *Margaret Fuller, American Romantic*, edited by Perry Miller; *Essays on Sex Equality*, edited by Alice Rossi; *A Room of One's Own and Three Guineas*, Virginia Woolf; *Adam's Rib*, Ruth Herschberger; *The Feminine Mystique*, Betty Friedan; *Born Female: The High Cost of Keeping Women Down*, Caroline Bird; and so on.

349
Hewer, Vivian H. and Neubeck Gerhard. ATTITUDES OF COLLEGE STUDENTS TOWARD EMPLOYMENT AMONG MARRIED WOMEN. *Personnel and Guidance Journal*, 1964, 42(6).

Maternal Employment. Sex Role Perceptions.

A questionnaire on the employment of married women was administered to 4,283 students (94 percent) of a college freshman class in 1959. Respondents suggested that the role of a married woman is to serve others, to work to put her husband through school, to pay bills, and to buy things for her family. The majority rejected having married women work because they owe it to themselves to make use of their abilities or because the home provides inadequate opportunity for the expression of intellectual interests. The study suggests that freshmen women in 1959 accepted the traditional role of women.

350

Howe, Florence. FEMALE STUDIES: NO. 2. Collected by the Commission on the Status of Women of the Modern Language Association, 1970. 165 pages.

Women's Studies.

This is a collection of syllabi submitted by various colleges and universities on the study of women, principally in literature.

351

Ickeringill, Nan. WHILE MOTHER WORKS, THE COMPANY TAKES CARE OF THE CHILDREN. *The New York Times*, 1970, August 26. Page 46.

Day Care. Business.

Several businesses have provided day-care services for the children of women employees. The business executives generally report positive results from the centers—lower turnover rates, less time lost because of sick leave, greater employee satisfaction, etc.

352

Singer, Stanley L. and Shefflre, Buford. SEX DIFFERENCES IN JOB VALUES AND DESIRES. *Personnel and Guidance Journal*, 1954, 38, 483-484.

Work Values. Sex Differences.

Boys desire jobs that offer power, in which they can profit and be independent, while girls are more inclined to have job values characterized by interesting experiences and social service. The sample included 373 male high school seniors and 416 female high school seniors.

AUTHOR INDEX

A

Almquist, Elizabeth M. 1, 2
Alpenfels, Ethel J. 289
Anastasi, Anne 3
Angrist, Shirley S. 1, 2, 4, 5, 6, 7, 83
Astin, Helen S. 8, 9, 10, 11, 101, 142, 249
Axelson, Leland J. 84, 85

B

Bailyn, Lotte 12, 86
Baker, Elizabeth F. 240
Bass, Ann T. 241
Bates, Jean M. 242
Bayer, Alan E. 142, 213, 249
Beck, Esther Lily 157
Bennett, Walter Wilson 166
Bernard, Jessie 143
Bernstein, M. Charles 252
Berry, Jane 242
Bird, Caroline 343
Blackwell, Gordon W. 330

Blood, Robert O. 87
Bohn, Martin J., Jr. 25
Bollman, Stephan R. 56
Boring, Edwin G. 103
Bott, Margaret M. 13
Bowers, John Z. 102
Bowman, Garda W. 167
Bradburn, Norman 94
Breytspraak, Charlotte Helfand 179
Broverman, Donald M. 214
Broverman, Inge K. 214
Brown, Donald R. 14
Brown, D. G. 215
Bryan, Alice I. 103
Bryce, Rose Ann 168
Bunting, J. Whitney 290
Bunting, Mary I. 291, 292, 331
Burns, Dorothy M. 158
Bynum, Caroline Walker 144

C

Cain, Glen George 243
Campbell, David P. 15, 36, 195

Carroll, Margaret S. 344
Cassara, Beverly B. 293
Centra, John A. 109
Clarenbach, Kathryn F. 332
Clark, Edward T. 16
Clark, Shirley Merritt 132, 155
Clarkson, Frank E. 214
Cless, Elizabeth L. 294
Collins, Orvis F. 178
Comstock, Peggy 186
Conway, Jill 244
Cook, Barbara Ivy Wood 17
Crowley, Mary Mulvey 345
Curtis, Elizabeth Ann 70
Cussler, Margaret 169

D

David, Opal D. 295
Davis, Ann E. 296
Davis, Natalie Zemon 18
Dawkins, Lola Beasley 170
Degler, Carl N. 245
Dennis, Lawrence E. 333
Dewey, Lucretia M. 171
Doherty, Sister Mary Austin 235
Dolan, Eleanor F. 334
Dolson, Miriam Terry 172
Dornbush, Sanford 216
Dudar, Helen 346
Dunlap, Carol 177
Dunn, Frances E. 81

E

Eddy, Edward D. 297
Edisen, Adele E. Uskali 104
Elton, Charles F. 19
Empey, Lamar T. 20
Entwisle, Doris R. 21, 41
Epstein, Cynthia Fuchs 105, 106, 180
Erikson, Erik 217
Erikson, Joan M. 246
Eyde, Lorraine D. 22, 23, 181

F

Falk, Ruth 247
Farber, Seymour M. 248
Farley, Jennie 24
Farmer, Helen S. 25

Faunce, Patricia Spencer 26
Featherstone, Joseph 298
Fidell, L. S. 182
Finkelman, Jacob Jack 88
Fischer, Ann 107
Flanagan, John C. 27
Flemister, Ida 311
Folger, John K. 249
Foster, Ann 173
Fox, David J. 236, 237, 238, 239
Freedman, Mervin B. 28, 218, 250
Frithiof, Patricia 108

G

Gallup, George 219
Galway, Kathleen 132
Gardner, Helen Rogers 174
Garland, Neal T. 89
Gehlan, Frieda L. 159
Gillette, Thomas Lee 90
Gilman, Richard 347
Ginzberg, Eli 251
Giuliani, Betty 109
Glancy, Dorothy J. 110
Goldberg, Philip 220
Golde, Peggy 107
Gordon, Michael 252
Gottlieb, Annie 348
Gover, David A. 91
Graham, Patricia A. 146, 292
Greenberger, Ellen 21
Greer, Germaine 299
Greyser, S. A. 167
Gust, T. 29
Gysbers, M. C. 29

H

Hahn, Marilyn C. 183
Harbeson, Gladys E. 111
Harmon, Lenore W. 30, 31, 32, 33, 34, 35, 36
Harris, Ann Sutherland 147
Hawley, Marjorie Jane 37
Heist, Paul 38
Helson, Ravenna 39, 221, 222
Henschel, Beverly Jean Smith 112
Hewer, Vivian H. 349
Hoeflin, Ruth M. 56
Hoffman, Lois Wladis 93
Honigman, Rhonda 113
Horner, Matina S. 40

AUTHOR INDEX

Houts, Peter S. 41
Howe, Florence 350
Hoyt, Donald P. 42
Hughes, Marija Matich 253
Hyatt, Jim 184

I

Ickeringill, Nan 351

J

Johnson, Ray W. 43
Johnston, J. A. 29
Jones, Paul W. 44

K

Kaley, Maureen M. 92
Kalka, Beatrice Symbol 223
Kammeryer, Kenneth 224
Kanowitz, Leo 254
Kaplan, Harold I 114
Karras, Edward J. 210
Katz, Joseph 186
Kaufman, Helen 149
Kay, Jane J. 160
Kelman, Steven 300
Keniston, Ellen 255
Keniston, Kenneth 255
Kennedy, Carroll E. 42
Klein, Viola 187
Knudsen, Dean D. 257
Komarovsky, Mirra 256
Komisar, Lucy 301
Kresge, Pat 188
Krueger, Cynthia 45
Kruger, Daniel H. 302
Kuvlesky, William P. 46, 225

L

Leland, Carole A. 47, 48
Letchworth, George E. 335
Lever, Michael 46
Levi, Joseph 237, 238, 239
Lewis, Edwin C. 49, 115, 304
Lifton, Robert J. 305
Liu, Phyllis Y. H. 336
Livingston, Omeda Frances 175

Lopate, Carol 116
Lovett, Sarah Lee 50
Lozoff, Marjorie M. 48, 186
Lubetkin, Arvin I. 51
Lubetkin, Barry S. 51
Lunneborg, Patricia W. 52
Lynn, David B. 226
Lyon, Ella Rhee 53

M

Maccoby, Eleanor E. 227
Malcom, Janet 306
Maraventano, Frances 247
Martin, Janet M. 144
Martin, Norman H. 178
Masih, Lalit K. 54
Maslow, Albert P. 189
Mattfeld, Jacquelyn A. 117
Matthews, Esther 55, 307
Matthews, Margie R. 118
Maule, Frances 161
McCarty, Edward R. 242
McClelland, David C. 228
McCune, Shirley 190
McGowan, Barbara 336
McGuigan, Dorothy Gies 258
McKiever, M.F. 191
McMurray, Georgia L. 119
Mercer, Marilyn 308
Merritt, Doris H. 176
Metzger, Sherrill M. 56
Millet, Kate 259
Mitchell, Elmer D. 57
Mitchell, Susan B. 192
Mooney, Joseph D. 150
Morrow, L. 120
Mueller, Kate H. 260
Myers, George C. 193
Myint, Thelma 11

N

Nager, Norma 95
Neubeck, Gerhard 349
Neuman, Rebecca R. 310
Newcomer, Mabel 261
Norfleet, Mary Ann 58
Nye, Francis Ivan 93

O

Obordo, Angelita S. 225
Oltman, Ruth M. 151
Oppenheimer, Valerie Kincade 262, 263, 264, 265
Orden, Susan 94

P

Painter, Edith P. 311
Parmelee, Rexford 125
Parrish, John B. 122, 123, 124, 163, 312, 313
Pavalko, Ronald M. 95
Payne, David 229
Pennell, Maryland T. 126
Perrucci, Carolyn Cummings 59
Peterson, Esther 266, 267
Poloma, Margaret M. 96
Powers, Lee 125
Pressman, Sonia 164
Preston, James D. 225
Psathas, George 60

R

Racz, Elizabeth 268
Ralph, Diane 247
Rand, Lorraine 61
Randolph, Kathryn Scott 337
Rappaport, Alan F. 229
Raushenbush, Esther 338
Reisman, David 316
Renshaw, Josephine E. 126
Rezler, Agnes G. 63
Robin, Stanley 64
Robinson, Lora H. 152
Roby, Pamela 153
Roe, Ann 194
Rose, Harriett A. 19
Rosenkrantz, Paul S. 214
Rosenthal, Evelyn 131
Rossi, Alice S. 65, 127, 154, 317, 318, 319
Rossman, Jack E. 195
Rostow, Edna 320

S

Safilios-Rothschild, Constantina 97, 98
Sandis, Eva E. 230
Sassower, Doris L. 128
Schab, Fred 66
Schaefer, Charles E. 3
Shearer, Lloyd 177
Schissell, Robert F. 67, 68
Schmalzried, B. L. 56
Schmidt, Marlin R. 69
Schuck, Victoria 129
Schwartz, Jane 269
Scott, Anne Firor 270
Scully, Malcolm G. 321
Searls, Laura G. 231
Senders, Virginia L. 339
Sharp, Laure M. 130
Shefflre, Buford 352
Siegel, Alberta Engvall 70
Simon, Rita James 131, 132, 155
Simpson, Lawrence Alan 156
Singer, Stanley L. 352
Smuts, Robert W. 271
Steinmann, Anne 229, 232, 233, 234, 235, 236, 237, 238, 239
Stolz, Lois M. 99
Suelzle, Marijean 272

T

Tangri, Sandra Florence Schwartz 71
Terrill, Hazel J. 242
Tiedeman, David V. 55
Tifft, Larry L. 155
Thomas, Martha J.B. 134
Thompson, Mary Lou 273
Torpey, W.G. 135
Trilling, Diana 323
Truex, Dorothy 324
Turner, Ralph H. 72
Tyler, Leona E. 73

V

Van Aken, Carol G. 117
Van Riper, Paul P. 178
Vogel, Susan R. 214

W

Walt, Dorothy E. 137
Warner, W.L. 178

Wasserman, Elga 292
Watley, Donivan J. 75
Weinberg, Ethel 138
Werts, Charles E. 76
Westervelt, Esther M. 326
Wetherby, Phyllis 139
White, Becky J. 77
White, James J. 140
White, Kinnard 141
White, Sylvia 327
Whitehurst, Robert Noel 209
Whitney, Mary E. 328
Wiesenfelder, Harry 125
Williamson, Thomas R. 210
Wilson, Kenneth M. 78, 79, 80, 81. 287
Wilson, Roger M. L. 248
Withycombe-Brocato, Carol Jean 82

Wolfe, Donald M. 87
Wolfe, Helen Bickel 211
Wolins, Leroy 49
Woodring, Paul 329
Worthy, N.B. 167

Y

Yelsma, Julie J. 49

Z

Zapoleon, Marguerite W. 288
Zytowski, Donald G. 212

SUBJECT INDEX

A

Academic reform 143
Academic prediction 44
Academic superiority 3
Achievement motivation 40, 41, 51, 58, 72
Adolescence 218
Adolescent employment 204
Advanced training 173
Advancement barriers 124, 167, 188
American Sociological Association 319
Anthropology 107
Antinepotism 155
Autonomy 48

B

Banking 168, 173
Barriers to raising status of women 272
Behavioral motivation 65, 177
Bio-medical sciences 62

Business 157, 161, 166, 167, 168, 169, 170, 176, 290, 308, 351
Business administration 168
Business education 175

C

Career achievement 38, 109, 117, 122, 125, 126, 130, 137, 244, 246
Career advancement 140, 142, 158
Career aspirations 17, 24, 56, 78, 79, 100, 189, 279
Career barriers 92, 101, 104, 105, 107, 108, 113, 116, 117, 122, 123, 128, 131, 166, 176, 180, 181, 185, 190, 192, 234, 251, 253, 302
Career commitment 9, 22, 23, 25, 56, 97, 141
Career expectations 46, 136, 210, 225
Career facilitators 309
Career-marriage conflict 25, 92, 115, 238, 256, 304, 320, 327, 339

239

Career motivation 2, 4, 5, 15, 16, 17, 19, 23, 29, 30, 37, 38, 42, 43, 54, 65, 73, 77, 101, 111, 112, 186
Career opportunities 201, 219, 245, 269, 276, 282, 307
Career patterns 59, 103, 109, 110, 121, 125, 127, 130, 159, 169, 172, 174, 175, 178, 189, 206, 251, 287, 345
Career planning 10, 18, 47, 111, 161, 170, 194, 269, 288, 310, 339
Career prediction 8, 10, 11, 23, 31, 33, 34, 35, 36, 50, 61, 67, 68, 70, 71, 73, 75, 112, 345
Career satisfaction 113, 122, 192
Changing role of women 271, 293
Chemistry 342
Child care 306
Clerical work 203, 210
College attendance 76
College teaching 163, 165, 208
Commitment prediction 30, 45, 63, 66
Consistency of feminine self-image 224
Continuing education 330, 331, 332, 333, 334, 335, 336, 338, 339, 340, 341, 342
Creativity 3, 39, 221, 222

D

Day care 298, 351
Deviance hypothesis 1, 5
Discrimination 101, 102, 103, 104, 107, 114, 115, 116, 120, 128, 131, 132, 133, 140, 144, 145, 152, 153, 155, 156, 164, 165, 166, 168, 176, 181, 182, 184, 185, 188, 190, 198, 199, 209, 219, 254, 257, 281, 283, 301, 308, 318, 321, 322, 324, 337
Doctoral degrees 192, 287, 292
Doctoral programs 337
Dual-career families 89, 96, 106, 162

E

Early dating 213
Economics 131

Education 112, 141, 256, 260, 267, 297, 315
Educational administration 149, 151, 158, 174
Educational aspirations 27, 69, 78, 79
Educational attrition 150, 153, 154
Educational barriers 62, 102, 192, 196, 241
Educational commitment 26
Educational counseling 14, 48, 81, 101, 118, 130, 233, 239, 279, 307, 310, 325
Educational facilitators 62, 102, 114, 118, 120, 135, 138, 146, 153, 247, 249, 251, 291, 292, 294, 309
Educational motivation 57, 81, 82, 196, 230, 335, 336
Educational patterns 192, 284, 287
Educational policy 291, 294, 309, 310, 312, 324, 330, 332, 333, 334, 337, 338
Educational prediction 41, 49, 80, 81
Effect of Functionalism 257
Elimination of sex role stereotypes 317
Employment 6, 9, 15, 27, 101, 136, 157, 161, 163, 183, 185, 187, 196, 197, 198, 200, 203, 204, 205, 207, 208, 238, 243, 245, 249, 263, 264, 267, 271, 272, 277, 285, 302, 309, 315
Employment facilitators 187, 242, 249, 266, 267
Employment legislation 184, 185, 188, 191, 202, 206, 240, 253, 254, 266, 275, 278, 280, 281, 286, 318
Employment motivation 74, 195, 196, 207, 211, 285, 344
Employment patterns 202, 203, 204, 208, 262, 274, 277, 284, 341
Employment trends 158, 163, 183, 184, 205, 240, 243, 245, 249, 262, 263, 264, 265, 269, 271, 276, 282, 302
Engineering 59, 64, 113, 122, 127, 134
Enrichment hypothesis 1
Equal pay 278
Executive careers 161, 162, 166, 167, 170, 175, 176, 178

F

Familial roles 90, 96, 97, 98, 106, 185, 209, 271, 320
Family responsibilities 53, 125, 163, 208, 303
Family size 24
Federal employment 164, 178, 189, 247
Female-dominated occupations 262
Feminine self-image 228, 229, 232, 237, 238, 239, 255
Feminism 65, 164, 273, 306, 317
Freudian theories on women 347

G

Goal deflection 46
Graduate education 51, 62, 82, 121, 123, 129, 130, 131, 146, 147, 148, 150, 196, 337

H

Harvard 144, 148
Health patterns 191
Higher education 4, 6, 7, 9, 11, 12, 14, 17, 18, 22, 23, 26, 27, 38, 39, 48, 49, 52, 53, 56, 57, 64, 66, 78, 79, 80, 81, 95, 100, 101, 103, 116, 121, 123, 124, 129, 130, 132, 133, 142, 143, 144, 145, 146, 147, 148, 151, 152, 153, 155, 156, 157, 158, 178, 192, 201, 218, 220, 224, 239, 241, 244, 245, 258, 260, 261, 284, 287, 289, 294, 295, 296, 304, 312, 313, 319, 321, 328
Hiring practices 182, 198
Historical biography 246
History 131
History of female employment 264
History of Feminism 244, 259
History of women's education 241, 258, 261
History of women's movement 268, 270
Hospital administration 172
Household employment 206

I

Income 139, 140, 142, 151, 199, 206, 274
Individual growth and development 218
Intellectual attainment 220
Intellectual development 227
Intellectual functioning 227

J

Job performance 200
Job restructuring 312, 313

L

Labor unions 171
Law 106, 110, 128, 140
Legislation needs 318
Leisure activity 83, 231
Librarianship 139
Life insurance 175
Life style aspirations 6, 7, 56, 70, 78, 100, 186, 225
Life style expectations 225
Life style influences 83
Life style motivation 55, 86
Life style prediction 48, 61, 69
Life styles 111, 228, 232, 251, 311, 316, 327
Life style satisfaction 29, 93, 94, 103, 231

M

Management 157, 160, 169
Man's "ideal" woman 223, 229, 236, 237, 238, 239
Manufacturing 168
Marital adjustment 84, 87, 91
Marital decision making 87, 88, 97, 98
Marital satisfaction 86, 94, 195
Marital status 17, 18, 25, 34, 59, 83, 131, 207, 229, 243
Marriage access 95
Marriage aspirations 4, 66, 320
Marriage counseling 236
Marriage stability 213

Maternal employment 74, 84, 86, 87, 88, 90, 93, 94, 96, 99, 183, 184, 193, 195, 209, 349
Maternal motivation 65
Mathematics 222
Mature women workers 263, 265
Medicine 102, 114, 116, 118, 120, 125, 126, 127, 138, 176
Methodologic issues 35, 44, 61, 98
Methodologic problems 13
Methodologic technique 31, 32, 34, 49, 67, 80
Methodologic validity 36, 79
Minnesota Plan for Women's Continuing Education 339
Minority status 59, 115, 127, 296

N

National policy on women's rights 314
Nineteenth-century marriage manuals 252
Nuns 235
Nursing 45, 95, 341

O

Occupational choice 1, 12, 16, 19, 32, 33, 46, 50, 53, 60, 69, 71, 194, 228
Occupations 240
Oppression of women 259, 299

P

Parental attitudes 234
Parental ambitions for children 230
Parental identification 226
Parental influences 233
Part-time employment 242, 329
Patriarchy 259, 299
Personality changes 69
Personnel 160
Political activism 270
Political science 129
Politics 159, 177
Pregnancy 191
Prejudice 220
Psychological counseling 237, 239
Psychological health patterns 214, 236
Psychology 103, 182

R

Racial differences 79, 85, 225, 236, 243
Radcliffe Institute for Independent Study 331
Radio-T.V. 168
Research needs 98, 101, 108, 216, 307, 310, 325
Role expectations 20, 28
Role influences 2, 6, 13, 39, 47, 77, 93, 224
Role perceptions 21, 37, 51, 88, 92, 223, 232, 326
Role/sex conflict 109, 118, 180, 190
Role theory 93, 326

S

Scholastic ability 75
Science 59, 104, 108, 117, 127, 142
Secondary education 11, 21
Sex differences 52, 54, 72, 76, 216, 217, 221, 222, 227, 228, 352
Sex labeling of jobs 262, 308
Sex role acceptance 179
Sex role development 215, 217, 226
Sex role differences 60, 64, 89
Sex role identification 43, 77, 179, 226
Sex role perceptions 41, 47, 50, 82, 84, 85, 89, 214, 215, 229, 233, 234, 235, 238, 244, 255, 349
Sex roles 4, 40, 96, 215, 216, 226, 300
Sex-role stereotypes 214, 255, 256, 299
Sexuality 65
Social work 119
Socialization practices 230
Social welfare activism 270
Sociology 131, 296, 319
Status 254, 257, 272, 275, 277, 289, 303, 315, 316
Student personnel administration 328

SUBJECT INDEX

Success avoidance 40, 110
Sweden 300

T

Technology 240, 276, 303
The French Revolution 268
The "ideal" woman 229, 233, 236, 237, 238, 239
The working wife 83, 85, 89, 91, 97, 162, 183, 234, 344
Three aspects of feminine image 305

U

University of Chicago 164
University of Maryland 165
University of Michigan 258

V

Value change 14, 250
Veterinary medicine 109
Vocational counseling 20, 31, 33, 63, 181, 197, 211, 212, 288, 325
Vocational theory 60, 212

W

Women's colleges 290, 291, 297
Women's liberation 273, 274, 301, 321, 322, 343, 346, 348
Women's magazines 186
Women's organizations 247, 273
Women's right to choose 311
Women in contemporary literature 323
Work values 22, 23, 189, 210, 211, 352